ROBERT the Bruce, King of Scots

Stewart

MARJORIE of Scotland d. 1315 ——— WALTER, 6th hereditary Great Steward of Scotland (whose father fought for Wallace), d. 1326 🏰 *Rothesay*

DAVID II Bruce, King of Scots, d. 1370 ——— MARGARET Drummond, *widowed Lady of Logie*

ROBERT II Stewart, King of Scots, as Great Steward saved the Scottish army after Nevill's Cross 1346, first Stewart king 1370, d. 1390 ——— ELISABETH Muir 🏰 *Rowallan*

ROBERT III, King of Scots, reigned but too injured by kick from horse to rule, d. 1406 ——— ANNABELLA Drummond 🏰 *Stobhall*

ROBERT, Duke of Albany, Regent of Scotland, d. 1420 🏰 *Doune*

MURDACH, Duke of Albany, Regent, beheaded 1425, ancestors of the Bonnie Earl of Moray and of the present Earl

ALEXANDER, Earl of Buchan, the 'Wolf of Badenoch'

ALEXANDER, Earl of Mar (natural son)

JANET m. Lachlan Maclean of Duart, ancestors of the present Lord Chamberlain 🏰 *Duart*

JOAN, m. Sir JOHN Lyon, Thane of Glamis 🏰 *Glamis* ancestors of Queen ELIZABETH the Queen Mother

JAMES I, King of Scots, assassinated 1437 ——— Lady JOAN Beaufort

Sir JAMES Stewart, 'the Black Knight of Lorn'

JAMES II, King of Scots, accidentally killed 1460 🏰 *Falkland*

JOHN, Earl of Atholl, ancestor of the Dukes of Atholl 🏰 *Blair*

JAMES III, King of Scots, beautified Stirling, slain by rebels 1488

JAMES IV, King of Scots, annexed Lordship of the Isles, killed at Flodden 1513 🏰 *Dunconnel*

JAMES V, King of Scots, beautified Falkland, d. 1547 ——— MARY of Guise, of House of Lorraine, Regent, embellished Holyroodhouse

Stuart

MARY, Queen of Scots (beheaded 1587) imprisoned at Lochleven 🏰 *Lochleven* ——— HENRY, King of Scots, previously Lord Darnley, strangled 1567

JAMES VI, King of Scots (James I, King of England), united the Crowns but not the countries, d. 1625

ELIZABETH, 'Winter Queen' of Bohemia ——— FREDERICK 'Winter King' of Bohemia

CHARLES I, King of Scotland (also King of England), beheaded 1649

SOPHIA, Electress of Hanover, d. 1714 ——— ERNEST AUGUSTUS, Elector of Hanover

Prince RUPERT of the Rhine, dashing Cavalier

CHARLES II, King of Scotland (also King of England), d. 1685

JAMES VII, King of Scotland (JAMES II, King of England), exiled 1688 🏰 *Holyroodhouse*

Hanover

GEORGE I, King of Great Britain, d. 1727

GEORGE II, King of Great Britain, last British Sovereign to command in battle, d. 1760

FREDERICK, Prince of Wales, kind to Flora Macdonald 1746, d. 1751

GEORGE III, King of Great Britain, driven frantic by porphyria, painted as a boy in Scottish Archer uniform, d. 1820

CHARLES, Duke of Richmond, natural son, ancestor of DIANA, Princess of Wales

HENRIETTA, Lady Waldegrave, natural daughter, ancestress of DIANA, Princess of Wales

ANNE, Queen of Great Britain, d. 1714

MARY II, Queen of Scotland (also England) m. WILLIAM of Orange, King of Scotland (also England)

JAMES, the Old Chevalier, 'King over the Water', d. 1766

CHARLES, the Young Chevalier, 'Bonnie Prince Charlie', d. 1788, saved by Rout of Moy 🏠 *Moy*

EDWARD, Duke of Kent (younger son), d. 1820

GEORGE IV, King of Great Britain, in 1822 wore kilt on Royal Visit to Scotland, d. 1830

WILLIAM IV, King of Great Britain, d. 1837

VICTORIA, Queen of Great Britain, Empress of India, d. 1901 🏰 *Balmoral* ——— ALBERT of Saxony, Prince Consort, d. 1861 🏰 *Abergeldie*

ELIZABETH FitzClarence, Countess of Erroll, natural daughter, ancestress of the Hereditary Lords High Constable of Scotland

Saxony

EDWARD VII, King of Great Britain, Emperor of India, d. 1910

LOUISE, Duchess of Argyll, m. JOHN, Duke of Argyll, Hereditary Master of the Household in Scotland 🏰 *Inveraray*

ARTHUR, Duke of Connaught

PATRICIA ——— Hon. Sir ALEXANDER Ramsay

ALEXANDER Ramsay of Mar m. FLORA Fraser, Lady Saltoun 🏰 *Cairnbulg*

Windsor

GEORGE V, King of Great Britain, Emperor of India (younger son, d. 1936) 🏠 *Birkhall*

ALBERT Victor, Duke of Clarence, d. 1892

LOUISE, Princess Royal m. ALEXANDER, Duke of Fife 🏠 *Duff House*

GEORGE VI, King of Great Britain, last Emperor of India, d. 1952 ——— Lady ELIZABETH Bowes-Lyon *Glamis* 🏰 *Mey* Queen ELIZABETH, the Queen Mother

Queen ELIZABETH II, Head of the Commonwealth ——— PHILIP, Duke of Edinburgh

CHARLES, Prince of Wales, Duke of Rothesay, Earl of Carrick, Baron of Renfrew, Lord of the Isles and Great Steward of Scotland, born 1948 ——— Lady DIANA Spencer, Princess of Wales

Prince WILLIAM of Wales, born 1982

To Dad.   1984.
Enjoy your literary journey.
    Yours, Jerry & Margaret.

Debrett's
Royal Scotland

Debrett's
Royal Scotland

Jean Goodman
in collaboration with
Sir Iain Moncreiffe of that Ilk, Bt

Debrett

Webb&Bower

For Simon James

TITLE PAGE: Balmoral Castle,
built in 1855 in near-white granite from neighbouring quarries.

FOLLOWING PAGES: The marriage of HRH Princess Louise
to the Marquis of Lorne in 1871, painted by Sydney Hall.
Note Disraeli in the right foreground.

First published in Great Britain 1983 by
Webb & Bower (Publishers) Limited
9 Colleton Crescent, Exeter, Devon EX2 4BY
in association with Debrett's Peerage Limited
73–77 Britannia Road, London SW6

Designed by Peter Wrigley

Picture research by Anne-Marie Ehrlich

British Library Cataloguing in Publication Data

Goodman, Jean
Debrett's royal Scotland.
1. Historic buildings—Scotland
2. Great Britain—Kings and rulers
I. Title   II. Moncreiffe of that Ilk *Sir*, Iain
941.1   DA760
ISBN 0-905649-59-1

Typeset in Great Britain by
August Filmsetting, Warrington, Cheshire
Printed and bound in Hong Kong by
Mandarin Offset International Limited

CONTENTS

Introduction
   by Sir Iain Moncreiffe of that Ilk   8

PART I
ROYAL CASTLES, PALACES AND HOUSES   15

Royal Stories in Stones   16

Dunbarton Castle   17
Dunadd and Dunstaffnage Castles   22
Scone Palace   27
Edinburgh Castle   33
Stirling Castle   38
Dunfermline Palace   46
Linlithgow Palace   51
Lochmaben Castle   57
Kildrummy Castle   58
Turnberry Castle   61
Stobhall Castle   62
Rothesay Castle   65
Rowallan Castle   67
Doune Castle   69
Blair Castle   72
Lochleven Castle   79
Tarbert Castle   80
Dunconnel Castle   82
Duart Castle   83
The Palace of Falkland   85
The Palace of Holyroodhouse   94
Moy Hall   104
Duff House   106
Cairnbulg Castle   110
Inveraray Castle   113

Balmoral Castle   120
Birkhall   132
Abergeldie Castle   136
Glamis Castle   140
The Castle of Mey   149

PART II
PAGEANTRY AND CEREMONY   157

The Honours of Scotland   158
The Royal Company of Archers   162
The Order of the Thistle   166
The Royal Household in Scotland   168
The Braemar Gatherings   173

PART III
ROYAL VISITS TO SCOTLAND   179

King George IV   180
Queen Victoria   183
King Edward VII   190
Prince Albert Victor, Duke of Clarence   195
King George V   198
King George VI   204
Princess Marina, Duchess of Kent   206
Queen Elizabeth   207
Prince Charles   211

Map of royal castles, palaces and
   houses in Scotland   217
Monarchs of Scotland since AD 1005   218
Bibliography   219
Acknowledgements   221
Index   222

There is scarcely a gentleman of any of the old Scottish families who cannot count kin with the Royal House: in this small country blood has so intermingled that far the greater part of our burgesses and yeomen are entitled to entertain similar pretensions.

SIR WALTER SCOTT

INTRODUCTION

SIR IAIN MONCREIFFE OF THAT ILK

The history of the foundation and consolidation of Scotland, as a very special country with a strong identity of her own, is the story of our continuing royal family. For Scotland is made up of many peoples, and it was our royal family who moulded them into one country which despite its mixed racial origins has ever since maintained its separate identity from the rest of Britain.

So it's impossible for a Scotsman abroad to say 'Yes' when asked by a foreigner 'Are you English?' My English friends seem to think this mere pedantry, and stare incomprehendingly when asked how *they* would reply to the question 'Are you Scottish?' Yet their attitude has this merit, that they are taught so little about us at school that they tend to have an open mind on Scotland.

Now, the Scots do not have an open mind about themselves. Most Scots are riddled with preconceptions that increasingly become misconceptions about their country's past: whether trendy left-wing, like much of our current historical 'scholarship', or starry romantick, like the Victorian novelists. So it was a pleasure to help Jean Goodman while she was writing this book; for she looked on Scotland with her fresh English eyes, prepared to see what was unfolded before her without having her vision already obscured by the bloody mists of bitter partisan feuding.

For, during the long years when our Royal Family temporarily abandoned us—no sovereign, except for the Old Chevalier, set foot in Scotland for nearly two centuries, between 1651 and 1822—Scotland became in many respects a land of nasty, petty squabbling, lowlander against highlander, clan against clan. I could still get a rise out of very many of my Scottish readers *if* I were to say for instance, that one of the most civilising influences on Scotland as a whole during much of that period was the dominance of the Campbells (note, equally, that I haven't said it one way or the other). But this tease would be lost on Jean Goodman, which gives her an immense advantage when she looks at the period through outside eyes.

It was perhaps the great and good Sir Walter Scott, above all, who gave Scotland back her self-respect. By his romances, which achieved European stature, he not only put Scotland back on the international map: he converted what had been squalid feuds into romantic episodes, changing real hatreds into what social anthropologists call 'joking relationships'. As a result of the Moncreiffes slaying a Jardine in 1578, for example, I was the guest of honour a couple of years ago at the Jardine Gathering. At the same time, Scott endeavoured also to reconcile the Highlands with the Lowlands: and to some extent canalised the tartan tradition to this end. Although originally highland, the use of tartan had spread to the lowlands before the Union with England, and by Sir Walter's time was already becoming the hallmark of Scots in foreign eyes.

Sir Walter Scott, from a painting by Thomas Lawrence.

In this great task of pouring oil on fresh waters rather than old flames, Sir Walter was magnificently assisted by the understanding and generosity of King George IV, whose famous visit to Edinburgh in 1822 was particularly addressed to reconciliation with the highlanders—he even had the good sense to ask very particularly for Glenlivet whisky—and who restored the actual presence of the monarchy to Scotland.

Of course, there can be too much of a good thing—even, alas, of Glenlivet—and there has been in recent years a reaction against what is known as 'tartan tosh'. Certainly, some of the tartan gimmicks for tourists are embarrassing, as is the garb of some Scottish football fans who, however, are only thoroughly enjoying themselves in identifying with their country. But I find the standard snide sniping by smart writers at King George IV himself for wearing highland dress mildly irritating as well as ungrateful: but for him, and his niece Queen Victoria, not just the Highlands but all Scotland might have continued to be a mere backwater called North Britain.

There is always something stimulating—a feeling of invigoration and renewal—about the presence among us of the royal house that gives unity and purpose to the nation: the Queen as Chief of Chiefs is the head of the whole family of Scots scattered throughout the world, even in countries where she is not also their Sovereign. The Royal Family is the nuclear family around which Scotland grew like a snowball.

For a glance at the endpapers of this colourful book will remind readers that Scotland has always had the same royal family. It shouldn't be, but it is, constantly necessary to emphasise this point, which has been obscured by the historians' convenient use of dynastic names to form as it were punctuation marks in the long chronicle of our national story.

Thus we learn of what happened under the House of Kenneth mac Alpin, the House of Atholl (or Dunkeld), the Houses of Balliol, Bruce, Stewart and Stuart, Hanover, Saxony and now Windsor: as though these surnames denote different royal families. They certainly denote different male lines, but our throne passes through women, and most people don't regard our royal family as having become a different one because the throne passed through Queen Victoria, for instance. Very few people think of Prince Charles as not belonging to the Queen's family: yet the historians' standard dynastic classification would make the Duke of Gloucester appear her nearest kin, and Prince Charles found a new branch of the House of Denmark.

So, at Jean Goodman's suggestion, I've prepared these endpapers to demonstrate the deep Scottish roots and flowing continuity of our Royal Family. The symbols for castles and palaces form only a rough guide, and are not tied to any particular consistency, but are intended to give some indication of the way the places about which the author has written were linked to this family. For instance, the modern palace at Scone is a creation of the Murrays, although it incorporates part of the earlier building in which both Charles II and the Old Chevalier stayed. But it's only a few yards from the Pictish royal inauguration mound on which so many of our kings were set on the Stone of Destiny or, later, crowned in state. Again, Dunstaffnage was originally a stronghold of the Lorn branch of the royal house of Dalriada, descended from King Lorn, brother of King Fergus the Great; and the existing ruin is itself that of a much later stone castle of the mediaeval period. But it seemed perhaps appropriate to set its symbol on the endpapers tree against Kenneth mac Alpin who united the Daldriadic Gaels with the Picts of Scone, since long-standing tradition connects him with Dunstaffnage and he falls midway between the two periods. So too, Stirling must have been fortified under the Pictish high kings, but is particularly mentioned early in the mediaeval building period in connection with King Alexander I.

These old names like Fergus and Kenneth mac Alpin and Alexander I may seem to many readers far more shadowy than George III or James VI or even Robert Bruce. But they were all flesh and blood, of the same royal kindred as today, real people who left a real mark on the making of our nation. What is strange, however, is the way that the different races over whom the royal ancestors ruled should have been so welded together as to form a peculiarly Scottish nation that was never assimilated by the English. Although we have now been British for two and three-quarter centuries—longer than

Queen Elizabeth receiving the Crown of Scotland from the 14th Duke of Hamilton and Brandon,
Hereditary Keeper of the Palace of Holyroodhouse, in St Giles' Cathedral on 24 June, 1953,
shortly after her Coronation in Westminster Abbey.
Painting by Stanley Cursiter at the Palace of Holyroodhouse,
on the great stair to the state apartments.

the United States have existed—we have retained a national consciousness within the framework of the United Kingdom that is quite different from that of, say, Virginia within the United States. Yet Scots is simply a form of the English language, and the great province of the Lothians was part of England until after the battle of Carham in 1018, while Edinburgh had still been an English city only sixty years before that.

Moreover, the Hebrides, including Skye and Mull and even Kintyre, were part of *Norway* until 1266. It was easier to sail from Norway to Kintyre than to ride there through bog and forest from Perth or Dunfermline. When my forefather Sir Mathew of Moncreiffe was living here under the shade of Moncreiffe Hill in the reign of Alexander II, he would have said he was voyaging to Norway, as indeed was true, if he had travelled to Skye to stay at Dunvegan with his contemporary the Norse prince Leod, ancestor of the MacLeods, or to Islay to visit his other contemporary the Norwegian local King Donald, progenitor of the Macdonalds. Now, the time between 1266 and the English Conquest of Scotland in 1296 is only thirty years: about the same as the interval between the death of King George VI and now. Furthermore, the Scottish royal house was deeply divided between its Balliol & Cummin v. Bruce branches. Yet Angus Macdonald of Islay and his so recently Norwegian Islesmen were among the staunchest supporters of Scotland's nationhood under Robert the Bruce. And the heroes of Bruce's patriotic army included, besides Gaelic chiefs like Campbell and Lennox, nobles of Flemish origin like Douglas and Murray, of Breton origin like the Stewarts, and Norman origin like the Hays and Bruce himself. Even Wallace means 'the Welshman'. It seems extraordinary that our inventive nation could be forged out of such mixed elements in so short a time. I put the achievement down to the tactlessness of Edward I of England, the Hammer of the Scots. He hammered us into an enduring nation in no time at all.

So it was that, unlike the kingdoms of Wessex and Mercia and Northumbria and even Cornwall, the realm of England never assimilated the realm of Scotland; although our own royal house had assimilated Caledonia of the Picts and Strathclyde of the Britons and Argyll (*Earr a' Ghaideal*, the Frontier of the Gaels) and even the Western Isles; England failed to take her chance to assimilate Scotland. Perhaps it would have succeeded had the Maid of Norway, King Alexander III's granddaughter and heiress to our throne, lived to marry her fiancé the future Edward II, and there therefore would have been no War of Independence. In the end, as everyone knows, a Welsh earl having conquered the English in 1485 and clinched that throne by marrying the Plantagenet heiress, their daughter eventually brought the throne of England to the Scottish royal family, who have held it ever since. It is by virtue of her Stuart royal blood that our Queen reigns over the whole United Kingdom.

Nevertheless, it isn't always realised that England and Scotland remained completely separate countries until 1707. They were still as separate as Canada is from Australia now. Sometimes England was at war with France when Scotland was not. Thus, in the North, Charles II was styled 'King of Scotland, England, France and Ireland' and not, as James VI and I had wished: 'King of Great Britain'.

And up here, the Queen still has her own ceremonial Scottish Royal Household, though she is accompanied for practical purposes by members of her ordinary Household wherever she may be in the worldwide Commonwealth of which she is the Head. The Scottish Royal Household, about which Jean Goodman writes, provides us colourful ceremonial with characteristically Scots economy. The hereditary Great Officers—such as the Lord High Constable, the Master of the Scottish Royal Household and the Royal 'Bannerman'—like the Keepers of the Palaces and Castles, perform their jobs for free, though the Banner Bearer does get a new Lyon Rampant banner at Coronations. The Archers of the Queen's Body Guard provide their own picturesque uniforms and parade at their own expense. The heralds and pursuivants also provide their own uniforms (except for the already existing stock of tabards), and perform their duties without a pay rise since the seventeenth century: the three heralds are each paid £25 a year—which is what I get as Albany Herald myself—while the three pursuivants each have to make do on £16 a year. The Lord Lyon, of course, is in a different position as he also functions as a judge and has to preside over Lyon Court, assisted by Lyon Clerk just as any other judge has a Clerk of the Court. The other positions in the Scottish Royal Household, however, such as the Historiographer, the Astronomer, the Royal Chaplains and the Painter & Limner, are also unpaid.

But all this beautiful though inexpensive ceremonial, in which we are able to mingle our hopeful present with our colourful future, would be meaningless if the Sovereign were never there to be its focal flame. The Lord Lyon as King of Arms may be called the custodian of the Spirit of Caledonia, but that spirit itself is metaphorically embodied in the Queen herself, with her radiant aura of goodness that is the true outward expression of inner majesty. And the Queen has paid more special Royal Visits to Scotland, quite apart from private visits to Balmoral, than any other Sovereign since her shrewd Stuart forefather James VI set out in 1603 to become, as he himself put it, King James the First of Great Britain: and to be placed at last on what was literally his rightful family seat, the Stone of Destiny.

Iain Moncreiffe of that Ilk.

Easter Moncreiffe, Perthshire

PART I

ROYAL CASTLES, PALACES AND HOUSES

The River Teith as it flows past Doune Castle in Perthshire.

ROYAL STORIES IN STONES

Five of the nine titles of the Prince of Wales are Scottish. Prince Charles Philip Arthur George is Prince and Great Steward of Scotland, Duke of Rothesay, Earl of Carrick, Baron of Renfrew and Lord of the Isles. His titles roll off the tongue with a flourish and evoke all the romantic glamour of a wild, untamed country, the mystery of moors and mountains, the clash of dirk and broadsword, the flash of tartan and the skirl of the pipes. They recall the glamour of the Stuarts, the ruthless courage of men like Macbeth, Robert the Bruce and Bonnie Prince Charlie who sometimes used the title Baron of Renfrew when travelling incognito.

The modern Prince's special affection for the rugged north is no coincidence. He descends from Mary, Queen of Scots, *twenty-two* times over: that is, by eight separate blood lines through King George V and Queen Mary, also fourteen more through Prince Philip, all from that tragic heiress of the Royal House of Stuart.

From the Dark Ages immortal stories of Scotland, intermingled with myth and legend, have been perpetuated by poets and writers so that they are often surrounded by considerable scholarly dispute. Yet time and again, seemingly far-fetched tales that challenge credulity can be substantiated in the derivation of a name, the insignia on a highland crest, a piper's doleful lament or a footprint carved in stone . . .

Interwoven with the stories are those of Scotland's castles and palaces, particularly those that have been associated with royalty. Down the centuries they have stood silent witnesses to feud and fighting and political controversy as groups of fearless peoples, divided by culture and heritage, gradually formed into one nation.

After the Romans withdrew from Britain in the fifth century four separate peoples struggled for living space in the north, beyond Hadrian's Wall. They were the Picts, including the Caledonians who, for some time, had settled in the land between Orkney and the Forth,

the Scots in Argyll ('Frontier of the Gael'), who were arriving from Dalriada in Antrim in Northern Ireland, the Britons who dwelt in Strathclyde, and the Angles who eventually conquered Lothian.

Each race had its own kings and traditions. Initially there were two main systems of succession—the Pictish matrilinear whereby males succeeded through their mothers or sisters, while the Scots inherited the throne by the rule of tanistry with succession by the senior member of the Royal Family such as a brother or a cousin, providing he fulfilled certain qualifications. These included having no physical blemish, being of age and yet not senile and having led at least one successful cattle raid.

In this second system the heir was known during the lifetime of the king and was called *tanaiste rig* ('second to the king'). The system survived until the twelfth century when the Scots adopted the present system of succession—primogeniture by direct descent. The change was imposed by King David I, for the method of choosing successors of the same generation, so that a king was succeeded by his brother or a cousin, had meant that in the first 160 years of a united Scotland the crown had changed hands no less than fifteen times.

As for the stories in stones: in the lowlands of Scotland early Norman nobles, who settled there by royal invitation and not by conquest, left mementoes in the shape of many motte-and-bailey establishments—natural or artificial mounds—surrounded by palisades enclosing domestic buildings such as kitchens or stables. Some of these developed into protective stone fortresses.

Further north, castles and towers were established as fortified homes by great Scottish families who were constantly at war with each other or in the King's name. In the seventeenth century many of these were influenced by the French châteaux. Often French masons, plasterers and decorators were brought over to embellish the castles with wings, turrets, decorative battlements or stone or brick projections from the walls to provide horizontal supports. This was the beginning of the Scottish Baronial style.

Down the centuries these homes and fortresses were more than symbols of feudal power. The owners protected their supporters and those who served them or worked for them. They gave them their name so that men with no original blood relationship became part of the clan. Today, the world over, Campbells regard their ancient home as Inveraray Castle; Kennedys, Culzean and MacLeods, Dunvegan. It is an extended family system that bridges frontiers and suggests a model relationship in a world in turmoil.

Gradually, the land of mountains and heather and flat peat-covered bog was studded with hundreds of castles—some fortified homes, others centres of administration or strategic strongholds in which royalty tended to consolidate their activities. The stories of some of those associated with royalty are, to a large extent, the story of Scotland and of a people who 'love Scotland better than truth'.

As far as possible, these palaces and residences have been selected and arranged in chronological order according to the parts they played in terms of their royal associations in the history of Scotland.

DUNBARTON CASTLE

Old King Coul was a jolly old soul,
And a jolly old soul was he,
Old King Coul he had a brown bowl,
And they brought him in fiddlers three.
And every fiddler was a very good fiddler,
And a very good fiddler was he.
Fiddel-didell, fiddel-didell, with the fiddlers three.

Useful Transactions in Philosophy,
William King, 1708-9

Dunbarton Rock, rising precipitously out of the sea at the junction of the rivers Clyde and Leven in Dunbartonshire, the province known as the Lennox, has been a centre of fortification since pre-Christian occupation. One of its earliest recorded rulers was King Ceretic whose family intermarried with that of the merry monarch of nursery-rhyme fame whose identity has long been a subject for speculation.

Some of the first recorded versions of the nursery rhyme are specifically Scottish and refer to Coel Hen (Coel the Old), who himself reigned in the country around Hadrian's Wall when the Romans left Britain, and was undoubtedly the earliest contender for the title of the immortal 'jolly old soul'.

Ceretic, or Coroticus as he was known in Latin, controlled the chain of little kingdoms in the West of Scotland from the fifth century AD, the last century of Roman Britain, and for the next 500 years his male descendants continued to rule there. However, towards the end of his reign he was upbraided by St Patrick for his evil ways: his subjects were Christians yet he caused a massacre and sold captured Christians to the Picts and Scots.

Speculation inevitably arises because the stories of those days were recorded by poets and minstrels rather than by historians. They wrote and sang of princes who fought with one another and held court, who hunted and banqueted and counted their wealth in flocks,

Coel Hen (Coel the Old) from an engraving in a children's toy book of 1858.

jewellery and splendid weapons. Accordingly, King Arthur, the fabled mythical hero who with his Knights of the Round Table led the Britons against the Saxons, is associated with Dunbarton Rock and is believed to have fought a battle at nearby Glen Douglas on Lochlomondside. Some writers support the legend that Dunbarton (the Fortress of the Britons) was 'Arthur's Castle' and maintain that his son 'Smerevie Mor' was born in 'The Tower of the Red Hall', possibly the red tower of the mediaeval castle which was repaired in 1460.

But the only visible remains of an early castle are a pair of gravestones dating from the tenth or eleventh century, which are kept in the Guard House. Prob-ably, however, dry stone ramparts and walls built at different levels defended the vulnerable rock slopes, while in the valley between the twin summits would have been most of the civil and ecclesiastical buildings of Strathclyde's 'capital', defended by a citadel sur-mounting the highest part of the rock. For in those days Dunbarton Rock was a city, not merely a fort. The separate town of Dunbarton did not exist until the thirteenth century.

By the ninth century, the male line of Ceretic came to an end when at least five peoples still occupied the land of mountains and mist and bog which would become Scotland. Meanwhile Kenneth mac Alpin, King of the Scots of Argyll through his father, successfully claimed the Pictish throne in the female line and united the two nations north of the Forth and Clyde. His descendant, Duncan I, was chosen to be King of the Cumbrians (Britons) and ruled from Dunbarton for sixteen years before he succeeded his grandfather as King of Scots. Eventually Strathclyde too merged into the united kingdom of the Scots. (As King of Scots, Duncan was duly slain by his cousin Macbeth whose wife Gruoch was also a claimant by royal blood.) His life was forfeited according to the old Gaelic system whereby a king expected to be slain by his rightful successor, unless he could manage to kill him first; a relic from pagan times.

After Macbeth slew Duncan in 1040, Duncan's sons Malcolm Canmore and Donald fled to England; but Macbeth was killed by Malcolm seventeen years afterwards. The fictionalized version of the story

Symbols of Pictish warriors on a stone
at Aberlemno in Angus.

embellished by poetic licence provides one of Shakespeare's greatest tragedies with immortal lines such as those spoken by Lady Macbeth after Duncan's murder:

> Will all great Neptune's ocean wash this blood
> Clean from my hand? No; this my hand will rather
> The multitudinous seas incarnadine,
> Making the green one red.

Duncan's youngest grandson, David the Saint, as Prince of Cumbria, held Dunbarton until he suc-ceeded two of his five elder brothers to the Scottish throne in 1124 and finally united the Britons of Strathclyde with the other peoples of Scotland. He also gained an earldom in southern England, Huntingdon, through his marriage to an English heiress and for this

David I of Scotland with his grandson Malcolm IV who succeeded him. An illuminated manuscript from the Charter of Kelso Abbey, 1159.

James I, the king-poet who, with his son James II, shed the Scottish monarchy's reputation for being weak and ineffectual. An engraving *c.* 1450.

he and his successors did homage to the King of England.

As economic, cultural and social relationships grew between the two countries, English rulers appreciated the increasing strategic importance of Dunbarton as a port of entry in the west of a united Scotland. Edward I took pains to secure it when he invaded Scotland in 1296. More than a century later King James I of Scotland, returning from his long captivity in England, asked the Clan Chief, Iain Colquhoun, 10th of Luss, to recover Dunbarton Castle from his enemies, the supporters of the former regent Albany. The castle lay in the territory of the ex-regent's father-in-law, the Earl of Lennox. Luss, according to the tale, replied '*Si je puis*' ('If I can') and cunningly pursued a stag with hounds past the castle. The garrison joined in the chase and gave the clansmen a chance to rush the castle and capture it. The story is reflected in the Colquhoun crest of a stag's head surmounted by the motto '*Si je puis*', and heraldic supporters of two hounds.

During Scotland's struggle for unity and independence Dunbarton Castle changed hands many times but always maintained royal associations. It was one of the few Scottish castles dating back to the English occupation which Robert Bruce did not order to be dismantled—presumably because of its inaccessibility to the enemy. After his death his son David II, at nine years old, sought protection there with his thirteen-year-old bride, Queen Joan, and eventually sailed from there to France.

The 'key of the realm' as Henry VIII described it, guarded the main western gateway to France and James V secured it in 1531 for several of his expeditions. His daughter, Mary, Queen of Scots, stayed there when she was five years old, while the treaty was drawn up for her marriage to the French Dauphin who, in return, promised to maintain the defence of Scotland and guarantee Scottish freedom and laws.

So in July 1548 Mary embarked from the great rock on the King of France's own galley accompanied by a suite of children and Scottish nobles considered appropriate for her new estate in France. It included her guardians, Lord Erskine and Lord Livingstone, her governess, Lady Fleming, an illegitimate daughter of

James IV, two of Mary's royal half-brothers—Lords Robert and John Stewart—her eldest half-brother Lord James Stewart, later Earl of Moray, and the four little 'Maries' of noble birth who were considered special children because they shared the Queen's christian name.

The weather was stormy and for a week the royal galley and her three escort ships lay at anchor in the Clyde in the shadow of Dunbarton. The weather had scarcely settled when they set off on a perilous voyage round the coast of the Isle of Man, Wales, the point of Cornwall and into the English Channel. Only Mary, it is recorded, was not seasick.

Sixteen years later she returned, a widowed queen, on the eve of her marriage to the ill-fated Darnley, son of the Earl of Lennox whose family had for so long been associated with Dunbarton Castle. It was a brief visit during her progress through Lennox and Argyll. Later, after Darnley's assassination and her deposition in favour of her infant son James, she vainly tried to seek refuge in Dunbarton, a key fortress still held for her, before fleeing to England and exile.

The castle, a pawn in the power struggle, appears again in her story when Queen Elizabeth demanded its surrender as a condition of Mary's liberation from imprisonment. It was the place where French help could be introduced into the country or, as had been proved, from which France itself could be reached in a desperate situation. Mary refused to surrender it, but fate, in the guise of a former soldier of its garrison, decreed otherwise.

In the spring of 1571 the soldier's wife had been ignominiously flogged for alleged theft, by order of the keeper, Lord Fleming. The soldier, determined on revenge, contacted a relative of the Earl of Lennox, regent for the young King James of whose regency Queen Elizabeth of England approved. He said he knew a secret route into the castle and was prepared to lead a party of soldiers to capture it. His daughter and son-in-law were held as hostages in case of a trap but on the night of 1 April, 1571, the soldier, true to his word, led a hundred men with ropes and ladders up the steep north-east side of the eastern peak, well away from the main defences, and at dawn captured the surprised garrison.

Frequently it changed hands and three years later the

An engraving of Dunbarton Castle, *c.* 1780, by an unknown artist.

young James VI of Scotland paid the first of many visits and in the years before he acceded to the English throne, he often went there to enjoy his favourite sport of deer hunting.

From then onwards piecemeal attempts were made to modernize the castle and stop its natural decay. Gun batteries and a sentinel box were erected along with towers and a guard house and in 1735 a Governor's House was built on the site of its most imposing recorded mediaeval building, a strong rectangular gatehouse with round corner towers. Most of these remain but there is no trace of the latest addition, an anti-aircraft battery erected in World War II. Fundamentally, the rock itself is its own fortress and in parts is so precipitous that no man-made defences are necessary. So, by and large, to see it today is to recapture its mood in the days of Druids and Romans, of kings and king-making.

Devoid of all but a few treasures or the trappings of kingship it is nevertheless still a royal castle and its Governorship an honour.

Its situation is very fine, [wrote Queen Victoria in her diary after her first visit on 17 August, 1847] . . . the rock rising straight out of the river, the mountains all round, and the town of Dunbarton behind it, making it very picturesque. We landed just below the Castle, and went with Charles [her half-brother] and the children in a carriage to the fort. There was a great crowd, but excellent order kept. We went to the battery, but had to mount steps to get to it. Wallace was confined there [Sir William Wallace, Scottish hero of the national rising in the late thirteenth century] and it was one of the last castles which held out for Mary Queen of Scots. From the battery there is a very extensive view of the Clyde and Dumbarton, and we ought to have been able to see Ben Lomond; but it was in mist.

Ninety years later when her great-grandson, King George VI, and Queen Elizabeth went there for the revived ceremony of handing over the keys of the castle to the reigning monarch the 'very extensive view' had been altered by the development of the burgh of Dunbarton and the establishment of the distillery built by the Canadian firm, Hiram Walker and Sons Ltd, the largest and most modern of that period in Europe.

However, when Queen Elizabeth and the Duke of Edinburgh attended a similar ceremony in 1953 the view of encroaching industrial development was almost obliterated by steady rain and a strong south-wester and the fortified rock must have seemed little changed from the days when the child bride Mary, Queen of Scots, waited impatiently to sail away to France.

DUNADD AND DUNSTAFFNAGE CASTLES

While King Ceretic ruled his kingdom of Strathclyde from Dunbarton, further north a small community of Scots from Antrim across the Irish Channel settled in the West Highlands and extended their kingdom of Dalriada to include Argyll, 'The Frontier of the Gael'. About AD 490 they established their first capital, Dunadd (the Fort of the Add), on an isolated rocky hill on the bank of the River Add where it meanders through the moss of Crinan.

The summit of the hill shows signs of having been strongly fortified while great stones and cairns on the moss around it indicate the many attempts to capture it.

The dauntless invaders spoke Gaelic, which would have been quite unintelligible to the Picts and Britons ruling others parts of the country, but from this language modern Irish and modern Scottish Gaelic evolved. The invaders were already partly Christians from Ireland where Patrick, a Briton, had attempted to spread the Gospel, even in pagan times.

The rulers of this small kingdom succeeded according to an Irish law which often assumed the form of an alternate succession from members of two families descended from a common ancestor. The first kings were Fergus Mor and Lorn, sons of Erc, and afterwards the succession alternated between the descendants of his two grandsons Gabran and Comgall and then Gabran's son Aedan. At the sacred inauguration of the Kings of Argyll they were required to place their foot in a footprint carved in the rock of Dunadd.

As the Dalriadic Kingdom pushed its frontiers north and eastwards, its first capital, Dunadd, was no longer ideally situated to administer to the extended realm and its importance declined.

It was superseded, it seems, by Dunstaffnage Castle (the Fort on the Point) on the Argyll coast, which the Dalriadic kings occupied. It commanded the principal route between central Scotland and a large portion of the western seaboard and had a safe anchorage.

A rocky hill in Argyll, 'the frontier of the Gael', where, *c.* AD 490, the Fortress of Dunadd, the first Scottish capital of the Kingdom of Dalriada, was established.

A footprint 11 inches long and 4½ inches wide carved in the rock at Dunadd, above the River Add.
In it Fergus the first Scottish king of Dalriada, clothed in white, set his foot at his inauguration, as did his
successors, symbolizing an oath to walk in the steps of their forefathers.

Its origins, like those of so many great Scottish castles, are shrouded in mystery (one theory is that the first castle on the site was built by a mythical King Ewin, who apparently reigned before the invasion of Britain by Julius Caesar). Later it must have been one of a series of strongholds erected along the Atlantic shore as bulwarks against Norse aggression and springboards for the conquests of the Isles. Its history is one of intrigue and bloodshed, sensed in the superb wild view from the battlements with forts and castles, woods, mountains and lochs gleaming in the distance.

King Robert the Bruce, born in the west and personally familiar with Argyll and the Isles, would never have doubted that a ruler of Scotland must command the western approaches and in 1309 he besieged and captured Dunstaffnage Castle. Normally it was his practice to demolish the castles he had conquered but in the case of Dunstaffnage he garrisoned it along with other castles on the western seaboard and made it over to his faithful supporter Arthur Campbell. His successor, David II, in the fourth year of his reign, dated a charter from there.

There were sieges and murder and bloodshed through the years of endless conflict and in 1490 King James IV seems to have twice visited the castle to pursue his policy of winning favour by personal contact with the wild chiefs of those parts. Never, because it had once been a royal castle, could it be given away, a fact established by Viscount Stair, 'Father of Scots law', in the seventeenth century in his *Institutes of the Law of Scotland*. It was decreed that even if a document purported to give a royal castle or palace away by royal grant or gift it could only resolve itself into an hereditary keepership. Thus Dunstaffnage still belongs to the Crown and the Duke of Argyll is its Hereditary Keeper.

It also, unlike many royal castles, has a Hereditary Captain because in the fifteenth century, the Earl of Argyll appointed an uncle to that position and his successors, on ceremonial occasions, wear a key over their lace jabot as insignia of office. A later Duke of Argyll, at the start of this century, tried to combine the two offices and took the case to court. He lost it however, because it was ruled that the hereditary duty of Captain could not be removed and the Captain

A carved slab from the second-century AD Antonine Wall, showing Roman cavalrymen.

today must still confirm his position by sleeping for three nights each year in a flat built in the ruins of the castle which was destroyed by a great fire in 1810.

On any one of those nights he might perhaps hear the ghost, a Glaistig or Elle maid, whose footsteps are as heavy as those of a jack-booted man. She is a female spirit who attached herself to the Campbell family when they lived there. Glaistigs were believed to associate themselves closely with the fortunes of families they adopted and announce, by cries of joy or wails of woe, the imminence of some happy or tragic event in the history of their family. They were not true fairies although they had many fairy traits including a love of green clothing, the ability to become invisible and the gift of being able to pass handicraft skills on to those they favoured.

Otherwise, the only visitors to the castle are the tourists and one or two fishermen who find the courtyard a convenient place for the peaceful occupation of mending their nets.

One persistent rumour surrounding Dunstaffnage is that the Stone of Destiny, now preserved in the Coronation Chair in Westminster Abbey, was kept there before it was transferred to Scone by Kenneth mac Alpin.

The remains of the fifteenth-century Dunstaffnage Castle.

SCONE PALACE

As we thus talked, our barge did sweetly pass
By Scone's fair palace, sometime abbey was;
Strange change, indeed! yet is it no new disguise
Both spiritual lands and men to temporise!
But palace fair, which doth so richly stand
With gardens, orchards, parks, on either hand.

From a seventeenth-century poem
by Henry Adamson

'The royal city of Scone', as the chroniclers described it more than a thousand years ago, is geographically and historically the very heart of a country of which it was once the capital. Today the only sign of former grandeur is its fairy-tale palace, a castellated Gothic-style building filled with treasures, home of the Earl of Mansfield whose branch of the Murray family have been Lords Scone since 1604. It dominates a great park, glimpsed through a mediaeval archway near the old market cross which once stood in the centre of the old city.

Just in front stands the dark tree-clad mound, Moot Hill, constructed in the Dark Ages, reputedly from earth brought from all parts of the realm. For when the Kings of Scotland were crowned at Scone and the Scottish chiefs and lairds came to swear allegiance, legend has it that before they left home they filled their boots with soil so that they could swear fealty to the new king standing on their own land. Afterwards they ceremoniously emptied their boots on the Moot Hill, or 'Every Man's Hill' or 'Boot Hill' as it also came to be known by the eighteenth century.

Other names for it were the 'Hill of Belief' or 'Hill of Credulity' as the meeting place of the earliest national councils ever recorded. From here too the High Kings of the mysterious Picts built up their mighty realm and in 710 their King Nectan 'embraced the customs of the Church of Rome'. Little is known about the Picts because their language died out but artistic symbolism is believed to show them as Painted Men, tattooed blue with marks of their rank and clan.

Royal succession was matrilineal, through the female line, and in pre-Christian times their princesses were allowed to mate with as many nobles as they liked, especially royal foreign ones. Queen Elizabeth reigns in Scotland today through her descent from Pictish princesses in an unbroken succession since at least AD 269 and probably longer.

'Scone of the High Shields' or 'Scone of the Melodious Shields', as it came to be known, was a very special place to the Picts. On arriving in the great hall the Celtic nobles would hand their battle-shields of thin beaten bronze to their shield bearers. Each shield gave out a slightly varying tone when struck as the shield bearer sounded it to announce his noble's arrival. The shields were then hung on the wall behind their owners, rather like name-cards, the High King's own shield being hung highest of all.

At such an assembly in Scone in the 800s, Kenneth mac Alpin, King of the Scots and son of a Pictish princess, united the Picts and Scots and became their first king, rumour has it by a blatant trick. He invited his rival, the Pictish king Drostan, and all his nobles to a banquet and after dining and wining them too well withdrew the bolts holding up the floorboards beneath them. The benches on which the Picts were sitting fell through, trapping the Picts up to their knees and, in the confusion, the Scots slaughtered them. In this way Kenneth mac Alpin's claim became the best and he declared himself King of the Picts and Scots.

The Kings of Scotland were inaugurated or 'enstoned' at Scone on the Stone of Destiny, a flat stone on top of the Moot Hill. The early kings, including Macbeth, were merely placed on the Stone and were not crowned or anointed. But in the year 1240 seven-year-old Alexander II was crowned there with a circlet of gold by the Bishop of St Andrews.

The Coronation Chair in Westminster Hall showing the
Stone of Scone beneath the seat.

The Stone itself has an obscure history: some see it as 'Jacob's pillow' on which he slept and dreamt of angels of God descending and ascending from heaven to earth and earth to heaven, or the stone the Belgic kings brought across the Channel from Antrim, while others believe it is an altar stone to some long-forgotten god. It was once claimed by the Scots to be the Stone of Destiny from Tara, brought with them from Ireland.

But that stone, the *Lia Fál*, is still in Tara and the Stone of Scone is of coarse-grained sandstone identical to the stone of the palace of Scone and the doorway of Dunstaffnage Castle from whereabouts it may also have come. It is 11 inches thick and measures $26\frac{1}{2}$ inches by $16\frac{1}{2}$ inches and is fitted with iron staples and rings at each end. Towards the centre back a small Latin cross is roughly cut.

The last king to be enstoned at Scone was John Balliol in 1292. Four years later Edward I of England defeated the Scots and carried the Stone of Scone off to Westminster Abbey to form part of the Coronation Chair. But with the token of Scottish humiliation went the ancient prophecy:

> Unless the fates are faithless grown,
> And Prophet's voice be vain,
> Where'er is found this sacred Stone,
> The Scottish race shall reign.

The prophecy was fulfilled in 1603 when James Stuart, son of Mary, Queen of Scots, and ancestor of the present Queen, became King of all Great Britain.

Only four times after that did the Coronation Stone leave Westminster Abbey: it went to Westminster Hall in 1652 for Cromwell's installation as Lord Protector; it was taken to safety during the two world wars and in 1951 it was temporarily abstracted by some enthusiastic young Scottish Nationalists in the reign of King George VI but was duly returned before the Coronation of the present Queen Elizabeth.

Meanwhile ten decisive parliaments were held at Scone, the capital of Scotland, between 1284 and 1401. Before the promulgation of any new law a great bell was rung and 'The Bell of Scone' became synonymous with the law of the land.

Sometimes Parliament was held simply to hear accusations of treason which were often settled in blood-stained trials by combat on a nearby marshy island: now the North Inch of Perth.

Without the Stone the Crown became the symbol of sovereignty and Scottish kings continued to be crowned at Scone, installed under hereditary right by the Earl of Fife, Chief of the premier clan of Scotland, the Clan MacDuff, to which also belonged the

Scone Palace from the south-west, the historic seat of the Earls of Mansfield
which was built between 1802 and 1812 by a site that has been, in turn, a place of ancient
tribal assembly and an abbey.

hereditary Abbot of Abernethy, ancestor of the Red Douglas and the Dukes of Hamilton. But in 1306, at the hurriedly arranged coronation of King Robert the Bruce, Scotland's saviour, the sixteen-year-old Earl of Fife was so under the power of England's Edward I that he was afraid to attend the ceremony. However, his twenty-year-old sister, Isabel, Countess of Buchan, had no such qualms and rode one of her husband's best horses at great speed to be there in time to place the gold coronet on Bruce's head at a specially arranged second coronation. For such 'mistaken patriotism' she was eventually to be inhumanly punished by being suspended in a cage from the walls of Berwick Castle by Edward I when he took her captive a few months later.

In 1329 Bruce's successor, his ten-year-old son David II, was the first King of the Scots to be anointed with sacred oil at his coronation at Scone. This ritual dates from pre-Christian times in Ancient Egypt when the new Pharoahs were anointed as if they were being embalmed or mummified, to seal within them a lucky part of the Divine Spirit on behalf of all their people.

The last coronation of a King of the Scots was the crowning of King Charles II at Scone in 1651, a time of great peril for Scotland. The English under Cromwell had invaded the country and beaten the Scots soundly at Dunbar. The Abbey of Scone, on the site of a mediaeval monastery, had been burned down by a maddened mob at the Reformation but the coronation was held in the church on the Moot Hill, built twenty-five years before. It was destined to be moved, stone by stone, to another site when the parish of New Scone was founded.

Meanwhile the last coronation at Scone was a splendid affair. The young King stayed the night at 'the

Allegorical engraving of Charles II (right) being crowned by the Marquis of Argyll at Scone in 1651. In the foreground he is shown being girded for war by Ireland while Scotland hands him a pistol labelled 'Revenge' and Douglas, in puritan garb, preaches on the text 'Let us swallow them up alive'.

The 1st Marquis of Argyll, Archibald Campbell.

House of Scone', which forms the main structure of the present-day palace. On New Year's Day 1651 he walked into the tapestry-bedecked church under a canopy carried by six eldest sons of earls, watched by the peers in state robes of crimson velvet or scarlet cloth according to their rank. A few heads nodded during a sermon by the Moderator of the General Assembly which lasted for an hour and a half. Afterwards the Lord Lyon King of Arms recited the monarch's genealogy sonorously and perhaps tediously back to Fergus, King of Scots in 490.

The Marquis of Argyll—descendant in the female line of the Clan MacDuff—crowned the King. Some believed that, ironically, he was the man who had betrayed the late King to the English Roundheads. Ten years later, however, when he himself was condemned to death for treason and refused a royal pardon he was heard to reflect: 'I had the honour to set

The Long Gallery at Scone, 168 feet in length, the floor inset with bog oak from the River Tay, survives from the Palace of 1580. Here, Queen Victoria was given a curling lesson.

the crown upon the King's head and now he hastens me to a better crown than his own.' Such swash-buckling courage, interlaced with intrigue and conspiracy, was the hallmark of the antecedents of the great Scottish families who still live in the fine castles and palaces of their country.

Through the years Scone Palace, restored and refurbished by a succession of distinguished owners, has entertained royalty down to the present day. Down the great gallery, nearly one-tenth of a mile long, the exiled Old Chevalier, James Stuart, once walked and, thirty years later, Bonnie Prince Charlie. In those days murals showing James VI of Scotland hunting with his courtiers covered the walls, but by the eighteenth century they were considered naive and were erased in favour of quiet Gothic grandeur.

There in 1842 Queen Victoria was given a curling lesson on the beautifully inlaid polished wood floor

The Earl and Countess of Mansfield. Lord Mansfield is wearing one of the two Murray tartans; the other is predominately green. They have two sons, Alexander, Viscount Stormont, and James Murray and a daughter, Lady Georgina Murray.

A bedroom at Scone Palace.

because it was not the time of year for ice. There in 1967 the present Queen Elizabeth planted a tree on the terrace overlooking lawns and park sweeping down to the River Tay.

It is not surprising to hear tales of ghosts who walk through the palace's 125 rooms, 90 of them bedrooms. The present owner, the 8th Earl of Mansfield, lives there with his wife and three children and regards it as a family home, not only a show-case for pictures by Van Dyke and Reynolds, for Chinese Chippendale and Adam furniture, old French clocks, Sèvres and Meissen porcelain and other splendid treasures.

These show-pieces are moved from room to room in the winter when the family occupy the whole palace but in the summer, when the palace is open to the public, they are restored to their appointed places and the family living accommodation is condensed into a portion of the building. But at any time of year the Countess of Mansfield accepts ghostly apparitions quite philosophically. She writes:

the distant sounds of children chattering and dogs scampering blend with other, stranger sounds. People from earlier centuries seem to continue their own ploys, oblivious of us.

I will mention but one in-house ghost. He is known as the 'Boring Walker'. He is heard but not seen, and walks down the south passage. When we walk down it, all the floorboards squeak and groan noisily; when he walks down it, which he does very frequently (always going east to west), there is the unmistakable regular pad of his feet—but on a *stone floor*! No squeaking floorboards! Is he a guard, a night-watchman, an ancient insomniac? Sadly, we cannot tell. I used to leap out of bed and peer nervously round the bedroom door but the noise of footsteps always continued unchecked, receding down the passage. He is typical of people from the past at Scone—heard but not seen!

EDINBURGH CASTLE

Edina; Scotia's darling seat,
All hail thy palaces and tow'rs,
Where once beneath a monarch's feet
Sat Legislation's sov'reign pow'rs!
From marking widely-scatter'd flow'rs,
As on the banks of Ayr I stray'd,
And singing lone with the ling'ring hours,
I shelter in thy honour'd shade.

From Robert Burns' *Address to Edinburgh*

Edinburgh Castle at sunset.

33

The history of Edinburgh Castle, a tale of siege and counter-siege, is almost the history of Scotland. From its beginnings as a fortress used by the early Scottish kings, its position as a strategic bastion near the frontier increased its importance and ensured its ever-growing significance as their territory extended from the Forth to the Tweed. The fortress, in turn, became a castle, a palace, a treasury, the home of the nation's records. It was a place of refuge for sovereigns during their minorities, a prison for their enemies, the last post of defence for lost causes.

Since the dawn of civilization there has been a fortification on the massive rock on the Firth of Forth over the North Sea. Successive alterations on the rock surface have obliterated any trace of the early ones, even of a castle rebuilt in AD 626 by Edwin, the Northumbrian King to whom the name of Edinburgh is sometimes attributed. It is also possible that it was already called Caer Eidyn by King Clinog Eitin, son of Cinbelin ('King Cymbeline') from whose sister our present Royal Family descends, when the Britons still held the country a century earlier. A reminder of Arthurian times when the rock was still British is Arthur's Seat in the Queen's Park at Edinburgh.

Edinburgh Castle was subsequently used as a fortress by Scottish kings including Malcolm III (Malcolm Canmore—Gaelic, *Ceann Mor*: 'Bighead'), son of Macbeth's victim Duncan. On Malcolm's death in battle in 1093 it was besieged by his brother Donald Ban (Gaelic, 'the Fair') who tried to get possession of Malcolm's son the young King Edgar ('the Peaceable'). Donald Ban held the throne for two short periods, before being blinded by his successor, but ten years and three kings later (the second king being his young nephew Edgar), the tower of the castle became a royal dwelling for the third of the kings, Edgar's brother, Alexander I ('the Fierce'). In 1124 he, in turn, was succeeded by another brother, David I, under whom it continued as a royal residence.

From then on it was the principal royal fortress in Scotland and the national records and the royal regalia were deposited there. But it was much coveted and was besieged and taken by the then Bruce in 1291 and frequently changed hands during the War of Independence. Eventually, it was completely demolished by King Robert the Bruce in line with his usual policy of leaving no place of strength standing which might prove useful to his enemies.

Edinburgh Castle on its rock which was formed by the core of an extinct volcano.

St Margaret's chapel, the only building to survive the destruction of the royal fortress by King Robert the Bruce. The chapel was built by Malcolm III's queen, Margaret, on the summit of the rock.

It was constructed mainly of timber and burnt easily. The only building to escape destruction was the beautiful little stone chapel on the highest point of the rock erected by Malcolm III's saintly queen, Margaret, and modified by her son, David I. The pious Queen Margaret virtually secluded herself in the tiny romanesque chapel to pursue her religious ideals. She died there after hearing of the death of her husband and eldest son at the Battle of Alnwick fighting the English

in 1093 and her body was smuggled from the little chapel by her other sons, to the safety of Dunfermline Abbey for burial before the castle was besieged by her brother-in-law Donald Ban.

Paradoxically, Queen Margaret led the country in secular as well as religious developments. She instigated cleanliness as part of knightly courtesy and introduced material luxuries into the court, such as gilded vessels at table, garments of vivid colours with splendid ornaments to adorn them and silk hangings to decorate the palace walls. The influence of these innovations ultimately benefited a primitive people whose houses and crude hearths had, until then, rarely attained even an elementary standard of cleanliness. Under her influence the Court moved closer to the rest of Christendom.

There's no lass in Scotland
Compared to our sweet Margaret

they sang, down the centuries, of the Queen who became Saint Margaret.

For the next two and a half centuries Edinburgh Castle changed hands many times and sheltered Scottish and English kings. But not until David II returned from long captivity in England after the battle of Nevill's Cross and in 1356 commenced rebuilding, did it begin to assume its present form.

Many tragedies were enacted there but none was more dramatic than the 'Black Dinner' of 1440. It was given for the proud sixteen-year-old William, Earl of Douglas, and his brother David, cousins to the young King James II who were considered to be a 'danger to the realm'. Despite warnings from their followers they attended the banquet in their honour and towards the end of the meal a black bull's head on a dish was borne high into the hall. It was the sign of the death of an enemy chief. The brothers recognized its significance and, with their supporters, vainly tried to escape. They were dragged outside; a hasty mock trial was held and they were beheaded despite a plea for mercy from the little king.

Such were the vicissitudes of royal accession that, in turn, James III was imprisoned there for three months in 1466 and thirteen years later he chose it as a prison for his younger brother Alexander, Duke of Albany, on

Malcolm III and his saintly queen, Margaret, from an early armorial manuscript.

An armorial seal of the 6th Earl of Douglas
who, with his brother, was beheaded after the 'Black Dinner'.
An engraving from the Douglas Book, 1885.

The statue of Robert the Bruce which embellishes one side of
the entrance to the gatehouse of Edinburgh Castle.

account of his frequent intrigues with England and his popularity in Scotland. Albany escaped, however, by means of ropes and secret instructions smuggled into the castle in barrels of wine he was allowed to buy from a French trader that appeared off-shore. He made the Captain of the castle and his men drunk on the wine; he and his boy killed the guard, escaped by means of the ropes and boarded the trader for France.

In the meantime successive kings had improved the royal accommodation but any additions that survive mainly date from the reign of James IV. Chief among them are the fortifications and the massive Great Hall, appropriate to the most important castle in the kingdom, by that time, and also the seat of government.

The palace was modified again for Mary, Queen of Scots, and her second husband, the beautiful Henry, Lord Darnley, created King Consort, four years her junior. Above a doorway is the date of their marriage, 1566, with the initials MAH (Mary and Henry), probably put there as a memorial by their son James VI. The marriage took place after Mary had returned, a widow, from France following the death of King Francis II, but it proved disastrous. Darnley, like his bride, had Tudor royal blood and was in line of succession to the English throne so Queen Elizabeth had made fruitless attempts to veto the marriage.

The outcome of Darnley's aspirations to receive the 'Crown Matrimonial' as well as being already 'King Henry' as Consort and to be co-ruler with Mary, resulted in the savage murder of Mary's secretary Riccio in Holyroodhouse, three months before Mary's first child, James, was born. The terrible tragedy aroused Mary's suspicions that her own and her unborn child's death were also intended. She moved to Edinburgh Castle, away from the scene of terror, and at the beginning of June began to make final preparations for the birth of her child.

James Stuart was born on 19 June, 1566, in a small cramped room in the south-east corner of the castle which can be seen today.

'Such a very, very, small room, with an old prayer written on the wall,' wrote Queen Victoria on her visit in 1842. Her ancestress had chosen blue taffeta and fine silk for the lying-in bed, ten ells of holland for the cradle and had supplied the midwife with a length of

The Edinburgh Tattoo which has taken place annually on the Castle Esplanade since 1947
when it was staged to coincide with the first Edinburgh International Festival.

special black velvet for a dress for the important occasion.

It was a difficult birth despite the efforts of Margaret, Lady Reres, who lay in bed trying to share the pains by witchcraft. Eventually, the baby was born with a fine caul stretched over his face—indicating, according to the old fisherman's lore, that he would never be drowned at sea. The mother's immediate reaction was

that she had been so badly handled she wished she had never been married; a sentiment to which her loss of feeling for Darnley may also have contributed.

A story goes that she was so anxious to have her son baptized in the old Faith that she lowered him in a basket from a window to retainers waiting to carry him to Stirling.

Between the time of her son's birth and Mary's next

visit to Edinburgh Castle came the murder of Darnley and her abduction by the Earl of Bothwell, the prime mover in an explosion in which the King Consort Darnley was strangled while escaping from the explosion. On 6 May, 1567, the day before Bothwell's divorce, the lovers rode up to the castle, he leading her horse by its bridle, she his captive. She stayed there for the next five days until their marriage in Holyroodhouse. A few weeks later Bothwell was in prison in Denmark and Mary, prior to her imprisonment in Lochleven Castle, was back in Edinburgh Castle to prepare for her abdication in favour of her son James VI.

From then on Edinburgh Castle remained a fortress, occasionally visited by the Kings of Scotland. During the reign of James VI there was a great deal of rebuilding. The room where he was born was redecorated and two men were hired to load and fire a salute to greet him. But they were scarcely used for his visits were fleeting and occasional.

His son, Charles I, spent the night before his coronation there and dined in the great banqueting hall constructed on the highest point of the rock—no mean engineering feat in those days. Its elaborate timber hammer-beam roof with carved human and animal masks at the end of each beam and with stone corbels portraying the symbols of Scotland including the fleur-de-lis, the thistle and a cherub's head, was just as it is today.

During the Jacobite Rising of 1745, Edinburgh Castle held out for King George II when the rest of the city was occupied for Bonnie Prince Charlie, one of whose officers stuck his dirk in the castle door.

Any additions made from that time were not designed to strengthen the castle's fortification but to confirm a new awareness of its historical importance. In 1846 St Margaret's Chapel was rediscovered and restored to its original twelfth-century form while the vaulted chamber in which the Scottish regalia known as 'The Honours of Scotland', consisting of the Crown, the Sceptre and the Sword, were stored and where they were walled up after the Act of Union of 1717, was reopened and the regalia placed on display.

Today Edinburgh Castle, still garrisoned, still marks the time of day by a gunfire salute across the city at 1300 hours. It remains a fascinating conglomeration of battlements and batteries, towers and gatehouses, prisons and a palace, showing how, down the ages, succeeding generations left their mark. This is never more apparent than at the annual tattoo on the esplanade when, as the light fades, the drums roll and to a barrage of gunfire the great castle slowly comes to light, gaunt and romantic, to dominate Scotland's capital.

STIRLING CASTLE

> The mighty Stirling Castle, high up on a rock which is like a gigantic figure of stone rising from the flat plains, dominates the town. . . . There is an absolutely wonderful view from the Castle out across the historically famous plains where the battle was fought between Edward II and Robert Bruce.
>
> Hans Christian Andersen, 1847

The Battle of Bannockburn of 1314, referred to by Hans Christian Andersen, is just one of many occasions when Scotland's gateway to the Highlands from the Lowlands changed hands. To look down from Stirling Castle, as that great story-teller did, and see the silvery River Forth where it is no longer

'Grey Stirling' being recaptured from the English by the Scots at the Battle of Bannockburn
where Edward II's vast feudal force was met and routed by Robert the Bruce in 1314.
From a fifteenth-century manuscript.

'The mighty Stirling, high up on a rock . . . like a gigantic figure of stone rising from the flat plains'
– Hans Christian Andersen in 1847.

navigable and where the first bridge crossed it in ancient time, is once again to be able to envisage history.

The rugged rock, towering 250 feet above the plains, attracted Roman soldiers in AD 81, but not until the twelfth century is the castle mentioned when Alexander I erected a chapel there. He died at his castle in 1124 but his brother, David I, continued the habit of often staying there.

It was a favourite resort of kings and in the reign of Alexander II extensive pleasure grounds were planned: the Sheriff was paid to feed the doves in winter; a foxhunter was engaged to destroy vermin and strong wooden palings were to be erected to enclose the parkland. But these leisure plans were interrupted by the fear that King Haakon of Norway might invade Stirling from the west and its garrison was strength-

ened. In the brief space of half a century during the Wars of Independence it changed hands seven times.

Edward I reckoned it was the strongest castle in Scotland, although it was mainly constructed of timber and, during the country's struggle for independence, he made a determined attempt to capture it. However, a garrison reduced to twenty-eight men withstood, for three months, the stones hurled at it from English catapults. Edward then ordered lead to be stripped from the roofs of the Cathedrals of Dunblane, St Andrews and Dunfermline Abbey to make heavier missiles to launch at the defenders. Nevertheless, the garrison's ultimate surrender was due to starvation rather than to the success of the missiles. For ten years the castle remained a symbol of English authority but was retaken by the Scots after the Battle of Bannockburn and from then on changed hands several times.

Edward I who seized 'the strongest castle in Scotland' and held it for ten years as a symbol of English authority
until his defeat at the Battle of Bannockburn, shown paying homage to the King of France.
From a fifteenth-century French manuscript.

Stirling, standing bleak and forbidding above Bannockburn, was within sophisticated and elegant. It was first designated a royal residence after the accession of the Stewarts. As an infant James II was hidden in a wooden chest and smuggled by his mother from Edinburgh Castle to Stirling Castle in 1439 to be warded there for a time in accordance with the habit of fostering out royal children to people of lesser rank—particularly in time of war.

The Stewart kings of Scotland were great builders and much building went on in the time of James II. There in 1452 was enacted the second Douglas tragedy of his reign. He heard rumours of a bond between the new Earl of Douglas and two other earls against him and summoned Douglas, under royal safe conduct, to attend him on the night of 22 February. After supper he taxed Douglas and charged him to break the bond. Douglas refused and in a moment of unpremeditated rage the King lunged at his throat with a knife and killed him.

On St Patrick's day, the murdered man's brother Hugh Douglas, Earl of Ormond, arrived at Stirling with six hundred men and denounced the King and his supporters by fixing their names to a board attached to a horse's tail and dragging it through the mud of the town. They then burnt and spoiled the borough. But the King had already left and in June he was exonerated of the murder by Parliament.

King James III of Scotland, who was born at Stirling, and his wife Margaret of Denmark whose father pledged Orkney and Shetland as a surrogate dowry on her marriage in 1469. From an early manuscript.

James III was born at Stirling Castle and it remained his favourite residence until his tragic death after the battle of Sauchieburn against an army of rebels nominally led by his eldest son. A story goes that after his defeat, his grey horse bolted and threw him and he sought refuge in a miller's house. He was so badly hurt that he asked for a priest and the miller's wife ran to find

one. A pursuer, hearing the King wanted absolution, masqueraded as a priest, was taken to the King and plunged a knife into his heart.

James IV could never disassociate himself from the idea that he was responsible for his father's murder and, until the day of his death, he wore an iron chain round his body as a reminder of his crime. He built a palace at Stirling and perhaps remorse frequently motivated him to go there. It is recorded—

> He daylie passit to the Chapell Royall . . . ewer sade and dollorous in his mynd for the deid of his father; [as a sign of repentance he] gart mak ane belt of irone and wore it dailie about him and eiket added to it everie zeir yewr during his lyfetyme certain once wyght ounce weight—as he thocht goode.

A less gloomy reason for his visits to Stirling was to indulge his passion for hunting. Deer and boar roamed the neighbourhood and wild white cattle, and sometimes as many as 300 huntsmen were accommodated in tents in the forest. In the castle grounds cranes and peacocks roamed, tournaments and jousts were held and the 'King's Knot', one of the earliest ornamental gardens in Scotland, was developed.

Revels were held, as was customary in many great houses and boroughs where an Abbot of Unreason was appointed annually to rule the revels during the six weeks between Christmastide and Candlemas. Midsummer brought strolling players to the court with minstrels, singers, acrobats and morris dancers from England and the Continent. There was hawking and fishing and the King encouraged the practice of alchemy there.

At this time when the Arthurian legend was popular Stirling became known romantically as Snowdoun. After this, one of the Scottish Royal Officers of Arms is still sometimes called Snowdoun Herald.

It was one of the most extravagant and picturesque periods in the history of the castle but the King also managed to pursue his complicated foreign policy. In 1495 he received, with regal splendour, a claimant to the English throne, 'Perkin Warbeck' masquerading as Prince Richard of England. The imposter almost

IACOBVS · 4 · D · GRATIA
REX · SCOTORVM

James IV, whose marriage to Margaret Tudor brought the succession of the English throne
to the House of Stuart.

involved James in war with the unwilling Henry VII. Fortunately this was averted for eventually James was to marry Henry's daughter Margaret Tudor, for political if not for romantic reasons.

Until his marriage in 1503, however, King James's mistresses often lived at Stirling Castle. Janet Kennedy, Lady Bothwell, took up residence there in 1499 and a year later a son named James, and created Earl of Moray, was born there. When he was three years old he was joined by a half-sister, the King's daughter by Margaret Drummond, known as 'the Diamond of Delight'.

Ten years after his marriage to Margaret Tudor, James was killed at the Battle of Flodden, attempting to invade England in support of France against Henry VIII. His year-old son, James V, was crowned at the Chapel Royal, Stirling.

Like his father the young King spent much time in the castle and when he was twelve he was warded there under the care of the Keeper, Lord Erskine. Later he extended the palace and often stayed there with his second wife, Mary of Guise, after the death of his first wife, Madeleine, also a French princess, who had died a few months after their marriage.

James V was particularly sympathetic towards his poorer subjects and often wandered about Stirling in disguise to study their conditions. But his reign too ended tragically and, after the loss of two sons in infancy, he died at Falkland Palace a week after the birth of his daughter, Mary, at Linlithgow.

When the infant Mary, Queen of Scots, was seven months old she and her mother were taken to Stirling because it was considered a suitable place to guard her. On 9 September, 1542 at nine months old she was crowned in the chapel with the minimum amount of ceremony and, apart from one short interval, lived there until she was five and went to Dunbarton where the arrangements were made for her marriage to the French Dauphin.

Fourteen years later she returned for a two-day stay during the first of her triumphant progresses through her kingdom but she had a lucky escape when a naked candle set fire to her bed curtains while she slept.

There were occasional visits and then a significant one in December 1567 when her eight-week-old son,

Margaret Tudor, daughter of Henry VII of England and wife of James IV of Scotland.

Prince James, was taken to Stirling from Edinburgh to be fostered in comparative safety by the Erskine family. The Queen made detailed preparations for his nursery: the buckets were of fine gold and silver, his room hung with tapestries and there were feather pillows in his blue plaid cradle. His baptism in the chapel when he was six months old more than compensated in grandeur for the austerity of his mother's coronation there. No expense was spared and the Queen paid for the nobles' garments so that they presented a splendid sight: '. . . some in cloth of silver, some in cloth of gold, some in cloth of tissue, every man rather above than under his degree.'

Costly gifts from the dignitaries and royalty of England and France included a magnificent gold font weighing two stone, from his godmother, Queen Elizabeth. The baby prince was christened from it according to the Catholic rite, except that his mother refused to allow the priest to spit into his mouth as was the custom in those days. After the ceremony, of which it was reported that the Queen 'did inhibit the use of spittle', there was supper followed by music and dancing and, two days later a banquet and a firework display. From all these rejoicings the baby's father, Darnley, was conspicuously absent although he was staying in the castle at the time.

A few months later, after the murder of Darnley, the King Consort, Mary's subsequent marriage to Bothwell and her abdication in July 1567, her son was crowned James VI in the parish kirk of Stirling, with the lovely Crown of Scotland, the oldest of all crowns still in use. Afterwards he was taken back to the castle where he was to spend much of his youth, surviving murderous intrigue, drama and dispute, plot and counterplot as Catholic and Calvinist nobles battled against each other with him as the prize.

At five years old he attended a Parliament held there, wearing gorgeous robes and a brand new crown. As he entered the unfamiliar building he asked what place this was and was told that it was a Parliament. While his paternal grandfather, the Earl of Lennox, the Regent, was making a speech the child's eyes noticed a gap in the roof:

'I think there's a hole in this Parliament,' he remarked solemnly, a comment that was deemed prophetic when five days later his grandfather was murdered before his eyes.

He proved one of the most intelligent of the Stuarts and his education was formidable: when he was seven a typical day started with prayers and a study of Greek and the New Testament before breakfast in his schoolroom on the south-east side of the palace. There was Latin until lunchtime and then composition, mathematics and science of the constitution of the world, including geography, astronomy, logic and rhetoric.

An astonished visitor at that time was invited to choose any chapter from the Latin Bible which James then translated into French and from French into English. Perhaps the fact that he caught smallpox when he was seven, during a local epidemic, gave him a short respite from his studies. He survived the illness along with other threats to his life.

King James VI's daughter, Elisabeth of Bohemia, 'the Winter Queen'. Her daughter, Sophia, married the Elector of Hanover. As the heir of the only Protestant line descended from the joint monarchy, she introduced the Protestant Hanoverian succession into the Royal Family of Great Britain.

In June 1583 at the age of seventeen, James became legally of age to assume the full government of Scotland and a year later he convened Parliament in Stirling Castle.

At twenty-three he married the fourteen-year-old Anne of Denmark and the birth of their first son, Prince Frederick Henry, at Stirling meant another elaborate baptism in the reconstructed Chapel Royal, to impress foreign visitors with the dignity and splendour of the Scottish court. Like his father, grandmother and great-grandfather, the young Prince Henry was fostered there under the guardianship of the Keeper of the Castle, the then John Erskine, Earl of Mar.

But the establishment of James VI of Scotland on the English throne ended the story of Stirling Castle as a royal residence, although John Erskine, Earl of Mar and Kellie is still its Hereditary Keeper on behalf of the

Queen. There were occasional royal visits: James returned for a few hours during a vain attempt to fulfil his promise to return to his native country every three years; Charles I spent two nights there and his son, Charles II, also paid a brief visit. But by then Stirling Castle and Palace, whose exterior shows probably the earliest example of renaissance work in Scotland, had reverted to its role, as in the Middle Ages, of a strategically important military stronghold and garrison, commemorated in Hanoverian times by Robert Burns, the patriotic Scottish poet in his verse 'On Stirling':

> Here Stuarts once in glory reign'd
> And laws for Scotland's weal ordain'd;
> But now unroof'd their palace stands,
> Their sceptre's sway'd by other hands;
> The injured Stuart line is gone,
> A race outlandish fills their throne.
> An idiot race to honour lost,
> Who knows them best, despise the most.

DUNFERMLINE PALACE

> The king sits in Dunferling toune,
> Drinking the blude-reid wine;
>   'O whar will I get a guid sailor,
> To sail this schip of mine?'

From the old Scottish
Ballad of Sir Patrick Spens

The ancient Scots ballad is said to have commemorated the 1281 expedition to take Margaret, the daughter of Alexander III, across the sea to marry Erik II of Norway. If so it undoubtedly signifies a tragic time in the history of Royal Scotland for two years later the young wife died giving birth to her daughter Margaret (the Maid of Norway). Two years after that her widowed father, King Alexander, who had already lost his two other children, married the beautiful Yolande, daughter of the French Count of Dreux, and was riding home to her from Edinburgh to Kinghorn on a tempestuous night when his horse stumbled and he was thrown over a cliff to his death. He was forty-five and had been married for five months.

It was the end of a mini-Golden Age of prosperity in Scotland and a Scottish poet lamented:

> When Alexander aur King was dede
> That Scotland held in love and le,
> Away was sonse of ale and breid
> Of wine and wax, of game and glee.

Alexander's three-year-old granddaughter became Queen of Scotland and by the time she was six Edward I had arranged a marriage between her and his son and heir. A year later she died from seasickness on a voyage home from Norway. With her died the house of Canmore.

There were thirteen candidates for the Scottish throne and Edward I, after persuading the competitors to acknowledge him as overlord of Scotland, was asked to decide the issue. He chose John Balliol.

Previously, for more than 200 years, Dunfermline had been the seat of kings, since Malcolm Canmore, Duncan's son, returned from exile in England with an army to overthrow his father's slayer, Macbeth, and claim the throne.

In Dunfermline he built a tower fortress on a 'hill by a winding stream', a site which gave the town its name but where only a circle of stones laid there in the eleventh century, remains to mark the spot. Margaret, his pious Saxon Queen, lived there and brought about the building of the country's first Catholic abbey

The inauguration of Alexander III in 1249
with the old Highland bard hailing the new king in Gaelic with the words *Benach de Re Albane Alex mac-Alex*
and reciting the genealogy of this French-speaking, Anglicized king back to Fergus I.
From a fifteenth-century manuscript of Fordun's *Scotichronicon*.

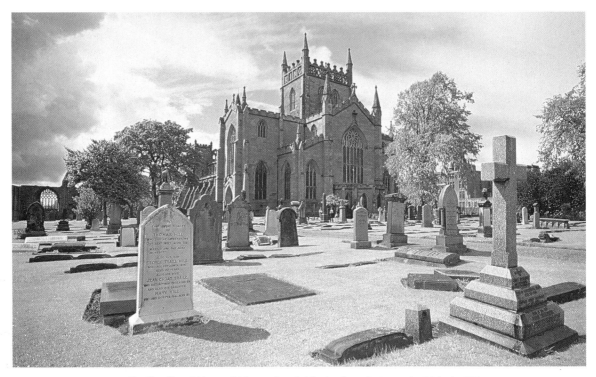

Dunfermline Abbey, which was founded in the eleventh century by Malcolm III.

church which became the wealthiest in the kingdom. It was a chief residence of her son Alexander I.

King Edward I spent part of the winter of 1303 in Dunfermline Abbey and when he left, he set fire to it and completely destroyed the buildings which had sheltered him and his army.

Afterwards Robert the Bruce built a royal palace to replace the tower fortress, restored the abbey and Dunfermline became the religious centre of Scotland. His son and successor was born there in 1323 and so were David II, James I and Charles I. Nearby are buried seven kings, four queens, five princes and two princesses.

Robert the Bruce is buried in the abbey beneath 'the fair tomb' which he ordered to be made in Paris; but his heart is interred in Melrose Abbey. It happened because the hero-king had always wished to take part in a crusade to fight the 'Saracens' in the Holy Land and on his death-bed he asked to have his heart taken from his body, embalmed and carried to the Holy Sepulchre by a warrior prepared to do battle with God's enemies.

The seal of King Robert the Bruce.

Robert the Bruce's 'fair tomb' which was made in Paris.
The King's body, without his heart, is interred in Dunfermline Abbey.
His heart lies in Melrose Abbey in Roxburghshire.

ABOVE: James, 4th Earl of Morton,
Regent for the young James VI.
Portrait attributed to Arnold van Brounckhorst, *c.* 1575.

LEFT: Anne of Denmark,
wife of James VI, in hunting costume.
Portrait by Belcamp after van Somer.

The honour was entrusted to his great friend Sir James Douglas, but on his way to Jerusalem via Spain, he was killed in a battle against the Moors near Granada. His bones and the heart of Robert the Bruce were taken back to Scotland for burial.

For the next three centuries Dunfermline fell from favour as a royal residence until James VI married the beautiful golden-haired Anne of Denmark and gave the town to his bride as a belated wedding present. She built a royal residence called 'The Queen's House' or 'Anne of Denmark's Building', now demolished.

There, most of her seven children were born but only three survived infancy. Among the survivors was her eldest daughter, Elisabeth, who became the famous 'Winter Queen' through her marriage to Frederick who for one winter was King of Bohemia. She had

thirteen children and the youngest daughter, Sophia of the Rhine, married the Elector of Hanover and introduced the Hanoverian succession from which stems Britain's Royal Family today. This came about with the death of James VI's great-great-grandson the Duke of Gloucester at the age of eleven, when the nearest Protestant heir descended from the joint monarchy, recognized by the English Parliament's Act of Settlement of 1701, was Sophia. Thirteen years later Queen Anne died leaving no surviving children and Sophia's son, great-grandson of James VI, was crowned George I.

Meanwhile, Dunfermline's long reign as a home of royalty had come to an end in 1603 when James VI of Scotland became James I of England. The French alphabet contains no 'w' and the Lennox branch of the family, so prominent in France, had altered the spelling of the surname Stewart (derived from the Great Steward of Scotland) and thus the House of Stuart was founded.

One more act of regal drama remained to be enacted at Dunfermline. There, in 1643, the Roundhead commissioners accepted that preposterous undertaking, the Solemn League and Covenant; a promise to impose a uniformity of doctrine, government and religion on the Church of Scotland, England and Ireland, through which English parliamentarians hoped to gain military assistance against King Charles I. Eventually the King was forced under duress to accept it.

In undertaking to establish Presbyterianism in England Charles II declared he was 'deeply humbled and afflicted in spirit before God, because of his father's opposition to the work of God, and to the Solemn League and Covenant, and for the idolatry of his mother'. From that day in Scotland when Charles had to malign the name of his father for his Protestant belief and his mother for her Catholic fervour, the humiliated and proud king is said to have regretted that he had ever been born.

Strangely appropriate, when the English writer Daniel Defoe visited Dunfermline Palace towards the end of the century he found there 'the full perfection of decay'.

LINLITHGOW PALACE

Of all the palaces so fair,
Built for the royal dwelling,
In Scotland far beyond compare,
Linlithgow is excelling;

From *Marmion* by
Sir Walter Scott

The palace in West Lothian, on the shores of Linlithgow Loch, midway between Stirling and Edinburgh, has been a favourite home of Scottish kings and queens since David I decreed Linlithgow town 'a Royal domaine with a residence and a church dedicated to St Michael'. In those times the Kings of Scotland had several houses to visit; partly to supervise the administration of the Crown estates and the neighbouring districts, partly to collect their rents (usually paid in kind) and partly for health reasons, for the primitive sanitary arrangements caused a residence to become unpleasant and unwholesome after a prolonged stay by a large household.

King David I's 'residence', situated in rich lowland country, represented one of the Crown's most profitable lordships. It was a manor house made of wood and, during the Wars of Independence, King Edward I of England often stayed there and fortified the place to use as an operational base for the siege of Stirling Castle.

It changed hands several times and in 1313 was recaptured for the Scots by a neat trick played by William Bunnock, a local farmer who often delivered hay for the use of the garrison. One day in late summer he concealed eight men under the hay in his wagon while a larger party lay in hiding nearby. Bunnock walked beside the wagon drawn by oxen to the castle; the drawbridge was lowered and the portcullis raised to admit him. He halted the wagon under it and at his pre-arranged signal 'Thief! ca' all! ca' all!' the servant leading the oxen cut the drawbridge ropes with a hatchet carried under his belt; Bunnock killed the porter; the eight men leapt from under the hay and attacked the guard and, with the help of those hidden nearby, captured the garrison. Bunnock was 'rewardit

Linlithgow Palace, on the shores of the loch, midway between Stirling and Edinburgh.

worthily', but the buildings were demolished by order of King Robert the Bruce.

Thirty years later King David II rebuilt the manor house and spent much time there as, in their turn, did Robert II and Robert III and the latter held a Parliament in the town. However, a quarter of a century afterwards the manor and part of the church were destroyed by fire.

Rebuilding was started a year later by James I, the accomplished poet-monarch who intended to turn the manor house into a palace. Building started on his return from captivity in England where he had grown up after being kidnapped at the age of twelve, on his way to France and safety. However, while in captivity, first under Henry IV in London and then under Henry V at Windsor, he became familiar with the work of Chaucer. He also fell in love with an English noblewoman, Lady Joan Beaufort, whom he eventually married. This romantic period of his life is reflected in his love poem *The Kingis Quair* (The King's Book).

The poem is a curious mixture of Scots and Chaucerian English. It has great charm and freshness of imagery and shows the influence of Chaucer's *Knight's Tale* and *Troylus and Criseyde* in such a verse as:

Gif ye a goddess be, and that ye like
To do me payne, I may it nocht astert;
Gif ye be wardly wight, that dooth me sike,
Why lest God make yow so, my derrest hert,
To do a sely prisoner thus smert,
That luvis you all, and wote of nocht but wo?
And therefore, merci swete! Sit it is so.*

James III, when he was fourteen, was captured at Linlithgow and imprisoned in Edinburgh Castle but later he and in turn James IV continued the improvements to Linlithgow Palace. In the latter's reign preparations for his many visits meant transporting plate for the royal table and also cords, hooks, rods and rings to fix French and Flemish tapestries to the bare walls for, apart from timber beds and trestle tables and forms, there were few permanent furnishings in the royal palaces.

At Linlithgow the conscientious James IV could

A surviving doorway to the palace, which dates from the reign of David I and was rebuilt by James I. Much of this magnificent building was destroyed by fire in 1746 and is now in ruins.

relax from the cares of government. He practised archery, played bowls and went hunting and hawking. In the evenings he played dice and cards and there was dancing and entertainments by the town choir or groups of travelling players. The royal table was provisioned with eels, pike and perch from Linlithgow Loch where the King often sailed his skin coracle.

In 1504 the chambers were carpeted with fresh rushes 'against the coming of the Queen'. Margaret Tudor, the fifteen-year-old daughter of Henry VII of England, arrived there after visiting the main towns of Scotland and remained there for most of her life. There her son James V was born and there, a year later, in 1513, she mourned the death of her impetuous, chivalrous husband, commanding the Scottish army at the Battle of Flodden —one of the blackest tragedies in Scotland's history. With him were slain one archbishop, two bishops, thirteen earls and countless unnamed soldiers, all commemorated in the haunting Scottish dirge, *The Flowers o' the Forest*, based on the words the messenger is said to have used when he broke the news to the Queen: 'The flowers of the forest are a' wede awae.' The lament has preserved the pain of Scotland down the centuries.

* astert = leap; dooth me sike = makes me sigh, lest = pleased; sely = innocent; wote = knows.

Engraving of interior of room in Linlithgow Palace where
Mary, Queen of Scots, was born.
J. Peterkin *c.* 1800

I've heard them lilting at our ewe-milking,
Lasses a'lilting before dawn of day;
But now they are moaning on ilka green loaning—
The Flowers of the Forest are a' wede awae.

At buchts, in the morning, nae blithe lads are
    scorning,
Lasses are lonely and dowie and wae;
Nae daffing, nae gabbing, but sighing and
    sabbing,
Ilk ane lifts her leglen and hies her awae.

We'll hear nae mair lilting at our ewe-milking;
Women and bairns are heartless and wae;
Sighing and moaning on ilka green loaning—
The Flowers of the Forest are a' wede awae.*

Before the Battle of Flodden there had been a haunting of a different kind in St Michael's Church where, it was rumoured, the Queen had been so afraid at the thought of her husband's determined attempt to invade England that she planned for an apparition of the Apostle John to appear while the King was at prayer in St Catherine's aisle, to warn him not to go to war.

Afterwards the grieving Queen retreated to 'the most perfect little room in the Palace', as the chamber at the top of the north-west tower has often been described. Known as Queen Margaret's Bower it is square within, hexagonal without and is reached by a spiral staircase. Sir Walter Scott records in *Marmion*:

*There are many versions of the ballad. This eighteenth-century lyric was written by Jane, daughter of Sir Gilbert Elliot of Minto, Lord Justice Clerk of Scotland.

His own Queen Margaret who, in Lithgow's
  tower
All lonely sat, and wept the weary hour.

Like his parents James V, 'the poor man's King',
loved Linlithgow Palace and in 1538 he spared no
expense to make it ready for his second wife, Mary of
Guise. She declared she 'had never seen a more
princely palace' and compared it very favourably with
the castles of the Loire. Four years later their daughter
Mary was born in a room on the west side of the
quadrangle. The King lay mortally sick in Falkland
Palace at the time, suffering, it was thought, a complete
nervous collapse perhaps partly caused by the deaths of
their first two infant sons or perhaps from porphyria*,
the malady that affected James VI. On hearing of the
birth of a daughter the thirty-year-old monarch
murmured: 'Adieu, farewell. It cam' wi' a lass, it will
pass wi' a lass,' remembering how the Scottish crown
had come into the Stewart family in the 1300s through
the marriage of Marjorie, daughter of King Robert the
Bruce, with Walter the Steward whose forefather had
been made Hereditary Steward of Scotland by King
David I. Six days later King James V was dead.

Mary, Queen of Scots, was baptized in St Michael's
Church and spent much of her young life in the palace,
surrounded by rumour and intrigue, before she was
taken to Stirling Castle for greater safety.

Some fourteen years later, as a widow, she returned
to Linlithgow for a two-day visit during a royal
progress through Scotland. On the journey she took to
bed with an unidentified pain in her right side which
some said was due to dancing for too long at her
twenty-first birthday but which, she maintained, was
caused by praying for too long in an icy chapel after
Mass. Whatever the reason—and it might have been
porphyria—it was the start of a pattern of ill-health
which persisted for the rest of her life.

Eighteen months later, after her marriage to Henry,
Lord Darnley, she was taken to Linlithgow Palace on
a litter to convalesce from another attack of pain in her
side. There she found she was pregnant with the future

The only known portrait of James Hepburn, Earl of Bothwell,
who aimed to replace Darnley as the consort of Mary,
Queen of Scots. After being involved in Darnley's murder
he abducted the Queen and married her.
Portrait by an unknown artist, 1566.

James VI who was born in June of the following year.

Ten months later she stayed at Linlithgow for the
last time. She had visited her son James at Stirling, ten
weeks after his father's murder, and was riding back to
Edinburgh when, once again, she was seized with pain
in her side and decided to spend the night at the
peaceful palace where she was born. The next
morning, riding on to Edinburgh with thirty horsemen, she was stopped at the Bridge of Almond, six
miles from the capital, by the Earl of Bothwell who
suddenly appeared with a force of 800 men. He rode up
to her, put his hand on her horse's bridle and led her to
the castle of Dunbar where he sexually assaulted her

*It appears that King George III went insane probably because he inherited porphyria from King James VI, who said that his urine was the colour
of Alicante wine and that he had inherited the malady from his mother, Mary, Queen of Scots.

Scottish silver coins (groats) showing the sovereigns' heads.
From left to right; Robert II, 1371–90; Robert III, 1390–1406; James III, 1460–88;
James V, 1513–42

and kept her prisoner until she had little alternative but to take him as her third husband. Four weeks later they were married.

After her abdication James VI continued the tradition of visiting the massive yet gracious palace where the original towers and walls had been built up and linked to form a large courtyard. When he was nineteen, two years after his formal assumption of power, he summoned Parliament to meet there rather than in Edinburgh, it being customary for Parliament to attend the king wherever he was in residence.

After his marriage to Anne of Denmark the second of their seven children, Elisabeth, was fostered when she was three months old to Lord Livingston, Keeper of Linlithgow Palace, a nephew of one of her grandmother's famous 'four little Maries' who had accompanied the young Queen Mary to France.

'The first dochtour of Scotland', as Elisabeth was 'cryed and called' by the Lord Lyon King of Arms at her christening in the chapel of Holyroodhouse, spent most of her childhood at Linlithgow. From the time she could walk she was dressed, according to the children's fashions of the time, in a stiff stay bodice, quilted ruff, fashionable head-dress and long-sleeved gowns with hooped skirts.

Until she was seven years old and the Crowns of England and Scotland were united under her father, the quaint little figure ran down the long gallery or the great hall, a hundred feet long and thirty feet wide with a minstrels' gallery, played with her dolls in the many fine withdrawing-rooms, said daily prayers in the chapel with its deep pointed windows and canopied niches, and walked in the fine park and gardens.

In the large square courtyard she must have been fascinated by the curious fountain built by her great-grandfather, James V. It was very tall and water tumbled through the mouth of a sun-face and then spurted out of the mouths of grotesque human and animal heads, less bizarre heads and the head of an angel. Incorporated in the design were a mermaid, a drummer, a whistler, St Michael, animals, three nude boys and two men holding their sides with laughter.

More than 140 years later, when Prince Charles Edward Stuart was entertained there on his way from Stirling to Edinburgh, his hostess, Mrs Glen Gordon, Deputy Keeper of the palace and a keen Jacobite, arranged for the fountain to run with wine. Soon afterwards it was irrevocably damaged when soldiers in the Duke of Cumberland's army, marching north, bivouacked at the palace and accidentally set fire to it. Mrs Glen Gordon had warned their Commander that the men's fires were too big but on 1 February, 1746, Linlithgow's magnificent stone palace was left to burn itself into a gaunt ruin.

It was a sad end to a palace which, according to the historian J. H. Plumb, illustrated the strange mixture that was Scotland of that time:

Half Catholic, half Calvinist, the battleground of bitter feuding actions where barbarism went cheek by jowl with wonderful Renaissance splendour. The castle where Mary, Queen of Scots, was born of a French princess, Mary of Guise, was built by her father and it illustrates the contrast perfectly. From across the loch the castle looks formidable, a great brutal fortress, but within, what do we find? The High Renaissance, an exquisite fountain that would grace Rome and a beautiful outside staircase that could come straight from the great Valois castle of Blois by the Loire.

LOCHMABEN CASTLE

The island fortress in Dumfriesshire became known as 'Bruce's Castle' after 1124 when the first Robert de Brus was granted the whole of the vast border lordship of Annandale by his comrade in arms, King David I. Despite his French-sounding name, Robert de Brus was a Yorkshire magnate whose ancestors had arrived in England with William the Conqueror from their home in Brix or Bruis, a few miles south of Cherbourg in Normandy. The first fortress he built on Castle Hill at Lochmaben guarded the natural western route to both England and Galloway.

The elder son of this first Robert Bruce, Adam, remained a staunch Yorkshireman but the younger son, Robert, took his place among the great lords of Scotland from his castle which was an important gateway to their country. His great-grandson, Robert Bruce the Old Competitor (so called because towards the end of his life he, with Balliol, was one of the two principal of the thirteen competitors for the crown in 1292), rebuilt Lochmaben Castle in the thirteenth century.

Until then the family's chief castle had been the Mote of Annan but in the twelfth century this had been half washed away in a deluge, some said because of a curse put on the Bruces by an angry Irish saint at the time of the second Robert Bruce.

This saint, St Malachy O'Morgair, was a guest in the castle about 1140 and asked for the life of a condemned robber to be saved. Bruce promised to reprieve the man and then secretly hanged him, whereupon St Malachy cursed the house of Bruce and the town of Annan in a 'thorough comprehensive and devastating way'. After St Malachy's death and burial in the abbey church of Clairvaux, Bruce the Old Competitor endowed the abbey with Annandale land to pay for an everlasting light on the Saint's tomb.

Bruce's new castle was built on a site across the lake and some of the stone used was from the original fortress. This was conveyed on a causeway just under the water, traces of which can still be seen. When completed the castle was recognized as the strongest fortress of the Border country.

Seal of John Balliol, 1292–6, the last king to be enthroned
on the Stone of Destiny at Scone.

Its owner was defeated, however, in his bid for the Scottish throne, by the strict rule of primogeniture. He was a grandson of Earl David, the youngest of King David I's three grandsons, and claimed the throne through his mother, Isabel, Earl David's second daughter. But on the decision of Edward I of England it went to a great-grandson of Earl David, John Balliol, because he was descended from Earl David's eldest daughter, Margaret.

Three years after Balliol was crowned at Scone, Bruce, the Old Competitor, died in Lochmaben Castle on Good Friday, 1295, at the age of eighty-four. Six years later Edward I spent the winter in Lochmaben after hammering the Scots into submission, and, as a symbolic insult, taking the Stone of Destiny from Scone to Westminster.

Like all Border fortresses, Lochmaben Castle changed hands many times and in 1304 it became a place of refuge for the future King Robert the Bruce, grandson of the Old Competitor. King Robert gave it to his nephew's family, but in the next century James II took it back and garrisoned it and from then on it belonged to the kings personally, or to their sons. James IV repaired and improved it and in 1504 stayed there during a progress through Southern Scotland. Subsequent royal visitors included Mary, Queen of Scots, and her King Consort, Darnley. Soon afterwards it ceased to be a dwelling place although it remained a royal garrison for another century until Border fortresses lost their purpose and it was allowed to fall into ruin.

Since then vandals have peeled away most of the walls and only massive remnants of masonry mixed with lime now mark the site, dominating the loch and rolling countryside, where 'Bruce's Castle' stood.

KILDRUMMY CASTLE

Another castle closely associated with Bruce is secluded Kildrummy in Aberdeenshire which has been called 'the Queen of Highland castles'. It is magnificent even as a ruin. The immense stone fortress on Donside, commanding the important pass between Mar and Moray, was built in the early thirteenth century by Gilbert of Murray, mason-bishop of Caithness, whose family took their name from the province of Moray. This seat of the Earls of Mar was closely linked, through family ties, with Robert the Bruce.

Robert the Bruce's first wife, Isabel, was the daughter of Donald, Earl of Mar, his grandfather's friend and ally. She died about five years after the birth of their daughter, Marjorie, but the ties were further strengthened when Bruce's sister, Christian, married Earl Donald's son, Earl Gartnait, and in time Bruce became guardian of their son and heir, his nephew the young Earl Donald of Mar. In this way Kildrummy became heavily involved in Bruce's struggle for the Scottish crown, first against England under Edward I and then against the claims of the House of Balliol.

In the first case, after Bruce's defeat at Methuen he took the remnants of his defeated army into the Western Highlands. At the same time he sent the new Queen of Scots, Elizabeth his second wife, his eleven-year-old daughter Marjorie, his sister Mary and other women of his household on horseback through the mountains of Atholl and Braemar to Kildrummy in the care of his youngest brother Sir Neil Bruce and the Earl of Atholl.

Throughout August and September 1306 the castle was besieged by Edward, Prince of Wales, and his forces. The garrison withstood the attack until a treacherous blacksmith set fire to a store of corn in the great hall. The story goes that for his part in the betrayal the English had promised him 'as much gold as he could carry' and they kept their word by literally

OPPOSITE: Robert the Bruce and his first wife Isabel of Mar. Their daughter Marjorie married Walter Stewart, the sixth High Steward of Scotland, and died giving birth to Robert, founder of the Stewart dynasty, in 1316. From the sixteenth-century Seton Armorial.

pouring molten gold down his throat. After the siege Sir Neil Bruce was executed by the English.

Before the siege began the Queen and her companions, including the Countess Isabel of Buchan who had ridden to place the crown on Bruce's head at Scone in default of her brother, the Earl of Fife, fled the castle but were taken captive by the English. The Queen and her sister-in-law Christian were banished to nunneries but Bruce's other sister, Mary, and the Countess Isabel received a full measure of Edward I's vengeance for which his reputed periodic attacks of paranoia may have been responsible.

Like animals they were placed in specially constructed cages of timber and iron hung from the walls of

OPPOSITE: The ruins of Kildrummy Castle, Aberdeenshire, once called 'the Queen of Highland Castles'.

Roxburgh and Berwick castles respectively. For months they were forbidden to communicate with anyone except the English who brought them food and drink, exposed to mockery or pity and allowed only the convenience of a privy. But somehow they survived the ordeal; the Countess was eventually released to a nunnery and Mary Bruce was transferred to Newcastle and freed after the Battle of Bannockburn.

King Edward had planned a similar fate for the child Marjorie, who was to be kept in a cage in the Tower of London and allowed to communicate only with the Constable. For some reason King Edward fortunately changed his mind and revoked this order and instead the child was sent to a nunnery. Eventually she married Walter the Steward and after a fatal fall from a horse gave birth to Robert the Steward, who became heir to the throne of Scotland.

TURNBERRY CASTLE

Here, rivers in the sea were lost;
There, mountains to the skies were toss't;
Here, tumbling billows marked the coast
    With surging foam;
There, distant shone Art's lofty boast,
    The lordly dome.

From verses evoked by the ruins of Turnberry in
The Vision by Robert Burns

Turnberry lighthouse in Ayrshire, its flashing light visible at a distance of fifteen nautical miles, marks the spot of two most significant episodes connected with Robert the Bruce. In the thirteenth century, in place of the lighthouse, stood a great stronghold washed by the sea on three sides and, to the south-east, overlooking a rich plain. This was the home of Neil, the powerful Earl of Carrick, the last earl to be a direct male descendant of Fergus, Prince of Galloway, in the reign of King David I. On his death in 1256 his heir was his

daughter Marjorie, wife of Adam, Lord of Kilconquhar, who later fell in the Crusades, *c.* 1270.

The story has it that one day, when the young widow was hunting in her domain, she met the then fifth Robert Bruce, Lord of Annandale, fell for his considerable charm, kidnapped him, took him to Turnberry Castle and married him a few days later. Some two years later their son, Robert Bruce, the future King of Scotland, was born. Turnberry is believed to have had the honour of being his birthplace.

On his mother's death he became Earl of Carrick—a title retained today by the Prince of Wales—and, from his father, he inherited the title Lord of Annandale.

A year after his enthronement as King of Scotland in 1306, followed by defeat and exile in Ireland, Robert the Bruce had gathered a force of Irishmen and Hebrideans and crossed from Kintyre via the Isle of Arran to the Carrick shore near Turnberry. From the surrounding hills he harrassed the enemy, spread panic among the English garrison in the castle and gradually recruited supporters until eventually he overcame the garrison.

In the campaign he lost two more of his brothers, Thomas and Alexander, Dean of Glasgow. Now of the five, only he and Edward Bruce, destined to be King of Ireland, remained. Alexander Bruce who was badly wounded in Galloway, was taken by King Edward's command to Carlisle where he was half-hanged and then beheaded. He had been the best scholar of his time at Cambridge and the Lincolnshire poet, Robert Manning said: 'No one who read arts at Cambridge before or since his time ever made such progress. He was a master of arts before his brother was King of Scotland.'

Sithen was never non of arte so that sped
Ne bifore bot on, that in Cantebrigge
[Cambridge] red.
   . . . Of arte he had the maistrie.

So Manning wrote in his epic poem *The Story of England*.

Gradually King Robert the Bruce recovered the Kingdom of Scotland and the English defeat was completed at the Battle of Bannockburn. The mood of his supporters from the time he came ashore near Turnberry has been recorded by Sir Walter Scott in part of his *Lord of the Isles*:

'The Bruce, the Bruce!' to well-known cry
His native rocks and woods reply.
'The Bruce, the Bruce!' in that dread word
The knell of hundred deaths was heard.
The astonish'd Southern gazed at first,
Where the wild tempest was to burst.
That waked in that presaging name.

Today the part that Turnberry Castle played in Scotland's history is commemorated by the most famous hole on the golf course where the castle once stood. 'Bruce's Castle', the ninth hole, is a 450-yard drive from a rocky tee over a chasm on to the green.

STOBHALL CASTLE

Joy was within and joy without
Under that wlonkest waw [wall]
Quhair Tay ran down with stremis stout
Full strecht under Stobshaw.

From *Tayis Bank*—a late fifteenth-century poem
which may have been written by James IV

There is a joyous feeling about the group of three small stone buildings set in a walled courtyard high on a ridge over the left bank of the River Tay, perhaps because they have played a romantic and strangely unwarlike part in Scotland's history. They have been associated with three ladies of such beauty that two of them, and very nearly the third, became Queens of Scots.

There has been a home here, rather than a fortress, probably since the twelfth century. Then it seems that Stobhall, situated some nine miles from Perth, belonged to a great Norman family, the Montfichets, to whom it was given by King William the Lion about 1190.

In the fourteenth century the Montfichets were forfeited but their heiress, Mary, married John Drum/mond, feudal baron and Clan Chief, who then became John Drummond of Stobhall. He was used to beautiful women for his sister Margaret, widow of the Thane of Logie, was a great beauty who became mistress of King David II, last of the Bruce dynasty. He was Scotland's first anointed king and at the age of four he had been diplomatically married to Edward II's daughter, Joan. It was a childless marriage which lasted for thirty/four years until Joan died in 1362. Then King David, much to the indignation of the great nobles, married Margaret Logie.

The new Queen, however, failed to produce an heir and the King tried to divorce her. His attempts failed for the Queen was as hot/tempered as she was beautiful and apparently justified the reputation perpetuated in an old Perthshire litany: '. . . from the ire of the Drummonds, good Lord deliver us.'

Meanwhile the Queen's niece Annabella, the feudal baron John Drummond's daughter who was equally beautiful, had married the heir to King Robert II who had produced twenty/one children, thirteen legitimate and eight illegitimate. The heir was his eldest son John Stewart, Earl of Carrick, who had been crippled by a kick from a horse and, on succeeding to the throne at the age of sixty/three, was advised to change his name to Robert III because of the unhappy association of the name John with the unlucky John Balliol. Despite the change, however, King Robert III fulfilled his own deepest fears when he told Annabella that he was 'the worst of Kings and the most miserable of men'.

Nevertheless his beautiful queen succeeded where her aunt Margaret had failed in producing heirs. Although her first/born, the unfortunate Duke of Rothesay, died in mysterious circumstances at Falk/land Palace, her second son, James I, became King of Scots while he was a prisoner in English hands and succeeded in restoring a measure of respect for the monarchy before he was murdered at Perth by conspirators vainly trying to claim the throne for his uncle.

By the time the third lady associated with Stobhall

Annabella Drummond,
mother of James I and wife of King Robert III
from the Seton Armorial.

had captured the attention of a king the Drummonds had built themselves a castle twenty/five miles away, indicating their increased power and influence after a later John Drummond, feudal baron in the time of King James III, had been raised to the peerage as Lord Drummond in 1487/8: a peerage still held by the Earl of Perth. From that time Stobhall became a dower house.

King James IV's true love 'The Diamond of Delight', another Margaret, Lord Drummond's daughter was for six years the mistress of the popular King and bore him a daughter. Some said they were married but certainly her presence was inconvenient to the party who wished him to make an English alliance by marrying Margaret Tudor, daughter of King Henry VII.

In 1502 this third Drummond lady, whose radiance assured her a place in history, died, together with her sisters Euphame, wife of Lord Fleming, and Sybilla, after all three had eaten a poisoned breakfast dish apparently intended only for Margaret and supplied by a group of scheming nobles. Their tomb/slabs in Dunblane Cathedral bear witness to the triple tragedy.

Part of the painted ceiling in the chapel of Stobhall, executed in 1642
and restored in the early nineteenth century.
It shows kings of many countries on horseback, surrounding
the Drummond arms.

There remains a strange contrast between that world of glittering intrigue and the sense of peace and enchantment inherent in the old stone buildings clustered round the green plot of grass in the courtyard that is Stobhall today. That it has survived as a home rather than a fortified castle may be partly due to the fact that its surrounding walls overhang a precipitous ravine on the north-east.

It may be partly due too, to the care with which successive owners have preserved and adapted the old buildings; the complex of buildings including the chapel and priest's house was rebuilt by 1578, and the present Lord Perth has made a library where there was once a kitchen, laundry or brew house.

A new dower house was built beside the new complex by the 2nd Earl of Perth, brother of the 4th

Lord Drummond who was created Earl of Perth in 1605. It was completed by the 3rd Earl, a gallant Cavalier who fought for King Charles. The 4th Earl of Perth and his brother were among the eight founder Knights of the Thistle, Scotland's own noble Order of Chivalry, and ruled Scotland under King James VII and II, Lord Perth as Lord Chancellor and his brother Lord Melfort as Secretary of State; both followed the King into exile whereupon he rewarded them for their loyalty in adversity and made them both dukes. In less troublesome times the 1st Duke of Perth is probably remembered in the name of the well-known Scottish country dance which ends with the characteristic 'reel of three' of that period.

In mid-Victorian times, when permissiveness was shrouded in discretion, the two small bedrooms of the former priest's house became a convenient retreat for an artistic *ménage à trois*. One of the Drummond family lent it to the painter Millais and to John Ruskin, the writer, artist and preacher and his wife Effie, whom Millais eventually married.

Today the beautifully restored dower house is the home of Lord and Lady Perth and their guests sleep in the former priest's house where the ceiling beams are painted with fruit, flowers, sea-serpents and mythical monsters. It is in keeping with the boldly painted ceiling in the chapel, executed about 1642 and restored two hundred years later. It depicts kings of many countries on horseback, including Charles I, Philip II of Spain and Gustavus Adolphus of Sweden, together with animals and other designs and over the doorway, the Drummond arms and motto 'Gang Warily'.

ROTHESAY CASTLE

From the days when the Scottish kings disputed the Norsemen's claim to Man and the Isles, Rothesay Castle on the Island of Bute has been in the forefront of battle. In the twelfth century Ragnhild, a Norse princess, married Somerled, local King of Argyll and from that day the royal blood of the Gaels and Norse was irrevocably mixed. But the right of their descendants to call themselves Kings in the Isles was still a cause for dispute until Norway ceded the Hebrides to Scotland in 1266.

In the next century an heiress of their line brought the Isles of Bute and Arran in marriage to the Steward of Scotland who, in 1230, successfully garrisoned their castle to withstand a siege by Norsemen trying to restate their claim. King Haakon's reply to the defeat was to attack Rothesay with eighty ships in the reign of Alexander III and capture it. Almost immediately, and a few months before King Haakon's death, the Scots recaptured it and negotiated with the new king Magnus of Norway who agreed to surrender Man and the Hebrides to Scotland for four thousand merks down and an annual payment of one hundred merks.

Rothesay Castle's fighting days were by no means over, however. During the wars between King David and King Edward it changed hands several times. In Stewart times it became a royal castle and a favourite residence of Robert II who made his natural son, Sir John Stewart, Hereditary Sheriff of Bute (and ancestor of the Marquis of Bute) Hereditary Keeper of the Castle. Robert III later created his own elder son David the 1st Duke of Rothesay, a title still retained by the Prince of Wales.

Robert III also visited Rothesay Castle often before he died in 1406 on 4 April, the very day that his son and heir James was captured at sea by the English on his way to be brought up in safety in France. As a result James I was brought up as an honoured prisoner in England instead.

Nearly a hundred years later, during the reigns of James IV and James V, it was an important military base during a time of internal feuds and turbulence, and both kings frequently visited the castle. After the reign of James V it again fell into obscurity until the Earl of Lennox, 'lusty, beardless and lady-faced', captured it for the English. In the seventeenth century its importance was again revived when it was held first by the Scottish Cavaliers and then by the English Roundheads who dismantled the building when they withdrew their garrison in 1659. Twenty-six years later any part that still remained habitable was burned by Argyll's highlanders during his rebellion. It remained a neglected ruin until, in the nineteenth century, the 2nd Marquis of Bute (the then Hereditary Keeper) removed the rubbish and repaired it. Throughout the century his successor continued the repairs and restoration.

Seventy years later Rothesay Castle returned to its original role of serving the townspeople. Originally its large fortified enclosure accommodated them with the garrison in times of trouble when they sought refuge

there in the four towers. Since 1970 the portcullis has remained raised and the townspeople are once again welcomed into the castle; for recreation if not for protection. This happened after the war when the Marquis of Bute entered into a guardianship agreement with the Ministry of Works to maintain the castle on behalf of the Secretary of State acting for the Crown. As a result the great hall has been restored and refurnished and, as a centre for functions and exhibitions, once more brings the castle more into the life of the town. Nevertheless, Rothesay remains a royal castle and Lord Bute is still its Hereditary Keeper and still wears the key of office.

In pride of place in the great hall is a bronze bust of the Prince of Wales, Duke of Rothesay. It is the first official portrait of Prince Charles wearing the coronet after his Investiture by the Queen in Caernarvon in 1969.

OPPOSITE: The gateway to Rothesay Castle on the Isle of Bute.

RIGHT: A bronze bust of the Prince of Wales, whose premier Scottish title is Duke of Rothesay, stands in the renovated great hall of Rothesay Castle. The sculpture, created by David Wynne, was the first official portrait of Prince Charles wearing the coronet after his Investiture by the Queen in Caernarvon in 1969. Only six casts were made.

ROWALLAN CASTLE

This little gem of a castle stands on a gentle bank of the Carmel River, near Kilmarnock. Its twin drum towers flank the entrance to the former home of the Muirs of Rowallan. Situated in what was then wild and mysterious country in the fourteenth century it was the home of Sir Adam Muir, head of the same family as that Muir of Auchindrane whose involvement centuries later in the murder of Sir Thomas Kennedy of Culzean is immortalized by Sir Walter Scott in his poetic drama *The Ayrshire Tragedy* and by S. R. Crockett in his novel *The Grey Man*.

It was Sir Adam's daughter Elisabeth who gave Rowallan Castle its royal connections by her marriage to King Robert II, the child who was born to Robert the Bruce's daughter, Marjorie, after her fall from her horse. But although Elisabeth Muir became the wife of this first of the Stewart kings she was never his queen because she died before he succeeded to the throne in 1371 at the age of fifty-four.

Elisabeth Muir was also the mother of the first of Robert II's twenty-one children, some of whom were born out of wedlock. Her son John, born in 1327, who

Rowallan Castle.

changed his name to Robert III, because, after the disastrous reign of John Balliol, John was thought to be an unlucky name. But when he succeeded to the throne, the change of name made little significant improvement to the king who reigned but never ruled. As soon as he was crowned in 1390, he retired to a monastery and allowed Scotland to be governed by his forceful brother, Robert, Earl of Fife, afterwards Duke of Albany.

Some say this most powerful figure in the Scotland of his day was responsible for the death in 1402, in a little vault of the tower of Falkland Castle, of his nephew and rival, Robert III's son David, Duke of Rothesay and Prince of Scotland, who was believed to have starved there to a piteous death. The mysterious tragedy forms the climax of Sir Walter Scott's novel *The Fair Maid of Perth* in which, at one stage, he describes the Duke of Albany's character:

If he had not courage, he had wisdom to conceal and cloak over his want of that quality, which, once suspected, would have ruined all the plans which his ambition had formed. He had also pride enough to supply, in extremity, the want of real valour, and command enough over his nerves to conceal their agitation. In other respects, he was experienced in the ways of the courts, calm cool and crafty, fixing upon the points he desired to attain, while they were yet far removed, and never losing sight of them, though the winding paths in which he trod, might occasionally seem to point in a different direction.

To protect his second son James, Robert III sent him to France but, on the way, he was kidnapped by some pirates and handed over to the English who kept him their prisoner for eighteen years. The very same day Robert III died leaving the Duke of Albany to rule for the imprisoned twelve-year-old James I, as Regent.

DOUNE CASTLE

He was a braw gallant,
And he play'd at the gluve;
And the bonny Earl of Murray
O he was the Queen's luve!

O lang will his Lady
Look owre the Castle Downe
Ere she see the Earl of Murray
Come sounding through the town.

From an old Scottish ballad,
The Bonnie Earl of Moray

This magnificent and unusually constructed castle, situated in Menteith on a tongue of land between the rivers Teith and Ardoch in Perthshire, was built on the site of its ancient 'dun' by Robert, Earl of Fife, Duke of Albany. He was Earl of Menteith in right of his wife, the Countess, towards the end of the reign of his brother, Robert III, and while he was Regent for his young nephew James I.

Many years later his castle was commemorated in the old ballad. For in the reign of James VI, the 'bonnie Earl' referred to, who met a violent death at the hands of the Gordons, was James Stuart who was both Lord Doune—his father, Captain of the Castle and direct descendant of the Dukes of Albany, received the title in 1570—and the 2nd Earl of Moray. He took the Moray title through his wife Elisabeth, Countess of Moray in her own right as the daughter of another James Stuart,

Earl of Moray, the natural son of King James V and half-brother to Mary Queen of Scots.

The 'lady' in the ballad, however, is presumably the Bonnie Earl's mother since his wife was already dead and, after her son's death, the Dowager Lady Doune extracted several bullets from his body and then ordered a portrait to be painted of his corpse showing his death wounds. They include two deep slashes across his face made by a Gordon ancestor of the poet Byron.

'You have spoilt a better face than your own,' the dying Earl is said to have told his assailant.

The unusual design of the castle was because it was intended for possible defence by mercenary men-at-arms rather than by trusted clansmen. For this reason, at a time when no man knew his enemy, the Duke's quarters were in a completely self-contained keep gatehouse with well-secured entrances. From there the

ABOVE: The ruins of Doune Castle in Perthshire.

LEFT: James, the 1st Earl of Moray, the natural son of King James V and half-brother of Mary, Queen of Scots.

A view of the Trossachs above the River Teith
and the Braes of Menteith.

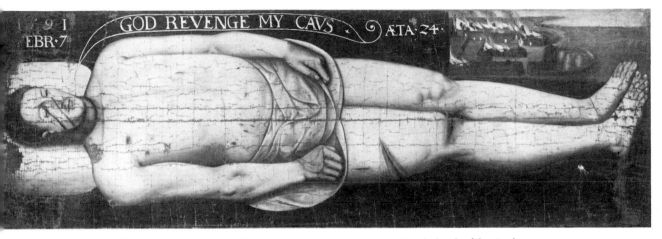

GOD REVENGE MY CAVS · ÆTA·24·

The 2nd Earl of Moray, the 'Bonnie Earl', who met a violent death at the hands of the Gordons.
When Gordon of Gight (an ancestor of the poet Lord Byron) slashed his face,
the dying Earl exclaimed: 'You have spoilt a better face than your own.'
The Earl's mother, Lady Doune (a Campbell of Argyll), extracted
several bullets with her own hands from her son's corpse and
ordered this portrait of his dead body to be painted.

portcullis was controlled and the garrison had no direct access to this part of the castle. It contained a secret room from which the Duke could observe everything going on in the huge lord's hall where the door is secured by a massive drawbar on the inside.

But all such precautions were ineffectual in the time of the 2nd Duke of Albany who, after the death of his father, acted as regent on behalf of the captive King James I for four years. He was a feeble, though well-meaning, ruler and was one of the first targets when the young king was released on a ransom of 60,000 merks.* He returned to a Scotland rent by feudal tyranny and swore: 'Let God but grant me life, the key shall keep the castle and the bracken bush the cow, though I myself lead the life of a dog in bringing it to pass!'

He was prepared to use all means to curb the power of the great nobles and one of his first acts to this end was to have the Duke of Albany, his son Alexander and his father-in-law, the Earl of Lennox, beheaded on the Heading Hill of Stirling within sight of the 'bannered towers of Doune'. They were deliberately beheaded in reverse order of age so that the eighty-year-old Earl could see his grandson die first.

From that time Doune Castle, under royal governors, was often used as a dower house by the Queens of Scotland. James II, tempted by the tall deer in the Braes of Menteith and the Forest of Glenfinlas, often stayed there for the hunting and his widow, like the widow of James III and the widowed Margaret Tudor, spent much time there and from the high towers surveyed, as Scott wrote in *The Lady of the Lake*:

mountains that like giants stand
To sentinel enchanted land.

Other royal occupants included Mary, Queen of Scots, and her son, the scholarly James VI, who wrote in one of his works:

at our last repairing towart our castell and place of Doune in Menteith we persavit the samin and feildis thereabout to be maist pleasant for our pastyme and verray commodious for our dwelling in the symmer seasonn.

Doune Castle has, since 1570, remained in the custody of the Earls of Moray, but gradually fell into a poor state of repair until 1883 when the 14th Earl began a careful restoration to bring it to its present position as the largest and best-preserved example of fourteenth-century domestic architecture in Scotland.

* A merk was worth 13s 4d.

71

BLAIR CASTLE

Wi' a hundred pipers an a' an' a',
Wi a hundred pipers an' a' an' a'.
We'll up an gie them a blaw a blaw
Wi' a hundred pipers an a'.

From a piping song written by
Caroline, Lady Nairne who lived near the Castle,
home of the last private army in Europe

There was a stronghold on this site in the kingdom of Atholl in Pictish times and one of its kings was drowned by the High King of the Picts for alleged treachery. In those pagan days, drowning was the Pictish method of execution, in obeisance to the goddess-spirit Bride or the legendary Boan, the Irish Goddess of the River.

Since those times, the fortress in the Strath of Garry between the Passes of Killiecrankie and Drumochter, and commanding the central route into the Highlands, has constantly been rebuilt, enlarged and remodelled to culminate in the fine treasure-house of today which is one of the oldest continually occupied great mansions in Scotland.

Atholl became an earldom as soon as earldoms started when the title Earl of Atholl was bestowed on a branch of the royal house descended from King Malcolm Canmore. The Celtic line of the Earls of Atholl, however, came to an end by the fourteenth century. The title was then held by various branches of the royal family including King Robert II and his son Walter, until 1457 when James II conferred it on his maternal half-brother Sir John Stewart of Balvenie, ancestor of the present Duke of Atholl.

The first recorded fortress was a great tower with walls fourteen foot wide in parts, erected in 1269, and succeeding generations added more living accommodation. In the sixteenth century it was more of a fortress than an ancestral home. James V and later Mary,

Queen of Scots, stayed there and were lavishly entertained in a whole new timber 'palace' erected for the occasion.

It was 1564 when the Earl of Atholl arranged a hunt in his forest to entertain the Queen. One of her suite, who was a young man at the time, recorded:

The Earl of Atholl had, with much trouble and vast expense, arranged a hunting match for the entertainment of our most gracious Queen. Our people called this a Royal Hunting.

Three thousand Highlanders, or 'Wild Scotch' as you call them here, were employed to drive to the hunting ground all the deer from the woods and hills of Atholl, Badenoch, Mar, Moray and the counties about. As these Highlanders use a light dress, and are very swift of foot, they went up and down so nimbly that in less than two months time they brought together two thousand red deer, besides roes and fallow deer.

The Queen, the great men, and others were in a Glen when all the deer were brought before them. Believe me, the whole body of them moved forward in something like battle order. The sight still strikes me, and ever will, for they had a leader whom they followed close wherever he moved. This leader was a very fine stag*, with a very fine head. The sight delighted the Queen very much, but she soon had occasion for fear upon the Earl (who had been accustomed to such sights) addressing her thus: 'Do you observe that stag who is foremost of the herd? There is danger from that stag; for if either fear or rage should force him from the ridge of that hill, let

---

*It was pointed out by the 7th Duke of Atholl that unless the habits of deer were different in those times surely it must have been a hind.

Blair Castle, at Blair Atholl, the ancient home and fortress of
the Earls and Dukes of Atholl, is one of the oldest continually
occupied Scottish great mansions.

everyone look to himself, for none of us will be out of the way of harm; for the rest will follow this one, and having thrown us under foot, they will open a passage to his hill behind us.'

What happened a moment after confirmed this opinion; for the Queen ordered one of the best dogs to be let loose upon a wolf; this the dog pursues, the leading stag was frightened, he flies by the same way he had come there, the rest rush after him, and break out where the thickest body of the Highlanders was. They had nothing for it but to throw themselves flat on the heath, and to allow the deer to pass over them. It was told the Queen that several of the Highlanders had been wounded and that two or three of them had been killed outright; and the whole body had got off, had not the Highlanders, by their skill in hunting, fallen upon a strategem to cut off the rear from the main body.

It was of those that had been separated that the Queen's dogs, and those of the nobility, made slaughter.

There were killed that day 360 deer, with 5 wolves and some roes.

In the mid-seventeenth century families were often divided by civil war. The Royalist stronghold was occupied until the Restoration by Cromwell's troops and in the next century the 1st Duke of Atholl's eldest son Duke William, Marquis of Tullibardine, was deprived of the dukedom of Atholl on his father's death after escaping into exile abroad after his part in the Jacobite Rising of 1715. Thirty years later the castle was engulfed in the '45 Rising after its owner the younger son, Duke James, abandoned it. The youngest son, Lord George Murray, the Jacobite General, also had some misgivings about where his loyalties lay and in a letter to his brother Duke James, he explained:

I was not a little difficulted when you left this place . . . for, to spake the truth, I was at that time resolv'd to take a step which I was certain you would disprove off as much when you knew it, as it would surprise you to hear it. I never did say to any person in Life that I would not ingage in the cause I always in my heart thought just & Righte. . . . My Life, my Fortune, my expectations, the Happyness

Lord George Murray,
the brilliant Highland guerrilla leader and Jacobite general, in his campaigning dress with sword, dirk and targe and a white cockade in his blue bonnet, symbol of the House of Stuart. He marched on foot with his men although, in order to be an effective general, he was mounted in battle.
At Culloden he led the charge of the Athollmen, galloping straight through to the rear of the Government army and then hacking his way back on foot through the enemy ranks to remount and bring on the second wave of Jacobites.

of my wife & children, are all at stake (& the chances are against me), & yet a principle of (what seems to me) Honour & Duty to King & Country, outweighs every thing.

Meanwhile Duke William accompanied Prince Charles Edward when he landed in Scotland in July 1745. The Prince is thought to have brought a personal letter to Lord George from his father King James, 'the King over the Water', which the recipient could not ignore. Accordingly in 1746 he sent out the Fiery Cross* for the last time in war to try to retake Blair, the

---

*In times of war the chief or chieftain sent out a charred wooden cross attached to a rag dipped in sheep's or goat's blood as a call to mobilization. It was a symbol of Fire and the Sword and was sent in relays through the countryside, each successive bearer shouting one word, the name of the Gathering Place, in this case Blair Castle.

Among the many family portraits displayed on the picture
staircase, built in 1756, is a study of John, 1st Marquis of
Atholl, by Jacob de Witt.
He is shown as Julius Caesar, in the classical French style,
and points to the Battle of Bothwell Brig being waged
in the background.

last castle to be besieged in Britain. It was occupied by
300 Hanoverian troops, but Lord George was resolved
to attack his old home although during the siege he
wrote to Duke William: 'If we get the Castle I hope
you will excuse our demolishing it.' His brother, the
staunch Jacobite, understood:

> Our great-great-grandfather's, and father's pictures
> will be an irreparable loss on blowing up the house,
> but there is no comparison to be made with those
> faint images of our forefathers and the more
> necessary Publick Service which requires he would
> sacrifice every thing.

The ancestral portraits were spared, however, because
the siege was abandoned and the battle of Culloden
was fought and lost. Lord George eventually died in
exile in Holland, and Duke William after being
captured died in the Tower of London. In 1746 Duke

James returned to Blair Castle, which he found so
damaged that he professed himself 'cured of all manner
of fondness' for the place.

The beautiful trees that he had taken such pains to
propagate and bring to perfection were no more and, in
his mid-fifties, he said he was too old to begin again. He
soon recovered from the shock, however, and spent the
rest of his life restoring the castle and its grounds. He
did away with its turrets and castellations—later to be
restored in Scots Baronial style by the 7th
Duke—lowered the roof line, planned the park and
added a ceremonial staircase within the house. Called
the 'picture staircase', its panelled walls are lined with
ancestral portraits including a fine study by Jacob de
Witt of the 1st Marquis of Atholl dressed as Julius
Caesar, in the classical French style of the period, with
the Battle of Bothwell Brig going on in the
background.

The beautiful Empress Eugénie, wife of Napoleon
III, saw none of the paintings or treasures when she
paid an unexpected visit to the house in 1860. She had
gone to Scotland to try and recover her health and
spirits after the death of her only sister. She was
travelling as the Comtesse de Pierrefonds and one
November day arrived with a small suite at the Birnam
Hotel. The following day the Duke of Atholl, hearing
that the Empress had driven through Dunkeld on her
way to see Blair, followed on a pony and, having
overtaken the party, was presented to her and invited to
join her in the carriage.

It was dark when they arrived at Blair and the castle
was dismantled for winter and could only be seen by
the light of a limited supply of tallow candles. The
Duke showed his guest into the housemaid's room
which was the only room with a fire. Afterwards they
had tea and chops at the hotel after returning to Birnam.
Her unscheduled visit was in marked contrast to the
carefully arranged one of Queen Victoria and Prince
Albert sixteen years previously.

It had been a memorable visit, for the royal couple as
well as for the occupants of Blair Castle. In a letter to a
friend at Coburg, dated 22nd September, 1844, Prince
Albert wrote:

> We are well, and live a somewhat primitive, yet
> romantic mountain life, that acts as a tonic to the

ABOVE: Furniture used by Queen Victoria and Prince Albert when they stayed at Blair Castle in 1844. The statuettes and busts of the Royal Family were among various gifts presented to the castle by Her Majesty.

OPPOSITE, TOP: Blair Castle in the time of the 6th Duke of Atholl who unexpectedly entertained the Empress Eugénie there. View looking towards Killiecrankie painted by William Evans showing the departure of the Duchess of Kent in 1850.

OPPOSITE, BELOW: A conversation-piece of the 4th Duke of Atholl with his first wife, the Hon. Jane Cathcart, and their family, painted by David Allan, hangs in the 4th Duke's Corridor on the second floor.

nerves and gladdens the heart of a lover like myself of field sports and nature.

Queen Victoria, writing in her *Journal*, was even more enthusiastic. She described drives in the pony carriage to see the 'wild and beautiful scenery':

'The air so pure and fine. . . . These Scotch streams, full of stones and clear as glass, are most beautiful: the peeps between the trees, the depth of shadows, the mossy stones, mixed with slate etc. which cover the banks are lovely; at every turn you have a picture . . . Albert in such delight; it is a happiness to see him, he is in such spirits.

She rode her pony into the hills and to the top of Tulloch:

. . . the most delightful, most romantic ride and

The Duke of Atholl still has his own guard of Atholl Highlanders, complete with pipers, the last private army in Europe.

walk I ever had. [She went deer stalking] . . . a long hard day's work, though extremely delightful and enjoyable, and unlike anything I had ever done before. I should have enjoyed it still more had I been able to be with Albert the whole time.

There were picnics and sketching parties and her entry for 1 October said they regretted leaving the beauty and wildness of Blair:

Every little trifle and every spot I had become attached to; our life of quiet and liberty, everything was so pleasant, and all the Highlanders and people who went with us I had got to like so much. Oh! the dear hills, it made me very sad to leave them behind!

It was the start of her life-long love for Scotland and by the time she returned, three years later, she had made up her mind to have a home of her own north of the Border.

Meanwhile the year after that visit to Blair Castle,

Colours were presented on her behalf to the Atholl Highlanders, the last private army in Europe. It is the sole survivor of the old custom whereby the Kings of Scotland had no army but relied on local chiefs to bring their clan forces to support them in time of war.

After the eighteenth century the Athollmen gradually changed their role when for those who wished to fight it became more common to join the regular army. Today, with the rank and file numbering about 100 and a celebrated pipe band, this private army is more of a ceremonial bodyguard for the Duke.

Their Colours are kept at Blair. Various others, a collection of weaponry and some fine portraits of earlier dukes and duchesses, are displayed in the huge ballroom, one of the latest additions to the castle, built in 1876 by the 7th Duke. It is one of thirty-two rooms alive with paintings, works of art and souvenirs where visitors can imbibe the history of a great Scottish family. The present Duke lives in a wing built in the eighteenth century.

LOCHLEVEN CASTLE

The dour little castle where Mary, Queen of Scots, was imprisoned for eleven months and where she miscarried with twins and abdicated in favour of her infant son, James VI, stands in ruins on a grassy island at the west end of the loch near Kinross. But at the time when it played its most important role in history, the waters of the loch lapped directly against its walls, as they did in 1257 when the sixteen-year-old Alexander III stayed there with his young queen, Margaret, daughter of Henry III of England.

On the night of 16 June, 1567, Mary, Queen of Scots, was rowed out to the castle of Sir William Douglas after surrendering at Carberry Hill to the rebels who objected to her marriage to Bothwell. They believed he had murdered her second husband, the King Consort Darnley. When Mary surrendered Bothwell galloped away and they never met again. Eleven years later he died insane in a Danish prison.

In Lochleven Castle Mary's gaoler was Sir William's mother, Lady Margaret, who no doubt relished the task: she had had a son by Mary's own father, James V, and was said to bear a grudge against the Queen for occupying the throne from which her own son was excluded because of his illegitimacy.

During the first weeks of her imprisonment the twenty-five-year-old Queen was physically and mentally ill and before the end of July she had miscarried. After that she gradually recovered her spirits and charmed the youngest son of the household, George Douglas, to such an extent that his mother had him expelled from the castle. He left behind an ally, however, an orphaned member of the family, eighteen-year-old William Douglas, and eventually these two admirers were able to engineer the Queen's escape.

Meanwhile Mary, Queen of Scots, dreamt of freedom. She asked for clothes for herself and her ladies including Mary Seton, favourite of her 'four Maries', who had been allowed to join her. A red satin petticoat trimmed with marten was sent to her, some satin sleeves, a cloak of holland, stockings, shoes and sweetmeats and a selection of false hairpieces. There was Spanish silk, and gold and silver thread for embroidery. She played cards, walked in the garden and even danced. She wrote letters which were smuggled out of the castle and made one abortive attempt to escape disguised as a laundress while Mary Seton took her place in the castle. But the boatmen recognized her by the whiteness of her hand holding the bundle of washing, and returned her to the castle.

The next attempt, devised by William Douglas,

A portrait of Mary, Queen of Scots, by the master miniaturist, Nicholas Hilliard.

The escape of Mary, Queen of Scots, from Lochleven Castle,
painted by Francis Danby.

involved scaling a seven-foot wall in the garden, but this was abandoned when her lady-in-waiting injured her foot during the rehearsal. Finally William Douglas stole the castle keys and, wearing borrowed clothing, the prisoner crossed the courtyard. William let her out of the gate and rowed her across the loch in a boat while she lay hidden beneath the seat. At the other side she was welcomed by the faithful George Douglas and by Mary Seton's brother, Lord Seton, with two hundred horsemen. But she had only exchanged a confined prison for a large one, for thirteen days later she was defeated at the Battle of Langside and fled to England where she remained a captive for the remaining nineteen years of her tragic life.

In time Lochleven Castle lost its forbidding aspect. Some of the loch water was sold by a later owner to an industrial undertaking and the lower water level allowed the ruins of the fourteenth-century tower and keep to be surrounded by a grassy island studded with trees.

TARBERT CASTLE

The ruins of Tarbert stand some sixty feet above sea level on the shores of a small creek called Loch Tarbert on the west side of Loch Fyne and about sixty yards from the shore. Its situation, on an isthmus, is one of the best strategic positions in the country and the name Tarbert is significant: it means 'drawboat', which was a place where the Vikings found they could drag a boat on rollers, as here between the Loup and Loch Fyne.

A view of Tarbert Castle in 1847,
from an engraving.

Here, in 1093, King Magnus (Bare-legs) of Norway agreed with King Malcolm (Bighead) Canmore, just before the latter's death during his fifth attempt to invade England, that the Hebrides formed part of Norway and the mainland belonged to Scotland. They decided that the test of what was rightfully Norwegian land was to be whether a ship with its rudder in position could sail round it. King Magnus, in this way, secured the peninsula of Kintyre, which he considered 'a large land and better than the best island in the Hebrides' by having his own dragon-ship dragged on rollers across the mile of dry land from east to west of Loch Tarbert, with himself at the tiller. Not until the late thirteenth century did Kintyre come under the suzerainty of the Scottish mainland.

Tarbert, held by the English during the Competition for the Scottish Crown, was handed over to John Balliol by King Edward I who placed him on the throne in 1292. His successor Robert the Bruce, towards the end of his reign, had the royal fortress inspected and repaired with the intention of using its strategic position to control the Highlands. He made a dwelling house within its structure, fitted up its hall and wine cellar, kitchen and brewery, had a moat built around it and added a mill and mill-dam, a kiln and a goldsmith's shop. He spent some time towards the end of his life there.

After his death it seems to have lapsed into a poor state of repair until James IV tried to restore it as part of his attempt to bring order to the remote western part of the country. Apparently the work was never completed because in 1525 the Earl of Argyll was granted hereditary 'custody of the Castle of Tarbert when it shall be built'. In turn, his descendants received the custody of the castle 'when it shall happen to be built'.

Like two other ruined castles in Argyllshire, Dunoon and Carrick, a favourite hunting lodge of Scottish kings, Tarbert has remained a Campbell stronghold, held for the Crown by the Clan Chief, their Hereditary Keeper, who is also Duke of Argyll and Marquis of Lorne by royal descent in the female line from the ancient local kings of Argyll.

DUNCONNEL CASTLE

On the northernmost and most precipitous of a chain of four rocky green islands called the Isles of the Sea or the Garvellach Islands in the Sound of Lorne, a heap of stones is all that remains of the fortress of Dunconnel built in the sixth century by Conall, a ruler of the Kingdom of Dalriada. The island consists of three separate rocky heights, so steep as to be almost inaccessible and where it is extremely difficult to land, even in fine weather. It was this King of the Scots from Antrim in Northern Ireland who gave the island of Iona to St Columba who established a monastery there in AD 563.

Legend has it that Conall's two brothers also had their own castles on his isle. The three lived so close to one another that every morning, on waking, Conall used to take a box from under his pillow, take a pinch of snuff-like powder and pass the box on to his first brother who, after using it, passed it to the second who, finally, returned it to its owner.

Records from the fourteenth century tell of the 1st Lord of the Isles, the great John Macdonald, ruler of the Western Highlands, whose installation ceremony imitated those of the Kings of Dalriada. Dressed all in white he put his foot in a hollowed footprint on Islay in a special stone as the Kings of Argyll did at their sacred inaugurations at Dunadd. He then received a white rod and a sword as symbols of power and protection. The ceremony was attended by at least one bishop, several priests and the leading chieftains from the Clan Macdonald. Mass was said, blessings and gifts were

An aerial view of the Isles of the Sea, known also as the Garvellach Islands, where Dunconnel became a royal stronghold in the sixth century.

given and everyone feasted for a week. Afterwards the ruler held his own council meetings round a special stone table and his autonomy was such that he issued his own weights and measures.

Lachlan Lubanach, the 5th Chief of the Clan Maclean, who claimed descent in the male line from the same royal house of Dalriada as King Conall, was related to this 1st Lord of the Isles and fell in love with his daughter, Mary, a feeling which she apparently reciprocated 'by her inclination of yielding'. Their romance, however, did not run smoothly and Lachlan and his brother, Hector, boarded the galley of her father and took him prisoner until he promised to allow the marriage in 1366. Even then, because of their close blood relationship, it was necessary to get special dispensation from the Pope before it could take place. It seems to have been a good marriage for, after twenty-four years, Lachlan's brother-in-law Donald, who was then the 2nd Lord of the Isles, gave Lachlan a charter granting him various lands and titles including those of Constable and Keeper of Dunconnel Castle. This descent from the ruling dynasty of the Isles was the fountain of Maclean power in the Hebrides.

In the next century John Macdonald, 4th Lord of the Isles, and also Earl of Ross which included the vast territory of Inverness-shire, was party to a treaty with Edward IV of England to divide up Scotland. Their plan never materialized but from 1474, when James III learned of it, there was constant suspicion and periodic outbursts of fighting between the Crown and the Lords of the Isles. This culminated in 1494 with the surrender of the last Macdonald Lord of the Isles after a family quarrel, followed by James IV's declaration, reinforced by strength, that all the territory of the Lord of the Isles now belonged to the Crown. Since that time the heir to the throne has always held the title of Lord of the Isles.

For the next two centuries the Chiefs of the Clan Maclean remained Constable and Keeper of Dunconnel Castle for the Crown but in 1691, during the period of insurrection and feuds preceding Union with England, the Isles of the Sea passed into Campbell hands. Recently the Keepership was recovered by Sir Fitzroy Maclean, 'the Balkan Brigadier', who, in World War II was parachuted into Yugoslavia to help Tito against the Nazis. He is a direct descendant of Lachlan Lubanach and the 15th Hereditary Keeper and Captain of the Royal Castle of Dunconnel in the Isles of the Sea.

DUART CASTLE

Come o'er the stream, Charlie, dear Charlie, brave Charlie,
Come o'er the stream Charlie, and dine with Maclean;
And though you be weary we'll make your heart cheery,
And welcome our Charlie and his loyal train.
We'll bring down the track deer, we'll bring down the black steer,
The lamb from the breckan, and doe from the glen;
The salt sea we'll harry, and bring to our Charlie,
The cream from the bothy, and curd from the pen.

From *MacLean's Welcome*—to Bonnie Prince Charlie,
representing heroes and warriors of all time

The great stone stronghold dominating the Sound of Mull, the second largest island of the Inner Hebrides, is the home of the Maclean Chiefs who were once Hereditary Keepers of Dunconnel Castle and from whom the Hereditary Keeper descends. Over Duart Castle flies the Chief's banner and among its quarterings is the Black Galley signifying its owner's descent from the old Norse sea-kings, although in the direct

Duart Castle on the Island of Mull, home of
Lord Maclean of Duart. It is separated from the mainland by the
Sound of Mull.

male line he springs from the ancient Gaelic Kings of Dalriada and, more recently, from Lachlan Lubanach Maclean, son-in-law of the 1st Lord of the Isles. From his brother-in-law, the 2nd Lord of the Isles, he received lands in Mull, including Duart.

In the fourteenth century he probably built the keep of the great castle standing high on the rock, separated from the mainland by the Sound of Mull. The name Duart is derived from the Gaelic words meaning 'Black Height'. The windowless curtain walls, thirty feet high and nearly ten feet thick, which protect the castle on the landward side, are probably older than the keep.

There is a rock just off shore known as 'Lady Rock'

where legend had it that in 1523 the then Lachlan Maclean of Duart left his barren wife to be drowned secretly by the rising tide. She was rescued by a passing fishing vessel and returned to her brother, the Earl of Argyll at Inveraray. Meanwhile, her husband carried out 'a good mock funeral for his much loved, much lamented lady'. The Earl being a 'mild and amiable man', took no revenge but years later, when Maclean was eighty years old, the Earl's younger brother, the Thane of Cawdor, entered his lodging house in Edinburgh and dirked him to death in bed.

In 1809 a dramatized version of this legend portraying the feud between the Macleans and the Campbells was written by the playwright Johanna

Baillie, a friend of Sir Walter Scott who wrote a prologue to it. It played to packed houses at the Edinburgh Theatre.

The tragedy represented the violence of clan warfare down the centuries which James VI, when he found himself backed by English power, determined to bring under control. In 1603 he sent a commissioner, backed by a naval force, to receive the submission of the Clan Chiefs, including the Maclean Chief. Duart Castle was delivered up but returned to the Chief's keeping under certain conditions and on his promise to surrender it when required.

The conditions imposed ensured that the Chiefs kept order in their territories and were held responsible for any outrage there. They were ordered to appear annually before the Privy Council, along with a stated number of their kinsmen. Duart, being an important castle, had to produce four kinsmen and was allowed to keep eight retainers in the household—the largest number allowed. Each chief was restricted to one galley of eighteen oar, firearms and two-handed swords were banned, there was compulsory education of his children under Privy Council direction and Maclean of Duart was allowed to import four tuns of wine a year—the largest sanctioned to any Hebridean chief—while the statutes banned wine to the clansmen.

Nevertheless there followed a century of civil and clan warfare culminating in the destruction of Duart Castle by the Campbells after the Jacobites were overthrown.

Not until 1911 were the ruins recovered by the Maclean Chiefs and restored to the home it is today, by the late Sir Fitzroy Maclean, 10th Baronet, a Hussar Colonel who had ridden with the Light Brigade in the Crimea and who spent his 102nd birthday at Duart. The present owner is Sir Charles Maclean of Duart, 11th Baronet, a life peer as Lord Maclean KT, who commanded a tank squadron of Scots Guards during World War II and is not only Lord Lieutenant of Argyll and former Chief Scout of the Commonwealth but also Lord Chamberlain to the Queen and head of Her Majesty's Household.

THE PALACE OF FALKLAND

Wes nevir in Scotland hand nor sene
Sic dansing nor deray,
Nouthir at Falkland on the green
Nor Pebillis [Peebles] at the Play.

From *Christis Kirk on the Green*
by King James VI and I

This palace, built alongside the site of an abandoned castle, is one of the most historically romantic buildings held by the Queen. In its turn, the thirteenth-century abandoned castle of Falkland was built on the site of an even older fortress that survived from the reign of Alexander I and which was afterwards held for Malcolm IV.

It is situated at the foothills of the Lomonds, in the most inland part of the sea-bound county of Fife and a long way from any great river, factors which made it of little military importance. But socially it was a palace that invoked the splendour of the Stewarts and was woven into the fabric of their lives and, even in its ruined state, this can be sensed in the air of luxury and lack of austerity it still preserves.

In the fourteenth century it had been the home of the Earls of Fife who had the right to enthrone kings at their coronations. Isabel, Countess of Fife in her own right, the last of the family, took as the second of her four husbands Walter Stewart, second son of Robert

II, who became the first of a long line of Stewarts to make their home at Falkland. Isabel had no children and she acknowledged as her heir Walter Stewart's brother, Robert, Earl of Menteith, the husband of her rightful heir. In 1398 he was created Duke of Albany, a title new to Scotland, which conferred on him a position of exceptional grandeur as it means Duke of the Scots or Duke of Scotland.

This introduced a sinister element to Falkland, despite its beguiling charm, for from that moment most of the royal Stewarts who lived there met with violent deaths, starting in 1402, even before the palace was built, with the handsome, unfortunate royal prince, David Stewart, Duke of Rothesay, heir to the throne and Albany's nephew. He was arrested on a wild stormy night, and disguised as a varlet in a coarse brown cloak, taken secretly to Falkland Castle by a strong guard of the Duke of Albany's mounted men-at-arms.

Some time before his arrest a fiery comet had appeared in the sky and Rothesay himself had remarked that such comets foretold the death of princes. Slowly the comet began to wane and at Easter the young prince died, some say by poison, some by starvation, thus lending credence to the ominous proverb that 'imprisoned princes do not live long'.

Throughout the reign of his elder brother, Robert III, the purely nominal king, the Duke of Albany had been Regent of Scotland and he continued while James I was an English prisoner. On his death the next Duke of Albany to own Falkland was his less effectual son, Murdach Stewart, who succeeded as Regent but was beheaded in 1425 after King James's return. The castle then passed to his uncle Walter Stewart, Earl of Atholl and contender for the throne, who was involved in the midnight assassination of his nephew King James I at Perth. He himself was then beheaded after suffering excruciating torture when he was forced to wear a red-hot crown in public, inscribed 'The King of Traitors'.

The first Stewart king to live at Falkland was James II, known as 'Fiery Face' from a large red birthmark. It

OPPOSITE: Falkland Palace, where the Stuart kings and queens went for relaxation.

James II, by an unknown artist who tactfully camouflaged his large red birthmark which led to his being called 'Fiery Face'.

was he who started building a hunting palace—far more of a royal home than a place of state. Here the kings and queens of that romantic royal dynasty came to relax. They spent their leisure in archery and tennis; rode out hawking into the hills with their hooded falcons; hunted stags through the glades and wild boar among the great oaks of the forest; cranes and peacocks strutted on the terrace above the beautiful gardens and the ladies of the court looked down at the knights in armour jousting in the tilt-yard below. At night they banqueted and played cards or chess to the soft music of flutes and lutes.

When the Sovereign was in residence, the gold-and-red lion rampant banner floated on its flagstaff high above the castle and the roaring of a great chained beast echoed from the 'Lion's Den' below, for the king of beasts was the royal mascot and travelled everywhere with the King of Scots.

In the twenty-third year of his reign James II was killed at the siege of Roxburgh Castle which was held

Scotland's only real (i.e. 'royal') tennis court, built by James V,
who made many improvements at Falkland.

for Henry VI of England. He was twenty-nine and his death was caused when a cannon he was supervising accidentally exploded.

His son, the bisexual James III, was nine years old when he succeeded to the throne. He grew up to love poetry and music and spent many evenings at Falkland listening to Foulis playing the harp, Lindores or James Rudman playing the flute or to Bennet, the fiddler. His short life ended when he was thirty-seven in a rebellion, nominally led by his own fifteen-year-old son, James IV, but motivated by the Scottish lords who, among other grievances, were appalled because the King had conferred a peerage on his new boyfriend, John Ramsay of Balmain.

Much of the Palace was built by James IV but it owes some of its beauty to James V who also had a tennis court built—the only real-tennis court in Scotland—and completed the Chapel Royal which had been started by his father. On the eves of his

marriages to his two French wives he introduced skilled French craftsmen to carry out extensive additions and alterations in the style of the French Renaissance. Typical of their skill are five pairs of beautiful medallions flanking the five great windows facing the courtyard.

Local tradition has it they are likenesses of the King's intimate household, portrayed with remarkable accuracy. They are said to show the King and his two queens, Madeleine of France who died within a few months of marriage, and Mary of Guise; his parents, King James IV and Margaret Tudor; his adviser, Cardinal Beatoun; his friend the Lord Lyon, Sir David Lindsay of the Mount, the satirical writer, and three charming mistresses from his premarital days. They are Elizabeth Schaw, daughter of the Laird of Sauchie, who bore him a son; Margaret, daughter of Lord Erskine, whose son by the King was the famous statesman James Stewart, Earl of Moray, destined to be

The restored bedchamber where James V died. The ceiling bears the crowned monograms of the King and his second queen, Mary of Guise.

James the fyft
began his raign
1514 He maryed fir
Magdelena dothter
of francis ye frst
k. of france.

This painting from the Seton Armorial shows James V with his first queen, Madeleine of France, who died within a few months of their marriage.

MARIA
D   G
SCOTIÆ
PIISSIMA REGINA
FRANCIÆ DOTARIA
ANNO
ÆTATISREGNIQ
36.
ANGLICÆ CAPTIVIT
19
S   H
1578

Mary, Queen of Scots, three times married yet a lonely figure in black velvet
who never saw her son, the future James VI, after he was ten months old.

shot whilst Regent of Scotland, and Euphame Elphinstone, daughter of Lord Elphinstone, by whom he fathered Robert Stewart, Earl of Orkney. It seems there was no space to commemorate Elisabeth Beaton, the attractive daughter of the Keeper of Falkland, by whom he fathered Jean Stewart, Countess of Argyll.

Sadly, before long, the 'King's Room', now completely restored, whose ceiling bears his crowned monograms, alternating with those of his queen, Mary of Guise, where the fireplace is dominated by a great armorial wall-painting and where the walls are hung with rich tapestries, held his death-bed. There he lay ill with melancholia (or possibly porphyria) when they brought the news that his daughter, Mary, had been born at Linlithgow on 8 December, 1542. He had longed for a son to replace the two who had been born at Falkland the previous years but who had both died within a year.

From that room when he was sixteen, he had escaped down the little private winding stair to the garden and, disguised as a groom, and attended by two loyal servants, he had ridden through the night to his castle at Stirling, rather than submit any longer to being a pawn of state while his stepfather, Archibald Douglas, Earl of Angus, the then Red Douglas, ruled in his name.

But he was thirty years old and the little winding stair no longer offered a means of escape from his problems. A few days after the birth of his daughter James V, surrounded by his friends and courtiers, signed his last will and testament. A framed replica of it hangs in the room but he was sinking so fast that there was some suspicion that he signed a blank paper which was filled in later, according to the dying man's wishes, by the cardinal.

At midnight, on 14 December, 1542 he

> . . . turned him back and looked and beheld all his lords about him and gave a little smile and laughter, syne kissed his hand and offered the same to all his lords round about him and thereafter held up his hands to God and yielded his spirit.

His widow, Mary of Guise, spent much time at Falkland Palace and, in turn, her daughter Mary, Queen of Scots, in her own widowhood went straight

A portrait of James VI, aged twenty, at Falkland Palace.

to Falkland on her return from France and tried to recreate the atmosphere of the French Court. She was only eighteen and loved outdoor sports. At Falkland she showed all her father's love of hunting and hawking. Nothing was left to chance to make sure the Court enjoyed good sport: roebucks and stags were carried in litters wherever the Court went and were temporarily released for the chase and then recaptured. But twenty-three years later this most passionate and romantic of the Stewarts to live at Falkland, also met with a violent death when she was executed for her involvement in plots against Queen Elizabeth.

Her son James VI, on his frequent visits to Falkland, subscribed to the allegation that he preferred hunting to preaching. The hunting palace came to be associated with plots and counter-plots, attempted murder and religious crises. From there, during the first part of his reign, he conducted affairs of state and held

The kitchen at Falkland Palace.

councils until the town was evacuated because of an outbreak of the plague in 1585.

A year later the Court was back and after his marriage in 1589 to Anne of Denmark (by whom he had seven children including the future Charles I) James conferred a lifetime tenure of the castle and palace on his bride.

Bullet marks on the gatehouse at Falkland mark the attempt in 1593 of the 'Wizard Earl' of Bothwell (nephew of Mary, Queen of Scots' husband) to seize the person of King James by force. But he was repulsed and accused of witchcraft and treason, eventually fled abroad and died in Naples after living there 'in poverty, supporting himself by feats of arms, fortune-telling and necromancy'.

However, when James VI of Scotland was crowned James I of England after the death of Queen Elizabeth, apart from one brief visit he left Scotland for

good and seemed to break the chain of violent deaths that befell the Royal Stewarts who lived at Falkland.

From that time there were only two brief royal visits to Falkland until the present reign: Charles I stayed there after his Scottish Coronation at Holyroodhouse and Charles II was there some time between his proclamation as King in 1650 and his crowning at Scone in 1651. On that visit he gave new Colours to the troops selected to guard him, a ceremony which is believed to have been the inauguration of the Scots Guards.

Two years later the east range of the palace was accidentally burnt when Cromwell's troops occupied the town and palace and over the next two centuries the palace became a ruin. In due course Sir Walter Scott suggested to an Hereditary Keeper that he should begin to restore it as 'a romantic ruin' but, fortunately, when John Crichton-Stuart, 3rd Marquis of Bute, became

Hereditary Keeper in 1877 his plans were considerably more ambitious: he had the gatehouse and the finely decorated Chapel Royal restored and the King's Room rebuilt. Since 1945 the palace has been redecorated and refurbished by an architect, Schomberg Scott, who set a standard of restoration and understanding of historic buildings that has never been surpassed. The King's Room was redecorated and at the same time the palace garden was recreated.

The late Hereditary Keeper, Major Michael Crichton-Stuart, in 1952 appointed the National Trust for Scotland to be Deputy Keeper and made over to it an endowment for future maintenance of the palace and its gardens. His son Ninian Crichton-Stuart is the present Hereditary Keeper and Captain of the Royal Palace of Falkland.

THE PALACE OF HOLYROODHOUSE

Thow suld have seen hir coronation
In the fair abbey of the Holy Rude,
In presence of ane myrthful multitude
On hors and fute, that tyme whilk suld have
    bene!

.From Sir David Lindsay of the Mount's poem on the crowning of James V's first queen, Madeleine of France, at Holyroodhouse on 1 January, 1537

A legend and a miracle relate to the foundation of the mediaeval Abbey of Holyrood, forerunner of the Palace of Holyroodhouse in the forest east of Edinburgh. The legend relates that in 1128, David I, King of the Scots, was staying at Edinburgh Castle and on 14 September celebrated the holy feast of the Exaltation of the Holy Cross. Afterwards, he was persuaded by his courtiers to go hunting rather than spend the holy day in contemplation.

The King soon became separated from the rest of the hunt and was attacked by a white stag and wounded in the thigh before being thrown to the ground with his horse. He raised his right hand to protect himself from the stag's horns but found himself clutching a wooden cross that suddenly appeared between its antlers. The stag vanished and the King returned to the castle.

That night he dreamt that a voice called his name three times and added, 'Make a house for Canons devoted to the Cross.' He obeyed and near the spring where he had first seen the stag he built the monastery of the Holy Rood (Holy Cross) and attached to it an Augustinian Abbey.

The miracle endorsed his action. It occurred when a joiner building the abbey roof fell to the ground and appeared to be dead. The abbot laid his body before the High Altar and the next day the King knelt and prayed beside it. He then ordered the Mass of the Holy Cross to be sung and, on uncovering the man's face, found him to be alive. In due course he made a complete recovery.

In the fourteenth and fifteenth centuries parliaments were often held there and a guest house adjoined the abbey which successive monarchs preferred to the comparative discomfort of Edinburgh Castle. James II was born there in 1430, crowned in the abbey when he was six years old, married there and was interred there after his accidental death at the siege of Roxburgh.

James III lived there and chose the abbey for his wedding to Margaret of Denmark and for her subsequent coronation. James IV and James V were

The main entrance to the Palace of Holyroodhouse, a magnificent seventeenth-century palace
used by the British monarchy. It grew from a guest-house attached
to a mediaeval monastery.

also married there and altered and enlarged the guest house to give this royal seat an air of greater magnificence. It was the former King, James IV, who decided that Edinburgh should be the usual capital of Scotland and that Holyrood should have a Palace.

For a start he built the north-west tower of the present building in time to welcome his bride, Margaret Tudor. He had planned a corresponding south tower, linked to the north-west one by an important architectural façade. But his premature death at the Battle of Flodden meant that a century and a half elapsed before

his design was completed by his great-great-grandson, King Charles II. During the interval the main events that were to secure Holyroodhouse its dramatic place in history, took place.

The most romantic tragedy enacted there concerned Mary, Queen of Scots, who returned to Holyroodhouse an eighteen-year-old widow of the King of France. Four years after her return she was passionately in love with her cousin the handsome Henry, Lord Darnley, two years her junior. They were married in the Chapel Royal at Holyrood on Sunday, 29 July,

Mary, Queen of Scots, and her King Consort Darnley.
They were married when he was only nineteen years old but less than
two years later he was murdered and Mary had married her third husband,
the Earl of Bothwell.

1565, without waiting for the arrival of the papal dispensation that was necessary because they shared the same grandmother, Margaret Tudor.

By the end of the year the Queen had discovered that her husband was a foolish, petulant youth who, not content with the title King Henry, grumbled perpetually because he had not the kingly authority he was incapable of using. Mary turned for advice, when she needed it, to the Piedmontese David Riccio, her secretary, 'a merry fellow and a good musician'. Soon he became her all-powerful minister, a situation which the jealous Darnley could not tolerate. On 9 March, using Darnley's private stairway, his confederates dragged Riccio away from the room where he was at supper with the Queen and butchered him in the outer chamber, leaving the King Consort Darnley's dagger in his body as a sign.

This bloody incident advertised the estrangement between the royal pair to the whole of Europe and the birth of their son a few months later did little to effect their reconciliation. Eleven months after Riccio's murder the King Consort Darnley was strangled escaping from an explosion that wrecked the Kirk o' Field, an abandoned church just outside the walls of Edinburgh, now the site of the University quadrangle. The Queen had persuaded him to stay there rather than at Holyroodhouse because he was suffering from a horrible disease which she was afraid would infect their son James VI, who inherited the throne after his mother had married one of his father's reputed

ABOVE: David Riccio,
Mary's Italian secretary
who played cards with the Queen until late
into the night, thus earning the
jealousy of her husband, the
King Consort Darnley.

LEFT: Mary, Queen of Scots,
in mourning costume,
with the royal arms of Scotland;
behind her on the right are her two ladies
who had waited on her to the
scaffold, Jane Kennedy and Elizabeth Curle,
and on the left a representation,
inscribed AVLA FODRINGHAMY, of the Queen's execution
at Fotheringay Castle on 8 February 1587.
It is probably a copy of the Memorial Portrait,
now at Blair's College, Aberdeen,
which is thought to have been commissioned
by Elizabeth Curle.

OPPOSITE TOP: Levinus Vogelaare's painting 'The Memorial of Lord Darnley', dated 1567, the year the infant James VI was crowned King of Scotland in the Church of the Holy Rude in Stirling: the one-year-old James kneels beside the tomb of his father Darnley; behind him are Darnley's parents, the Earl and Countess of Lennox, with their younger son Charles, all praying for vengeance on Darnley's assassins. The Queen is shown (in the indistinct inset picture, lower left) surrendering to the Confederate Lords at Carberry Hill.

OPPOSITE, BOTTOM LEFT: The coat of arms of King James V.

OPPOSITE, BOTTOM RIGHT: Bonnie Prince Charlie painted between 1739 and 1745. He wears the Star and Ribbon of the Garter on his red jacket.

ABOVE: A late eighteenth-century painting of the French school showing Bonnie Prince Charlie, the 'Young Chevalier', in July 1745 landing on Eriskay in the Outer Hebrides from the French brig *Du Teillay*. From here he went on to raise the clans in the ill-fated '45 Rebellion.

murderers, James, Earl of Bothwell, and been forced to abdicate.

From the age of twelve the young King spent more time in the Palace of Holyroodhouse than any other monarch until he travelled south in 1603, King of England as well as Scotland. Fourteen years later he returned to the palace and stayed for a few weeks.

In June 1633, eight years after his accession, Charles I was crowned King of Scotland in the Abbey of Holyrood and his last visit was in 1641. His son Charles II was crowned at Scone ten years later and never visited Scotland after the Restoration, but on his instructions much of the Palace of Holyroodhouse was rebuilt by the architect, Sir William Bruce of Kinross, in a Palladian classic style—the first major example in Scotland of this pure design. It was left to his brother James, Duke of Albany and York (later King James VII and II), to appreciate the restoration on his intermittent visits before his accession as Lord High Commissioner or Viceroy of Scotland from 1679 to 1682. Then, for a time, royalty took little interest in the palace which was mainly occupied by the Hereditary Keepers, the Dukes of Hamilton.

But in 1745 Bonnie Prince Charlie arrived to give levées, entertainments and a grand ball in the great picture gallery hung with the framed portraits of one hundred and eleven Scottish kings, legendary and real, from Fergus I to Charles II who commissioned the Dutch artist Jacob de Witt to paint them at two pounds a time in 1684.

'A lot of bad portraits,' commented the story-teller Hans Christian Andersen who visited the palace in 1847, and added:

> It was only when I entered Mary Stuart's bedroom that it became Holyrood House for me. The tapestry there represented 'the Fall of Phaeton'* so that is what she always had in front of her eyes; it was almost like a forewarning of her own fall. In the little room at the side, the unfortunate Riccio had been dragged to be murdered; spots of blood are still to be seen on the floor.

Queen Victoria, on her second visit to Holyroodhouse, showed neither the story-teller's vivid imagination nor indulged in his poetic licence. She wrote in her *Journal*:

> We saw the small secret staircase which led up in the turret to Queen Mary's bedroom, and we went up another dark old winding staircase at the top of which poor Riccio was so horribly murdered—whose blood is still supposed to stain the floor. . . . Thence we were shown into poor Queen Mary's bedroom, where are the faded old bed she used, the baby-basket sent her by Queen Elizabeth when King James I was born, and her work-box. All hung with old tapestry, and the two little turret rooms; the one where she was supping when poor Riccio was murdered, the other her dressing-room.

The revival of royal interest in the Palace of Holyroodhouse began when George IV visited it in 1822 and for the last hundred years it has been regularly occupied by successive kings and queens during their visits to Edinburgh. The abbey that preceded it was desecrated by English raids in the sixteenth century. The abbey church was burnt by a mob during the Whig Revolution of 1688; only its ruined nave remains with, at one end, the burial vault containing the earthly remains of many kings and queens who lived in the palace.

ABOVE: The Palace of Holyroodhouse, by Robert Murray, 1882.

RIGHT: Queen Mary's closet, from an engraving by W. H. Bartlett *c*. 1800.

OVERLEAF: Prince Albert, the Prince Consort, in the west drawing room at the Palace of Holyroodhouse. Later, all the walls were oak-panelled from a single tree from Yester, East Lothian. From a painting by G. M. Greig.

* The mythological son of Phoebus the sun god, who caused much of the earth to be parched and barren until he was transfixed by a thunderbolt by Zeus.

MOY HALL

A blue bonnet and a canopy bed draped in tartan hold pride of place at Moy Hall, home of The Mackintosh, reminders of one of the family's most distinguished visitors who arrived unexpectedly on the bitter cold night of Sunday, 16 February, 1746. He was Charles Edward Louis Casimir Stuart, alias the young Chevalier, alias Bonnie Prince Charlie, who arrived in advance of his army to stay at the mainland house by Loch Moy, the second Moy Hall which since 1442 had replaced the island castle of Malcolm M'Kyntosh, the Clan Chief.

The laird was away on Government service but the Prince was entertained by The Mackintosh's lady who had raised the clan for his father, the old Chevalier, and

The Mackintosh of Mackintosh examines some of the treasures of Moy Hall before the bed in which Prince Charles Edward slept in 1746.

ever since has been known as 'Colonel Annie'. Only a few servants and retainers were within easy call and, while the Prince slept, his hostess was worried about his safety. Privately she ordered Donald Fraser, the blacksmith, and four of her own servants to post themselves beyond the guards and sentries along the road to Inverness from where trouble might be expected.

Some two miles from Moy Hall they saw a great body of men approaching. It was a Government force of 1500 men led by Lord Loudoun. The story goes:

> The blacksmith fired his musket and killed one of Loudoun's men, some say the piper. . . . The four servants followed the blacksmith's example, and is thought they too did some execution. Upon this the blacksmith huzzaed and cried aloud 'Advance, Advance, my lads . . . I think we have the dogs now' and raised the slogans of various clans.

Darkness concealed their number and the Hano-verians, thinking they had come upon a strong body of the Prince's supporters, retreated to Inverness. Mean-while the young Lachlan Mackintosh was sent to warn the occupants of Moy Hall.

This engagement, which took place two months before the Prince's disastrous defeat at Culloden, became known as the Rout of Moy. Only one man was killed, Donald Ban MacCrimmon, paragon of pipers, who was with the MacLeods in the Government force. Before he left home he had a presentiment of his death and composed the famous pipe tune known as MacCrimmon's Lament.

That haunting dirge and the four-poster bed where Prince Charles Edward slept are reminders of the second Moy Hall which was accidentally burned down in about 1800 and was succeeded by a third Moy Hall that became riddled with dry rot and was destroyed in the 1950s. Its namesake, a two-storey,

Two months after Bonnie Prince Charlie had
escaped capture at Moy Hall came his disastrous defeat at the
Battle of Culloden.
This eighteenth-century engraving shows one
of the final incidents in his army's defeat by forces
commanded by His Royal Highness,
the Duke of Cumberland.

RIGHT: King George V
who visited Moy Hall seven times between
1905 and 1923.

pleasant stone house, now the family home, was built
in 1957 by the late Vice-Admiral Lachlan Mackintosh of Mackintosh CB, DSO, DSC who in World War
II was on the aircraft carrier HMS *Eagle* when she was
sunk by the Germans, but he was subsequently
rescued.

This house, the last of several to be built on the shore
near the site of the original Moy Hall, also displays a
souvenir of another royal visitor: a walking stick
presented by the Prince of Wales (afterwards George
V) to The Mackintosh. It is bound with silver
engraved with the number of grouse shot on his visits
there between 1905 and 1923. On the seven visits the
King shot a total of 4363 birds.

DUFF HOUSE

This massive Palladian building on the bank of the River Deveron in Banffshire claims to be neither castle nor palace, despite its one-time royal associations, but owes its existence to a wily merchant from Dipple in Morayshire. William Duff, or 'Dipple' as he was known, 'dealt in salmon, meale and grain and greatly in malt,' slept in his mill, drank two bottles of claret every day and amassed a huge fortune. He married twice and he had nine children but his only surviving son, William, inherited his flair together with a good deal of his father's land and became the 1st Earl Fife. In 1753 he commissioned William Adam, father of the

more famous Adam brothers, to design Duff House as his family seat.

The central block was completed at a cost of £70,000 when a crack suddenly appeared in the fabric. The Earl went to law with the architect and, after an embittered quarrel, refused to live in the house and whenever he drove past it the blinds of his carriage were drawn.

His descendants, however, who already owned Balmoral and other extensive estates, had no such scruples about living in one of the handsomest examples of the baroque style in Scotland. It was modelled on the famous Villa Borghese in Rome but the two wings which would have given it an oblong shape were never added and it remained a large quadrangular four-storied building decorated on the outside with vases and statues.

Gradually as the family fame and fortune increased the Earls Fife acquired other homes in London and elsewhere in Scotland but invariably they all spent some time at Duff House. In 1883, the 6th Earl, an Eton-educated wealthy politician, entertained there the Prince of Wales (later King Edward VII) and six years later he married his guest's eldest daughter, Princess Louise, whereupon he was created Duke of Fife and Earl of Macduff. The latter title lent weight to the family's unproved but not impossible claim to be a branch of the great Clan Macduff, the premier clan among the Gaels of mediaeval Scotland whose chiefs had the right to enthrone the Scottish Kings at Scone.

The only son of their marriage was still-born but the daughters, Alexandra and Maud, born in 1891 and 1893, were declared Princesses by their grandfather, King Edward VII in 1905. In 1913 the elder, Her

OPPOSITE: Duff House, which was designed by William Adam, father of the more famous Adam brothers. From an engraving by J. C. Varrall c. 1790.

RIGHT, ABOVE: William Duff, 1st Earl Fife, who commissioned Duff House but refused to live in it. From a painting by William Smith.

RIGHT: James Duff, 2nd Earl Fife.

ABOVE: Group at the wedding of Princess Louise of Wales
and the Duke of Fife, 27 July, 1889.
From left to right; standing: Princess Victoria of Wales,
the bridal couple, Princess Mary of Teck, Princess Marie
Louise of Schleswig-Holstein, Countess Feodore Gleichen.
Seated: Princess Maud of Wales, Countess Helena Gleichen,
Countess Victoria Gleichen, Princess Helena Victoria
of Schleswig-Holstein.

RIGHT: Queen Alexandra, aged 68, in 1913,
the year her granddaughter Princess Alexandra married
Prince Arthur of Connaught.

Highness Princess Alexandra, Duchess of Fife since the death of her father in 1912, was married to His Royal Highness Prince Arthur of Connaught.

It was a romance that delighted the bride's grandmother, Queen Alexandra, for the handsome soldier-prince was the only son of the Duke of Connaught, her husband's younger brother. The couple had fallen in love in the summer of 1913 and were married at the Chapel Royal, St James's, on 15 October. Ten months later the birth of their son* made Queen Alexandra a great-grandmother. She was sixty-nine but this was hard to believe and an old friend, Sir Maurice de Bunsen, a former Ambassador to Portugal

*Alistair, Earl of Macduff, the only child of the marriage. On the death of his father, in 1938, he succeeded his grandfather as 2nd Duke of Connaught and died in Canada in 1943, leaving all his vast Scottish estates to his cousin, Captain Alexander Ramsey of Mar (grandson of the 1st Duke of Connaught) who, on the decision of the Queen is considered very much a part of the Royal Family.

and Spain, described her as looking 'like a young girl'.

Meanwhile in 1906 the bride's parents had paid their last brief annual visit to Duff House. In 1906 they gave it, with 140 acres of land, to the towns of Banff and Macduff to put to the best use in the interest of the beneficiaries. In turn it became an hotel, sanitorium and a World War II prisoner-of-war camp. In 1935 it was passed on to the State and is gradually being restored by the Department of the Environment who open it to the public during the summer months. The grounds contain an 18-hole golf course as well as a fine park.

CAIRNBULG CASTLE

While a cock crows in the North
There'll be a Fraser in Philorth.

This is a legend imputed to Thomas the Rhymer which must have been a prophecy, because its author died a good sixty years before the first Fraser came to the North. Neither does it seem applicable to this land-locked castle of Cairnbulg, one of a chain built in the thirteenth century by the Earls of Buchan for coastal defence against the Norsemen. It stands, large and impressive, high and dry, separated from the town of Fraserburgh, two miles away, by the lonely sand dunes. But closer examination shows that at this point on the Aberdeenshire coastline, the sea has receded over the last few hundred years and the castle was originally strategically sited at the mouth of the tidal estuary to the water of Philorth which gave it its old name.

In those days the Comyns, Earls of Buchan, held all the land in this part of Aberdeenshire but in the Wars of Independence they sided with the English against Bruce. Afterwards their mistake proved costly for in an operation called the 'Harrying of Buchan' their estates were confiscated, the earldom forfeited and their castles destroyed by Bruce so that they could never again be held against him.

Today the restored castle, whose royal associations were consolidated when the present owner, the Right Honourable Flora Fraser, Lady Saltoun, married Captain Alexander Ramsay of Mar, a great-grandson of Queen Victoria, is also indebted on other scores to the military victories of King Robert the Bruce.

Firstly Thomas the Rhymer's prophecy became more appropriate when a hero of the Battle of Bannockburn, Sir Alexander Fraser, Chamberlain of Scotland, married Bruce's widowed sister, the Lady Mary, who had been imprisoned in a cage by King Edward I. Subsequently the Comyn's confiscated estates in Buchan were given to the Earl of Ross as a

Sir Alexander Fraser, aged fifty-six, in 1597, 8th Laird of Philorth and builder of the town and university of Fraserburgh.

Cairnbulg Castle from which the sea has receded so that it no longer commands the tidal estuary
as it did in the thirteenth century.

Group at the wedding of the Hon. Flora Fraser (now Lady Saltoun)
and Captain Alexander Ramsay in 1956. Queen Elizabeth the Queen Mother sits beside the bride's mother Lady Saltoun,
while Queen Ingrid of Denmark sits next to the bridegroom and his mother
Lady Patricia Ramsay.

reward for throwing in his lot—rather tardily—with Bruce. In 1375 the earl's younger daughter and co-heiress married Sir Alexander Fraser, grandson of the Chamberlain of Scotland and the former Lady Mary Bruce.

In 1380 they set about restoring the castle which eventually became known as Cairnbulg instead of Philorth. They built the main tower, a massive keep rising four storeys high, and a courtyard and outbuildings. One of these buildings probably contained the kitchen which, at that time, was usually well away from the main building to minimize the danger from fire.

The powerful Frasers lived there until the late sixteenth century and built the town of Fraserburgh

and a new castle, now the Kinnaird Head lighthouse. In the sixteenth century King James VI, by royal charter granted to the Frasers of Philorth, confirmed the unique right for them to have their own university at Fraserburgh. The right still continues but nearby Aberdeen University was so jealous that during the first few years of its existence they sabotaged it by luring away all its leading dons.

Ironically that did not obliterate the establishment of the Fraser clan's name in the academic world. In 1964 the Simon Fraser University was founded in British Columbia, named after the intrepid Canadian explorer, a descendant of Sir Simon Fraser, the brother of Sir Alexander Fraser, Bruce's Chamberlain of Scotland.

Meanwhile, by the beginning of the seventeenth century, Sir Alexander Fraser, 8th of Philorth, after building a town, a university and a new castle, was heavily in debt and was obliged to sell his old castle and a good deal of land. His son married the heiress of the great Lord Saltoun, a peerage of 1445 which the Frasers duly inherited. Not until 1934 was the original castle bought back for the family by the 19th Lord Saltoun who modernized it and in 1966 gave it to his daughter, the present owner, Lady Saltoun. That was ten years after her marriage to Alexander Ramsay, a member of the present Royal Family as grandson of Prince Arthur, Duke of Connaught, Queen

Victoria's third and favourite son. (The Sovereign's personal decision determines who is considered a member of the Royal Family.) The bridegroom's mother was Princess Patricia of Connaught, who became on marriage Lady Patricia Ramsay, known as 'Princess Pat', Colonel-in-Chief of the famous PPCLI, 'Princess Patricia's Canadian Light Infantry' in the First World War.

The marriage took place at St Peter's Church, Fraserburgh and among the guests were the Queen of Denmark, a first cousin of the bridegroom, and Queen Elizabeth, the Queen Mother, who spends many of her happiest days in her own Scottish homes.

INVERARAY CASTLE

What I admire here is the
total defiance of expense.

Samuel Johnson, 24 October, 1773

Nearly thirty years separate two of Queen Victoria's entries in her diaries recording her visits to Inveraray Castle, the seat of the Dukes of Argyll, Chiefs of the Clan Campbell. During that interval the vast baronial mansion, that replaced a fifteenth-century fortress and had taken almost one hundred years to build from the year 1744, had achieved a new royal status, in addition to its owner's royal descent in the female line from the ancient kings of Argyll.

On 18 August, 1847, Queen Victoria wrote:

The weather was particularly fine and we were much struck by the extreme beauty of Inveraray—presenting as it does such a combination of magnificent timber, with high mountains, and a noble lake.

The pipers walked beside the carriage, and the Highlanders on either side as we approached the house. Outside stood the Marquis of Lorn, just two years old, a dear, white, fat, fair little fellow with reddish hair, but very delicate features like his father and his mother; he is such a merry, independent little child.

The following year Princess Louise, the sixth of the nine children of Prince Albert and Queen Victoria was born. The next time the Queen stayed at Inveraray Castle she was a widow. Her diary entry for 22 September, 1875, describes the very special welcome she received where the duke's property began, five or six miles before Inveraray:

... where the Duke's property begins, four of our own horses were waiting, and here dear Louise and Lorne met us, looking pleased and well. Lorne rode, and dear Louise got into her pony carriage and drove after us. ... In front of the house the volunteers in kilts and red jackets, and the artillery volunteers in blue and silver, of whom Lorne is the colonel, were drawn up, and a good many spectators were assembled. The Duke and Duchess of Argyll and their six girls were at the door.

The Duke and Duchess took us upstairs at once to our rooms, part of which are Louise's: very comfortable, not large but cheerful, and having a beautiful view of Loch Fyne. It was one when we arrived and we lunched at two, only Louise, Beatrice, her youngest daughter, and Lorne. ...

Inveraray Castle, Argyll, was built in the eighteenth century, based on a design by Sir John Vanbrugh
the dramatist and untrained architect who, with his artist's imagination, also built
Blenheim Palace and Castle Howard.

By then the Queen had learned that the 'dear, white, fat, fair little fellow' of her first visit spelt his name with an 'e'. Four years previously he had become her son-in-law and was destined to be Governor-General of Canada.

By agreeing to her daughter's marriage Queen Victoria had set a precedent for royalty marrying commoners. It must have been a hard choice for the Queen, for 'The Maiden all for Lorne', as the princess was known, had threatened to go into a convent if she did not get her way. She had fallen in love with the talented, artistic, handsome, fey Marquis with the immense violence sometimes envinced by members of the Royal Family. The Queen had taken Lord Lorne on one side and told him of the hostility to such a break with tradition, particularly from the Prussian royal family who took the deepest exception. Lorne replied, 'Ma'am, my ancestors were kings when the Hohenzol-

lerns were parvenus.' The matter was settled but the marriage was not a happy one.

Almost one hundred years before Queen Victoria's first visit to Inveraray, the 3rd Duke of Argyll had started an amazingly ambitious scheme to replace his crumbling fifteenth-century castle on the bank of the River Aray with a building of unprecedented size in the West of Scotland. He also planned to remove the old town surrounding it to a new site and transform the existing parks into a fine landscape.

The new and impressive power house of the West from which the successive Earls of Argyll acted as Crown agents in the long struggle to bring the whole of the Western highlands and islands under control—and in the course of doing so they caused a good deal of trouble—was based on an original design by Sir John Vanbrugh, the English baroque architect and drama-tist. It was reminiscent of a French château with its four

This painting of HRH Princess Louise, Duchess of Argyll,
by Koberwein, after Winterhalter, hangs in the Victorian Room
of the castle.

The 5th Duke of Argyll;
a portrait attributed to Cosway.

The Duke and Duchess of Argyll with their son Torquhil
Ian, Marquis of Lorne, and their daughter Lady Louise
Iona Campbell.

corner towers capped by conical roofs of gleaming slate. The theatrical design was developed by a London architect, Roger Morris, and building started in 1744.

The 3rd Duke never lived to occupy it although he visited it every autumn until the year of his death in 1761. Work was then suspended since his successor, a cousin, was not interested in the scheme for the castle or the town and only when he was succeeded by his son, the 5th Duke, in 1770, was the great work resumed.

Soon afterwards Dr Johnson visited the castle with Boswell and professed himself 'much struck by the grandeur and elegance of this princely seat', but he felt it might be improved by the addition of another storey. His comment was strangely prophetic because a century later the roof of the central hall was destroyed by

fire and during the repair a third storey with gabled dormer windows was added by the 8th Duke.

Today, a tour of the castle with its fine collection of tapestries, furniture, pictures and an armoury which houses the dirk handle and sporran belonging to Rob Roy, the Highland character immortalized by Sir Walter Scott, evokes the long warlike history of the Campbell clan. The small gentle Victorian room typifies its latter-day connection with royalty. It contains the dainty maplewood writing desk inlaid with blue, given by Queen Victoria to Princess Louise on her marriage, a charming portrait of the Princess when she became Duchess of Argyll, painted by Koberwein after Winterhalter and, between the windows, a large canvas of her wedding in St George's

One of the rooms in Inveraray Castle.

A corner of the Victorian Room showing the maplewood
writing desk given by Queen Victoria to her fourth daughter,
Princess Louise, on her marriage in 1871.

Chapel, Windsor, by Sydney Hall in which most of the sixty or so spectators are easily identifiable.

It is not surprising that this castle which looks like one out of a fairy tale, has its fair share of ghosts and portents, some older than the home to which they have attached themselves. Flocks of ravens, 'ominous birds of yore', wheel about the castle before the death of a Chief of the Clan Campbell. Niall Campbell, the 10th Duke, told H. W. Hill, one-time secretary of the English Church Union, that he believed in the tradition. He also described a more mysterious sign that had appeared just prior to the death of his father, Lord Archibald Campbell, brother of the 9th Duke, Queen Victoria's son-in-law, which was seen by many witnesses. This was a galley which sailed over Loch Fyne and then continued its voyage overland to vanish at a spot associated with St Columba, which had been given to the Church by the Campbells. It was shaped like the ship on the Campbell coat of arms and had three figures standing on board.

The castle is also haunted by a phantom harper, the ghost of one who was executed by order of the Marquis of Montrose in the seventeenth century when he drove the Marquis of Argyll from his castle. It seems the squint-eyed Archibald had abandoned the traditional

Rob Roy's sporran, belt and dirk handle are on display in the 95-foot high Armoury Hall.

loyalty of his family to the Stewart kings as successors of the Bruces. He led the extremist Convenanting party that sought to impose religious control on the state and, after being defeated by Montrose whose men ravaged Argyll, he was ultimately victorious. He personally crowned King Charles II at Scone but was beheaded at the Restoration for having collaborated with Cromwell.

The ghostly harper, who is described as a 'harmless old thing', appears in Campbell tartan and apart from playing his harp he makes a noise in the green room as if books were being flung about. But when anyone goes to investigate every book is in place and the family portraits, including some particularly fine ones by Gainsborough, Sir Peter Lely and John Opie, are in perfect order.

Down the centuries the great physical courage and ability of the Campbells has brought them much glory but, not surprisingly, their success has engendered considerable romantic unpopularity and even hatred amongst the clans they worsted. Perhaps Robert Burns' *Epigram Written at Inveraray* expresses the animosity mildly:

> Whoe'er he be that sojourns here,
> I pity much his case,
> Unless he come to wait upon
> The Lord their God, his Grace.
> There's naething here but Highland pride,
> And Highland scab and hunger;
> If Providence has sent me here,
> 'Twas surely in his anger.

BALMORAL CASTLE

. . .our dear Balmoral.

Queen Victoria, 24 August, 1867

In the same way that Queen Victoria's agreement to the marriage of her daughter, Princess Louise, to a non-royal personage broke Hanoverian royal tradition, so did her decision to have a home in Scotland. Apart

from George IV's brief stay in Edinburgh in 1822 no reigning British monarch had been to Scotland since Charles II, nearly two hundred years previously.

Queen Victoria and Prince Albert made three visits

Queen Victoria and Prince Albert arrive at Granton in 1842 on their first visit to Scotland.
The journey by sea from Woolwich on the *Royal George*, accompanied by eleven
other steamboats, took two-and-a-half days. Painting by an anonymous artist.

in the first eight years of their marriage and these convinced them that they needed a home of their own there for regular autumn holidays. The Queen's *Journal* shows that the 'great peculiarity about the Highland and Highlanders' fulfilled a real need in her life;

> . . . they are such a chivalrous, fine, active people. Our stay among them was so delightful. Independently of the beautiful scenery, there was a quiet, a retirement, a wildness, a liberty, and a solitude that had such a charm for us.

Here the role of sovereign could be subjugated to that of a young wife and mother still very much in love. For her wish to have a Scottish home and for Albert's interpretation of it, later generations of royalty have had cause to be grateful.

Its location was largely influenced by the health of the royal couple. Both suffered from twinges of

rheumatism and their chief physician, Sir James Clark, a Scotsman and a recognized authority on the influence of climate on health, was emphatic that Deeside was the place for them. His own son had been convalescing from an illness at Balmoral, the home of Sir Robert Gordon, a distinguished diplomat, where he had found an unusual purity in the air and plenty of sunshine and a report showed it to be one of the driest places in the country.

The sudden death of Sir Robert enabled the Royal Family to lease his property in 1848. After her first visit the Queen confided to her *Journal*:

> It was love at first sight. . . . All seemed to breathe freedom and peace and to make one forget the world and its sad turmoil.

After four years' tenancy the estate of 17,400 acres was brought by Prince Albert from the Fife Trustees for

The drawing room with its tartan carpet, curtains and upholstery. Watercolour by J. Roberts.

A late Victorian painting of a bedroom at Balmoral, by J. Roberts.

Bringing the stags home to Balmoral after a day's hunting. Oil painting by Carl Haag, 1854.

The gillies' ball at Balmoral in 1859.

30,000 guineas. Balmoral, as it was, was too small for the growing Royal Family, their guests and members of the Court, and an Aberdeen architect, William Smith, was engaged to design a larger castle, just one hundred yards away. Balmoral entered into a new phase in its long history.

Its story began in 1484 when as 'Bouchmorale', a beautiful home situated on a curve of the River Dee, it was leased to Alexander Gordon, second son of the Earl of Huntly, for £6 8s 6d a year. He lived at the nearby castle of Abergeldie and the combined estates gave him a secure footing on Deeside until 1662 when his powerful neighbours, the Farquharsons, foreclosed on some debts and acquired Balmoral.

Their ownership lasted little more than a century for they were ardent Jacobites and after the defeat of the Young Chevalier they had to sell the heavily mort-gaged estate to pay the fines imposed by the Hanov-erians to ensure the end of Stuart claims to the throne. The purchaser was James Duff, 2nd Earl Fife, a wealthy politician whose father had built Duff House.

He never lived at Balmoral but, with his extensive estates in Morayshire and Banffshire, it meant that by the end of the eighteenth century he was reputed to be able to control elections in three counties. He let it to a succession of tenants and in 1831 the wheel of occupancy turned full circle when it was leased by Sir Robert Gordon, a descendant of the Gordon family who had first lived there. On acquiring it he built a small new castle, Balmoral II.

From the start Balmoral III was Prince Albert's creation. The Scottish Highlands reminded him of his Saxon homeland and he felt able to express himself more spontaneously than he had ever been able to do in England. When the castle was finished in 1856 Queen Victoria wrote:

> Every year my heart becomes more fixed in this dear Paradise and so much more so now, that *all* has become my dear Albert's *own* creation, own building, own laying out . . . and his great taste and the impress of his dear hand, have been stamped everywhere.

The 'creation' was not a palace nor an official residence but a laird's house that happened to be the Scottish home of Great Britain's reigning sovereign which it has remained through six reigns. Built of white granite quarried on the Balmoral estate, its gleaming Scottish baronial-style towers and turrets are set in landscaped grounds surrounded by deep woodland. Terraces and courts of small formal gardens surround the castle with beds filled with flowers chosen as far as possible to bloom during the owners' autumn visits, like the late raspberries which are specially cultivated as a Septem-ber crop. Great trees, poplars and pines brought by Prince Albert from his native Coburg, help to ensure privacy.

The splendid views of the Scottish scenery from the windows were matched by the Scottish flavour inside for the new castle's interior was designed like a Highland shooting box and clad in tartan from floor to ceiling: the carpets, curtains and upholstery were of Royal Stuart tartan and green hunting Stuart. For contrast there was some chintz with a thistle pattern, Highland weapons and trophies and Landseer paint-ings on the walls. The Queen wore her own Victorian tartan while Prince Albert designed a Balmoral tartan of black, red and lavender on grey for deer stalking.

His enthusiasm for this sport needed some subtle curbing and of the day when he shot nineteen deer it was written:

> Then from the scene that viewed his warlike toils
> The blood-stained victor hastens with his spoils,
> And laid them humbly at Victoria's feet—
> To such a Queen most intellectual treat.
> So on the grass plot—to a shambles changed—
> The gory things were scrupulously ranged,
> Before the windows of the Royal guest,
> Famed for the woman-softness of her breast.

This appeared following a report that deer were driven past the Prince at Balmoral, so that he might get some practice and show his skill. There were no recurrences.

Like all family homes Balmoral witnessed its share of happiness and sorrow, much of which is commemo-rated in cairns, memorials and plaques sited in the policies or on the sky-line of the hills. There was much to celebrate. Three days after the Royal Family arrived in their newly completed home a great bonfire was lit to celebrate the fall of Sevastopol; two weeks later their eldest daughter, fourteen-year-old Princess Victoria, became engaged to Prince Frederick William of Prussia, after he had plucked her a sprig of white heather on their ride up Craig-na-Ban.

Memorable to the family were the 'Great Expeditions' when they set off on ponies to explore the wild countryside, riding for days at a time in the saddle or in the carriage, sometimes covering a hundred miles a day. They stayed in simple inns in remote villages, slept in sparsely furnished rooms and chatted unrecognized to the friendly villagers. Sometimes they travelled incognito and at least once, the Queen recalled, her disguise was nearly penetrated when, as she reported in her *Journal*, she heard a woman observe:

'The lady must be terrible rich,' as I had so many gold rings on my fingers!

At Balmoral the gillies' ball was an annual ritual with the Queen and her guests joining in a rowdy Hooligan dance with the best. Days of shared pleasures were interspersed with ones when Victoria and Albert followed their separate interests. On such evenings the castle courtyard would suddenly be illuminated with flares to welcome the hunters back with their kill after a day's stag hunt and after a good day's stalking the keepers and gillies would take part in a torch-light dance. Later, after dinner Victoria would show her husband the gentle little watercolours she had painted on her excursions into the hills she loved and where she was mindful of the drawing instruction given to her by the painter Sir Edwin Landseer. It was hardly surprising that, on returning to England in 1858, she wrote to her daughter: 'The heartache I suffer each year, on leaving Balmoral and coming here, is most distressing.'

On Wednesday, 16 October, 1861, there was not a cloud in the sky when Victoria and Albert and three of their daughters set off before nine o'clock for a day's expedition. They drove and rode and walked for five hours to picnic on the edge of the valley of Cairn Lochan. The Queen wrote in her *Journal*:

We sat on a very precipitous place, which made one dread anyone moving backwards; I made some hasty sketches; and then Albert wrote on a bit of paper that we had lunched here, put it into a Salters-water bottle, and buried it there, or rather stuck it into the ground. . . . We went back on our side of the river; and if it had been a little earlier, Albert might have got a stag — but it was too late. The moon rose and shone beautifully, and we returned at twenty minutes to seven o'clock, much pleased and interested with this delightful expedition. Alas! I fear *our* last great one!

It proved a strangely prophetic comment for two months later Albert was dead from typhoid fever at the age of forty-two.

He bequeathed Balmoral to the Queen who, in turn, arranged that it would always remain the property of the reigning Sovereign. The following year a 35-foot cairn was raised on Craig Lowrigan inscribed:

To the beloved memory of Albert the Great and Good Prince Consort, raised by his heartbroken widow Victoria R.

Closer to the castle the Queen erected a 10-foot high bronze statue of the Prince depicted by William Theed, wearing Highland dress and the Garter, with his retriever by his side. It was a replica of a marble statue inside the castle which was sculpted in his life-time.

Otherwise Queen Victoria made few changes at Balmoral during her long widowhood except to implement the ideas Albert had instigated. On 24 December, 1861, she wrote to her uncle, the King of the Belgians:

my firm resolve, my *irrevocable decision*, viz. that *His* wishes, *his* plans about everything, *his* views about *every*thing are to be *my* law. And no *human power* will make me swerve from what *he* decided and wished. . . .

As the years passed her spring visits became annual occurrences in addition to the extended autumn ones and eventually the Queen spent one third of the year at Balmoral. It seemed as if only in the seclusion of the home Albert had created, could Victoria come to terms with her loneliness. She rebuilt the head gardener's cottage and conducted affairs of state from this unusual 'audience chamber', guarded by her faithful Highland attendant, the enigmatic John Brown.

There her prime ministers were in attendance including Gladstone who, on his first visit, walked a precise 24¾ miles and then complained bitterly of stiffness. However, the next day he did a modest nineteen miles up Lochnagar and felt 'fresh as a lad'. Disraeli, on the other hand, passed the time more sedately, wandering in the gardens, comparing them with his own garden at Hughenden, and complaining that 'carrying on the Government of a country six hundred miles from the Metropolis doubles the labour'.

In time Queen Victoria recaptured some of her old gaiety and zest for living and during the last twelve years of her life visitors were warmly welcomed at Balmoral. Often her daughter-in-law, Princess Alexandra, was there to help to entertain the distinguished personages who alighted from the royal train at Ballater station.

Three years before Prince Albert had finished building his new Balmoral, the Royal Deeside Line, the first complete railway line in Aberdeenshire, had been built to run along the Dee Valley from Aberdeen, following the course of the River Dee through some of the most beautiful scenery in Scotland. For 113 years—until it was overtaken by the competition of motor travel—it ran through the lowlands to the gateway of the old highland kingdom of Mar at Ballater station. It seems the reason why it was never extended beyond Ballater to Braemar was because Queen Victoria objected to a railway along the edge of her Balmoral estate, disturbing the privacy.

However, the Queen used the railway regularly to travel to and from her Highland home and her despatches were conveyed daily by a special messenger train—a very colourful affair with its engine painted tartan and one or two royal coaches in purple and gold with the royal cipher on their sides.

It proudly bore distinguished royal visitors including Queen Elizabeth of Roumania who wrote poetry, prose and plays under the name of Carmen Silva and had a particular interest in her native folk-lore. In 1889 the Shah of Persia arrived for a three-day visit. He presented a striking figure:

dressed in a dark military uniform ... over which he wore a flowing military cloak sufficiently open to display the large emeralds worn on his breast. In his Astrakhan cap the Shah wore a large Persian crest richly encrusted with diamonds.

In 1896, the Emperor Nicholas II, Czar of all the Russias, came with the Empress Alexandra Feodorovna of Russia. They were accompanied by such a large staff that a special village had to be built to accommodate them for the ten-day visit. Even then four laundrymaids had to share a bed and the footmen's quarters were as packed full as the hold of a ship.

The beautiful empress was the Queen's grand-daughter 'Alicky', the youngest surviving daughter of Princess Alice, Grand Duchess of Hesse, and she received a warm welcome but the Czar himself was greeted with little enthusiasm. It was a time when, as a result of events in Turkey, Russia was hated in Britain and the Press noted:

He is a political personage whose unlimited power exceeds that of any monarch on earth.

Nevertheless his cool reception was lost in the warm glow at Ballater Station decorated in the imperial colours of yellow and black, where electric lighting had been especially installed for the occasion and lit the square as well as the station and the road as far as the burgh boundary. It was powered from a generator with steam from a Great North engine in the station.

Despite strong security arrangements everything had been planned to be as spectacular as possible to try and impress Russia and foster good relations. A hundred men of the Black Watch formed the guard of honour at Ballater station when the Czar, wearing the uniform of the Scots Greys, was received with the Czarina by the Duke and Duchess of York. The visitors were accompanied by the Prince of Wales, in the uniform of Colonel-in-Chief of the 25th Dragoons of Kiev, who had joined the royal train at Ferryhill.

Bonfires blazed from every hill and church bells rang out as an escort of Scots Greys led the cavalcade of carriages through the night along the Deeside road lit by blazing torches held high by Highland troops and, at the approach to the castle, the queen's pipers added their music to the welcome.

Arrival of Czar Nicholas II and his wife, Queen Victoria's granddaughter at Balmoral
accompanied by the Prince of Wales and the Duke of Connaught, 23 September, 1896.
From a painting by Orlando Norie.

Queen Victoria at work in the Garden Cottage, Balmoral, 1882. Watercolour by W. Simpson.

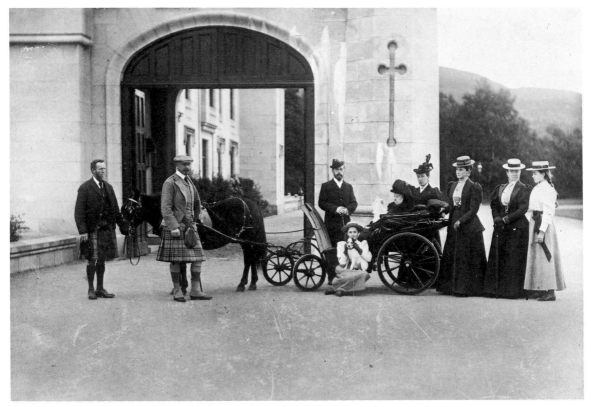

A still taken from the first moving picture of royalty by the new cinematograph process in 1896.
Czar Nicholas II stands behind Queen Victoria in her pony carriage.
Next to the Queen are her granddaughters, the Duchess of Fife
and the Czarina, the Duchess of Connaught and Princess Margaret.
In the foreground is Princess Patricia of Connaught.

The visit coincided with the date on which the Queen had reigned longer by a day than any other English sovereign—nearly sixty years—and also with the first time a moving picture had been taken of royalty by the new cinematograph process. Evidently the Czar enjoyed his visit because, on leaving he handed the Master of the Household £1000 to be distributed among the servants.

By then Queen Victoria had added the Ballochbuie Forest to Balmoral at a cost of nearly £100,000. It is a forest that has one of the largest areas of natural Caledonian pine left in Scotland. The story goes that it was once sold to the Clan Farquharson by the Clan MacGregor for a tartan plaid. When it became part of the Balmoral estate Queen Victoria had a stone erected there inscribed 'The bonniest plaid in Scotland'.

Successive generations of the Royal Family have been inclined to agree.

They have all contributed to Balmoral's history. King Edward VII and Queen Alexandra spent a month of every summer holiday there when, from Queen Alexandra's letters, it appears she felt her mother-in-law's influence very strongly and made little changes in the castle. King George V and Queen Mary spent about eight weeks of every summer there. Their affection for the place is reflected in the gentle additions they made to the gardens, notably a formal pansy garden and the construction of a low semi-circular wall of rocks planted with alpines leading to a fountain surrounded by flower beds. Known as 'Queen Mary's garden', the entrance is through a pair of wrought iron gates monogrammed 'GR' and 'MR'.

Queen Elizabeth reviewing a Highland Regiment at Balmoral in 1955.

At Balmoral during his short reign King Edward VIII entertained Mrs Simpson but the castle soon regained its more conventional image as a family home when King George VI received a spontaneous heart-warming welcome there on his first visit as king with his family in 1937. He wrote to his mother:

> When we got to the gate here, about 100 of the employees here pulled the Balmoral Victoria with us four in it and Ross on the box all the way to the Castle, in silence except for the pipers, who marched ahead playing. . . . It was their own idea.

It is a family home too with sentimental memories for Queen Elizabeth and the Duke of Edinburgh, for there in August, 1946, they became unofficially engaged. In the eight weeks or so they spend there each year from mid-August and sometimes occasional weekends, they too continue its ongoing story. New trees have been planted, there is a water garden devised by the Duke of Edinburgh who has also extended Queen Mary's garden, and in line with maintaining an efficient and modern estate of 24,000 acres, there is a fold of pedigree Highland cattle and a herd of Luing cattle instead of the old Ayrshire dairy herd.

Most of the stables have been converted into garages but two blocks remain to house ponies and riding horses for the Royal Family. Several traps, dog carts and game carts are still used and a four-wheeled Balmoral dog cart presented to the Queen in 1966 is often driven four-in-hand by the Duke of Edinburgh using stalking ponies.

Another of the Duke's activities is reflected inside

Queen Elizabeth at Balmoral at the time of her Silver Wedding in 1972.

The Prince of Wales returning to Balmoral with his gundog Harvey, after fishing the River Dee where it runs through the estate.

Prince Charles at Balmoral with his cousin,
Lady Sarah Armstrong-Jones, in 1972.

Prince Philip and Princess Anne at an informal family
barbecue at Balmoral.

the castle where Queen Victoria's beloved Landseer paintings are far outweighed by a large collection of Antarctic pictures by Edward Seago who accompanied Prince Philip, as he then was, on his trip to Antarctica in 1956 and, at the Prince's suggestion, became the first painter to work there.

Today, more than ever, in the late summer Balmoral comes into its own as one of the few places in the kingdom where the Queen and her family are able to relax in the greatest privacy and a seclusion they can hardly ever find anywhere else.

A local supplier of fishing tackle.

BIRKHALL

I had a little whisky and water, as the people
declared pure water would be too chilling.

Queen Victoria after her ascent of Ben Muich Dhui

The atmosphere of a beautiful little dower house pervades Birkhall which looks east over Glen Muick and is too small to be considered a royal residence. Yet, as such, it has served the past four generations of royalty. Prince Albert envisaged it as an ideal Scottish home for his eldest son and bought it in 1849 with its estate of 6500 acres from the Fife trustees from whom, three years later, he purchased the adjoining estate of

Balmoral. It was bought in the name of the eight-year-old Prince of Wales who stayed there only once, in 1862, the year before his marriage to HRH Princess Alexandra of Denmark. However, in time it was to play a rather more important part in his mother's life although she too never actually lived there.

The house, surrounded by tall and graceful birch trees from which it derives its name 'Birk Ha'', was built by Captain Charles Gordon, a rather reluctant Jacobite, in 1715, the year of the first Jacobite rising. He deserted shortly before the Raising of the Standard but, swayed by local enthusiasm, returned in time to see his feudal superior, the Earl of Mar, declare for the Stuarts.

Birkhall: 'too small to be considered a royal residence'.
From a painting by Henry Fisk,
1849.

Later Birkhall became the home of the youngest of his three sons, Joseph, who took part in the '45 Rising, and after the Battle of Culloden, was forced into hiding nearby. Elizabeth, his wife and staunch Jacobite, sheltered two other refugees from the battle. They were the Oliphants of Gask, father and son, who concealed their identity under the names of Brown and Whytt until their hostess arranged their escape to Sweden. Their choice of names illustrates a theory that after 'the '45' it was dangerous to bear the name of a family associated with the Rising so that 'Macs' reappeared from hiding with undistinguished names like Brown or White.

Although Queen Victoria never stayed at Birkhall, while she was at Balmoral she visited it regularly for it was usually occupied by friends and members of her Household. Her physician, Sir James Clark, was a regular occupant and in 1856 Florence Nightingale, tired and ill after the Crimean campaign, stayed there and the Queen called on her daily. They walked in the gardens 'plotting and planning' for the start of an Army Medical Service which became the foundation of the Royal Army Medical Corps.

Birkhall was also the stepping-stone to two of Queen Victoria's favourite haunts. Beyond it the road to Loch Muick, the largest sheet of water in the district, led through the wilderness to a cottage called Alt-na-guithasach, near the eastern end of the loch. It took its name from the burn which poured down from Lochnagar to join the River Muich. The 'bothie' or the 'hut' as it was known, had two sitting-rooms and a bedroom and dressing-room for the Queen and the Prince, a small room for the lady-in-waiting and one for the maid. A few yards away a primitive little house was constructed for a small staff. There was no mention of a bathroom in either place.

Queen Victoria and Prince Albert stayed there regularly from 1840 until his death and both revelled in the freedom and isolation. The Prince learnt Gaelic from the gillies who rowed them over the loch to net trout and took them on expeditions into the hills, on foot or on horseback, in all weathers. The Queen was indefatigable. One less hardy member of the party commented ruefully that the trout and midges of Loch Muick were 'each superlative in their way'.

Alt-na-guithasach – the 'Hut' at the eastern end of lonely Loch Muick,
where Queen Victoria and Prince Albert spent some of their happiest days.
From a painting by C. Bossoli.

After Prince Albert's death the Queen found Alt-na-guithasach too vivid with happy memories for her to stay there again. Seeking more solitude and a temporary withdrawal from the life she had so enjoyed, she built 'the Widow's House' as she called it, in an

John Brown, Queen Victoria's personal attendant.

even more remote position at the lonely western end of the loch. It had a sitting-room, bedroom, dining-room, kitchen and maid's room on the ground floor and above, a room for a lady-in-waiting and an occasional guest, and three rooms for her faithful John Brown, for the cook and another servant. Here in her husband's favourite spot where he had often promised he would build himself a cottage, she could be out of touch with the rest of the world for days on end.

Its real name was the 'Glassalt Shiel'—the shiel 'of the grey burn' and, at first, the heartbroken Queen had a strong feeling that there she would find her husband. The first night she spent there she wrote:

> I thought of the happy past and my darling husband whom I fancied I must see, and who always wished to build here, in this favourite wild spot, quite in amidst the hills. At Altnaguithasach I could not have lived again now—alone. It is far better to have built a totally new house; but then the sad thought struck me that it was the first Widow's house, not built by him or hallowed by his memory. But I am

sure his blessing does rest on it, and on those who live in it.

Her Private Secretary, Sir Henry Ponsonby, was one of many who deplored her disappearance to this inaccessible retreat but he had to admit that she always returned 'the better and livelier for it'. And as the years passed she gradually found the strength to come to terms with her loneliness and rediscovered a degree of happiness. Perhaps the foundations for her recovery were laid in those quiet days when, forgetting that she was queen, she strolled along the sand and pebbles beside the lonely loch whose name, she learned appropriately enough, meant Darkness or Sorrow.

In 1885 Queen Victoria bought Birkhall from her son and, for the rest of the century, it was frequently occupied by her young widowed daughter-in-law, Princess Helena, Duchess of Albany, and her two children. The princess had married Queen Victoria's youngest son Prince Leopold, who died suddenly at the age of thirty-one in 1884. Their eldest child Princess Alice (who later married the Earl of Athlone) wrote of Birkhall in her memoirs:

> Here we spent some of the happiest days of our lives. It was a small place in those days. We loved the sloping garden full of fruit and sweet peas and, at the bottom, a chain bridge, heavenly to jump upon, which spanned the rushing little Muich where we loved to play.

And it was as a family holiday home that Birkhall came into its own again during the reign of King George V when his second son and his wife, the Duke and Duchess of York, and their daughters, Princess Elizabeth and Princess Margaret, found it was one of the few places where they could enjoy a quiet family life. However, their plans for altering the gardens were interrupted by the Duke's accession to the throne in 1936 when Balmoral became their official Scottish home and their visits to Birkhall ceased until 1939 when the two princesses were installed there for a time with a governess, on the outbreak of World War II.

In peace-time Princess Elizabeth took over Birkhall and in 1947 part of her honeymoon was spent there. In 1952, on the death of King George VI, mother and

Princess Helena, Duchess of Albany,
and widow of Prince Leopold, Queen Victoria's youngest son.
The Princess spent much time at Birkhall with her
two children.

daughter changed their Deeside homes and Queen Elizabeth, the Queen Mother, energetically embarked on supplementing some of the plans she had made for Birkhall nearly twenty years before. A new wing was built to accommodate guests—including Prince Charles when, as a schoolboy at Gordonstoun, he spent many of his weekend exeats with the grandmother who shared and encouraged his interest in fishing.

In the garden, alpines were planted among miniature rocks surrounding the new wing, a rose garden was made and masses of early-flowering bulbs and plants were introduced to bloom a welcome to greet the Queen Mother when she arrives for the spring fishing season on the River Dee.

ABERGELDIE CASTLE

Bloody-thirsty Dee
Each year needs three,
But Bonnie Don
She needs none.

The verse refers to a superstition surrounding the stately Gordon stronghold that, for five centuries, has dominated the south bank of the River Dee, about three miles from Balmoral. It derives from the fact that the Dee, with its tendency to severe flooding from the melting snows of the Cairngorms or after prolonged rainfall, is likely to kill three people a year.

The estate lies between Balmoral and Birkhall and the castle was described in the sixteenth century as one 'of most respect'. It stood in a commanding position by a track running north and south and by a ford through the Dee. For additional protection a loop was made in the river to form a moat.

The most interesting and ancient part of the castle is

A watercolour of Abergeldie Castle
on the banks of the River Dee
by W. Wyld.

the high rectangular tower with a crow-stepped gable roof with a rather elaborate angle turret. This tower forms the nucleus of the whole structure and many alterations and additions were made to it at later dates.

From the time it was built, in the sixteenth century, Abergeldie was a Gordon stronghold, having been acquired by Sir Alexander Gordon of Midmar, second son of the 1st Earl of Huntly, and had embarked on a long and stormy history.

The Gordons, Cavaliers and Jacobites, were not a family to miss a war. They fought and were killed at the battles of Pinkie, against the invading English, and at Glenlivet in 1594, when the Catholic Gordons were in revolt against the forces of King James VI. They fought with Montrose, and also with Dundee at the Battle of Killiecrankie, the first Jacobite rising in Scotland which few men of consequence chose to join. The outcome was that, eventually, the victorious

General Mackay garrisoned their castle in an attempt to preserve discipline on Upper Deeside. So the Gordons created new homes and in 1715 built Birkhall, while waiting to reclaim Abergeldie.

The 'Gey Gordons' as they were called was not because of their gaiety, for *gey* was used in the sense of a 'a bit too much'. This might certainly have been the case when seven sons were slain by their hereditary enemy, the Clan Forbes, while digging peats. The claim of the River Dee to kill three people a year palls by comparison.

This average number of river deaths was subscribed to until the last century probably because the only means of crossing the river from Abergeldie was by a wooden cradle or basket consisting of three narrow planks connected by iron bands. It ran on two iron wheels along a roped cable thrown across the river and wound round a sort of windlass on either bank. The

Prince Albert Victor and Prince George of Wales (later King George V) crossing the River Dee at Abergeldie
by way of the old wooden cradle, once the only means of getting across.
From an oil painting by S.P. Hall.

Alexandra, Princess of Wales, at Abergeldie *c.* 1870
with her children, Prince Albert Victor (right),
Prince George, Princess Louise (left)
and Princess Victoria.

cradle was large enough to seat two people and the castle gardener usually worked it. He placed one leg across the knees of the passengers to keep them steady, let the cradle run down the slack of the cable to the middle of the river and then hauled it up, hand over hand, to the other side.

One wild night early in the last century, a young couple used it after being entertained in the castle kitchen on their wedding day. The bridegroom, Willie Frankie, a gamekeeper, was taking his bride, pretty Ba'bie Brown, home in the cradle after their wedding festivities when suddenly the spoke of a windlass gave way, the cable uncoiled and sprung back violently and the unfortunate pair were pitched into the surging river and drowned.

The tragedy happened long before Prince Albert tried to buy Abergeldie Castle to add to his Deeside

estate but although the Gordons gave him a long lease, regularly renewable, they always refused to part with the freehold. Since Prince Albert and Queen Victoria acquired Birkhall and Balmoral, however, Abergeldie Castle has welcomed many royal visitors.

First to the dour little castle with its single sitting-room came Queen Victoria's mother, the Duchess of Kent, for annual autumn visits from 1850 to 1858. Patricia Lindsay, daughter of the local doctor, a schoolgirl at the time, recalls many evenings spent at the castle. She particularly enjoyed the dances given to the tenants and servants on the Duchess's birthdays. Nearly fifty years later she wrote:

The Duchess and her party sat on a raised platform at the end of the long dining-room which was cleared for dancing as soon as we left the dinner-table . . . from the walls the rather grim Gordons of earlier generations looked down upon the revelry. On these occasions the Duchess always wore white, and though at this time she must have been approaching seventy, it was still becoming to her. At these dances we girls and the younger ladies in attendance on the Duchess always wore silk or satin tartan scarves, fixed on the shoulder, Highland fashion, over our white or black dresses. We had the privilege of selecting our partners from among scarlet-coated, powdered footmen and kilted keepers and ghillies; and reels, country dances, and the 'everlasting jig' succeeded each other in quick succession to the inspiring strains of the bag-pipes or Willie Blair's fiddle. . . .

Until Queen Victoria's death the Prince of Wales and Princess Alexandra spent their Scottish holidays at Abergeldie Castle and the Empress Eugénie was a frequent visitor. She first stayed there after the death of her son Louis Napoleon, the Prince Imperial, who was killed fighting the Zulus in South Africa.

From 1902 to 1910 it was a holiday home for the future King George V whose wife, Princess May (later Queen Mary), made considerable improvements to the gardens. Meanwhile their young sons, when they could escape from their tutor, made straight for the foot suspension bridge that had supplanted the wooden cradle across the river and, on windy days, raced across it as it swayed—an eight-year-old Prince and his younger brother relishing the sense of danger.

A fishing expedition near Abergeldie, September 1904.
From left to right: Lady Katharine Coke; Victoria Mary, Princess of Wales;
Princess Mary of Wales; Cameron; Prince Edward of Wales; Sir James Reid.

However, even on holiday these future Kings of England, Edward VIII and his brother George VI, were subjected to strict schoolroom discipline. Of the Abergeldie holiday in 1906 Prince Edward wrote:

Experience had taught Bertie and me to associate my father's return home with a tightening of the screw of our schoolroom discipline. . . . Since his heart was set on our entering the Navy and as mathematics was of course one of the principal bases of naval education, he inquired into my progress in arithmetic with particular attention. The results in my case and Bertie's had been hardly what he had hoped for; and, concluding that mathematics was not Mr. Hansell's (their tutor's) forte, he decided to test our knowledge on the subject by presenting us with practical problems of his own devising. For example, the number of stags, with their weights, he had shot at Balmoral the previous stalking season was carefully recorded in his game book. One morning at Abergeldie he handed us a copy of this record, commanding us to strike the average weight of the stags he had killed over this period. The problem was more complicated than it sounds; for the reason that our system of weights and measures includes the stone of fourteen pounds. My father maintained that *anybody* over ten years old should be able to solve so simple a problem; but on returning to the schoolroom Bertie and I found that we had been given a task of brain-racking complexity. The day was spent at our desks, adding and dividing, while Mr. Hansell, who had been instructed not to help us, paced about the room or stood at the window staring meditatively out across the Dee. Unhappily for Bertie and me, the results of these agonized calculations, influenced less by logic than by desperate hope, failed by a wide margin to tally with those my father had independently arrived at.

As a result a special tutor, a master from Tonbridge School, was engaged to teach the brothers nothing but mathematics during the holidays.

Prince Edward also had other, more exciting, memories of Abergeldie. He wrote in his *Memoirs*:

Its ancient granite walls were covered with a gritty white stucco that could be ripped off with one's finger nails. Its most conspicuous architectural feature was a tall stone tower surmounted by a wooden cupola infested with bats and haunted, we were led to believe, by the ghost of Kittie Rankie, an unfortunate creature who had been burned at the stake as a witch on the hilltop overlooking the Castle.

Patricia Lindsay recalled how she used to play in Kittie's dungeon in one of the castle cellars where the witch was said to have been kept for a time before being taken to Craig-na-Ban to be burnt. The child described the delightful fascination of the place:

. . . with its little door just high enough for a child of ten to stand upright on the threshold . . . and though frequently visited with pleasure by day, was much to be avoided after dark. Old Effie, the first housekeeper I remember at the Castle, used to tell us blood-curdling tales of mysterious noises and bell-ringings, supposed to augur misfortune to the Gordon family.

But the ghost of Abergeldie was nothing compared to those who inhabited the two other royal Highland castles of Glamis and Mey.

GLAMIS CASTLE

Glamis hath murder'd sleep, and therefore Cawdor
Shall sleep no more, Macbeth shall sleep no more!

From *Macbeth*, William Shakespeare

Shakespeare's creation of Macbeth as Thane of Glamis and his choice of the castle, one of the oldest inhabited dwellings in Great Britain, as the setting for his great tragedy, may be poetic licence but it certainly contributes to the sinister atmosphere of this acknowledged home of more spectral appearances than any other building in the British Isles.

Yet when the sun shines this soaring edifice of pinky-grey stone is breathtaking in its beauty. Its rounded towers, conical turrets and battlements rise as from a fairy tale against the far-off backcloth of the snowline of the Grampians. Ghosts are banished. This family home of Elizabeth, the Queen Mother, is both the stuff of history and the fabric of dreams.

Inside it is a more chilling story with rooms called 'Duncan's Hall', 'Hangman's Room' and 'Prince Charlie's Room' making it easy to sense the ghosts of previous occupants drifting through the corridors.

Even before the first rocks and stones were laid in the eleventh century for the foundations of this royal keep or hunting lodge, the story goes that the fairy-folk interfered. Building was started on the top of nearby Hunter's Hill in a place called Fiery Pans ('pan' being the Pictish word for head or heights), but every morning the workmen found the stones they had built up during the previous day were scattered about—presumably by the fairy people. To humour them—and to prevent more unpleasant happenings—Glamis was built on the flat low-lying level of the great vale of Strathmore in Angus, ten miles north of Dundee.

In 1034 King Malcolm II, grandfather of Duncan I

and Macbeth, is believed to have died there of wounds received in the moment of victory at the Battle of Hunter's Hill. In the chamber built on the site centuries later, called 'King Malcolm's Room', a large faded bloodstain was proudly displayed on the stone floor until this century when the owner of the castle, unable to remove it, covered it up with an oak floor.

King Malcolm was the first of a steady stream of royal visitors culminating with the birth of Princess Margaret there on 21 August, 1930. She was born on a wild night of thunder and lightning and it was the first time an heir in direct line to the British throne had been born in Scotland since the children of James VI of Scotland and I of England.

Queen Elizabeth when she was Princess Elizabeth
at Glamis with her mother
and her sister, Princess Margaret.

Glamis has been owned by one family, the ancestors of Queen Elizabeth, the Queen Mother, since 1372 when Sir John Lyon, Thane of Forteviot, was knighted by King Robert II and made Thane of Glamis with baronial rank. He was known as the 'White Lyon' because of his fair complexion, and gained his castle for a tribute of 'one red falcon to be delivered yearly on the Feast of Pentecost'. Five years later, as Chamberlain of Scotland, he married Joan, the king's widowed daughter, but five years after that he was murdered in his bed by the Lindsay Chief, in the course of a long blood feud.

His successor, his only son John, eventually strengthened the ties with the Royal Family by marrying his cousin Elizabeth, Robert II's great-granddaughter, and embarked on further reconstruction of the castle. After his death his widow continued the improvements and built the beautiful Gothic chantry chapel which is part of the Church of Glamis. In 1445 her son was created the 1st Lord Glamis.

The close association between the owners of Glamis Castle and the Royal Family continued until James V became King. Then, because of his almost paranoic hatred of the Douglases—his step-father's family, he seized the castle for the Crown. He accused the beautiful twice-widowed Janet Douglas, Lady Glamis, a sister of his step-father, of witchcraft and of mixing deadly potions for him and he imprisoned her and her young son, the 7th Lord Glamis in Edinburgh Castle. Meanwhile the King and his Queen, Mary of Guise, held court at Glamis and ransacked it of its valuable furnishings and silver.

Lady Glamis with her son was found guilty of the trumped-up accusation. On 17 July, 1537, after a long imprisonment in the dark dungeons, which left her almost blind, she was burnt alive as a witch on the Castle Hill of Edinburgh, 'with great commiseration of the people, being in the prime of her years, of singular beauty, and suffering all, though a woman, with a manlike courage, all men conceiving that it was not this fact, witchcraft, but the hatred which the King carried for her brothers'.

Lord Glamis, aged about sixteen, was compelled to witness 'the agonies of his clansmen who were put to the torture of the rack in the vain attempt to extort from

Glamis Castle,
the entrance front.

Lady Elizabeth Bowes-Lyon (Queen Elizabeth the Queen Mother),
aged nine, playing at dressing-up with her brother David at Glamis Castle.

One of two known paintings depicting Christ with a hat. It is
by the Dutch artist Jacob de Witt who supplied all the pictures
for the walls and ceiling of the chapel at Glamis. He also
painted the portraits of all the Kings of Scots in the long gallery
in the Palace of Holyroodhouse.

Mary, Queen of Scots, dined and slept at Glamis on
her way to quell Huntly's rebellion. With her were her
four Maries and her half-brother, Lord James Stewart,
whom she had created Earl of Moray. By doing so she
had caused the breach with the House of Huntly who
had already been granted the lands of the Earldom of
Moray.

It was dreadful weather when they arrived at
Glamis, with the roads nearly ankle-deep in mud, but
the Queen's spirit was undaunted. She told the English
Ambassador that her only regret was that she was not a
man

> . . . to lie all night in the fields, or to walk upon the
> causeway with a pack, a Glasgow buckler, and a
> broadsword.

Gradually, Glamis was restored to something of its
former splendour and in the time of the 9th Lord
Glamis, who was one of James VI's Privy Coun-
cillors, the King was a frequent visitor and in 1606
created Lord Glamis the 1st Earl of Kinghorne. At the
Court in London Lord Glamis probably met Inigo
Jones who was invited to design plans for the castle's
extension.

Visitors were many and varied. Cromwell quar-
tered troops there, left it in a dreadful state and when the
young Earl Patrick, the 3rd Earl, and his bride
returned, once again the place was empty of treasures
and the estate was loaded with debt. Doggedly the Earl
set to work to renovate and improve his home between
1670 and 1680 and 'by prudence and frugality' paid off
most of the debt of £400,000. With considerable help
from local craftsmen he built the present chapel,
furnished and decorated the rooms and relandscaped
the policies until 'Glamis House', as he chose to call it,
was one of the finest castles in Britain, its elegant
improvements echoing some of the architecture of the
châteaux of the Loire.

Its 'Hangman's Room' was invariably occupied for
it was the responsibility of the Thanes and Lords of
Glamis to maintain justice, law and order throughout
the wide lands of Angus and so a private hangman
became an essential part of the household.

On a more spiritual level the chapel contains one of

them words which would implicate his mother'. He
was threatened with similar treatment and condemned
to death but he was reprieved until he came of age,
although he was kept a close prisoner until the King's
death. Then, on the accession of the child Mary,
Queen of Scots, his peerage and his nearly empty castle
and his ruined lands, were restored to him.

Not surprisingly, however, the ghost of his murdered mother, surmounted by a bright halo, has been
seen floating above the castle clock tower. Sometimes,
strange knockings are heard in the castle at dead of
night and these are believed to be the ghostly echo of
hammering at the building of her scaffold.

Patrick, 3rd Earl of Strathmore and Kinghorne, wearing flesh-coloured armour, with his sons.
He is pointing to the castle as it was until 1770, with double walls
and seven gates up the approach. These were demolished when the
grounds were remodelled by the landscape architect 'Capability' Brown.

only two known paintings showing Christ wearing a hat, a realistic interpretation which was quite unusual in those days. It was painted by Jacob de Witt and local gossip suggests that the artist depicted Christ in contemporary guise to annoy the Earl because he had not been paid. Actually, the reverse was the case because de Witt had promised to do all the work himself and then broke his contract by employing inferior painters from Dundee to help him.

Another example of this painter's work is a family portrait dominating one end of the drawing-room, once the great hall, where there is a particularly fine plaster-work ceiling created by Italian workmen. The portrait shows the 3rd Earl of Strathmore and Kinghorne pointing out, with an expression of justifiable pride, his magnificent castle to his three sons. In this room is also displayed a jester's suit of motley

and set of bells, for the Strathmores were the last family in Scotland to maintain a jester.

'Earl Patrick', as he was known, obtained a new charter of his peerage, stating that he and his heirs should in future be styled Earls of Strathmore and Kinghorne, Viscounts Lyon, Lords Glamis, Tannadyce, Sidlaw and Strathdichtie. Unfortunately his grandson, the 5th Earl of Strathmore, was slain by a dragoon after being wounded and taken prisoner as a Jacobite at the Battle of Sheriffmuir in the 1715 Rising.

Two months after the death of the 5th Earl the Old Chevalier visited the castle and was entertained by the new Earl, another boy of sixteen. On that visit eighty-eight beds were prepared for the gentlemen accompanying him and he 'touched for the King's evil' in the castle chapel. Sufferers came from miles around and it seems that every person touched by him was cured.

When he went he left his silver watch and sword behind and these are still on view. Thirteen years later the 6th Earl was killed by a neighbouring laird in a brawl in the streets of Forfar.

Forty years later the family name became Bowes Lyon when the 9th Earl, 'the beautiful Lord Strathmore', married Mary Eleanor Bowes, a wealthy heiress of an old North of England family. They were quite unsuited and the unhappy marriage lasted nine years, until he died. They had five children but her flirtations, including her affair with a smooth scoundrel and her abduction by a fortune-seeking rogue, justified her being known as 'the Countess of Tragedy'. In May 1800, wearing her wedding dress, she was buried in Westminster Abbey. There 123 years later, in April 1923, her descendant Lady Elizabeth Bowes-Lyon, youngest daughter of the 14th Earl of Strathmore and Kinghorne, married HRH the Duke of York, who was to become King George VI.

It is hardly surprising that the family home of Queen Elizabeth, the Queen Mother, so touched by history, should be heavily associated with ghosts. Sir Walter Scott, after a visit there in 1793 when he was about twenty-two, commented:

I was conducted to my apartment in a distant part of

Lady Elizabeth Bowes-Lyon (Queen Elizabeth the Queen Mother) with her father, the 14th Earl of Strathmore, and her eldest brother Lord Glamis, just before her marriage to the Duke of York (later King George VI) in 1923.

Mary Eleanor Bowes, a wealthy heiress, daughter of George Bowes of Streatlam Castle and Gibside, who married the 9th Earl of Strathmore in 1767 and brought the additional surname of Bowes into the family. Since then the family name has always been Bowes-Lyon.

the buildings. I must own that when I heard door after door shut, after my conductor had retired, I began to consider myself too far from the living and somewhat too near to the dead. . . .

He was not alone in his apprehension. The Dowager Lady Granville, elder sister of the Queen Mother, recalled that when she lived there children often awoke at night screaming because a huge bearded man had leant over their beds and looked at them.

There was one story, however, which Lady Granville admitted they were never allowed to discuss when they were children and which her father and grandfather absolutely refused to speak to her about. This was the story of the Castle Monster, an eldest son of the family born in a hideous form with a massive body covered in matted black hair, tiny arms and legs and a head sunk deep into his barrel chest. Obviously such a creature could not inherit the title and he was kept in a secret room and exercised on the roofs at night. He was believed to have lived to be well over a hundred and died in the early part of this century.

To keep the dreadful secret only four men at any one time were allowed to know of the Monster's existence. They were the Earl, the family lawyer, the agent to the estate and the eldest son who was shown the Monster, the rightful Earl, on the day that he came of age.

The Duke and Duchess of York visiting the Isle of Skye in 1933.

Certainly many secret rooms were constructed at Glamis at the end of the seventeenth century where the Monster could have been kept and an entry in *Debrett's Peerage* of 1841 which conflicts with entries in other reference books poses the unanswered question. It concerns nineteen-year-old Lord Glamis, heir to the 11th Earl, who in 1820 married Charlotte Grinstead. Certain reference books state that their first child was a son, Thomas, born in 1822 but the entry in *Debrett* reads differently:

GEORGE LYON, Lord Glamis, b. 6 Feb. 1801, m. 21 Dec. 1820, Charlotte, da. of Charles Grinstead, esq. and d. 27 Jan. 1834, leaving issues, 1. a son, b. and d. 18 Oct. 1821; 2. THOMAS GEORGE, Lord Glamis, b. 28 Sept. 1822, in the army; 3. Claude, b. 19 June 1824.

It is possible that the first son did not, in fact, die on the day he was born. His parents were very young, and if he was born deformed, many reasons, such as emotion or reception into the Church, may have prevented the kindest course being taken. There has been consistent evidence of some strange being imprisoned in the castle. For instance the local slater was repairing the castle roof when suddenly he rushed down the ladder and, with ashen face, began to tell his workmates of a terrible sight he had seen. At that moment the agent to the estate rushed up and hurried him away. It is said that the slater, on swearing never to reveal what he had seen, was given a pension and sent to Australia.

Even less credible is the story of Lord Glamis and his old enemy the 'Tiger Earl' of Crawford who gambled with dice late on Saturday night. An old

ABOVE: Lady Elizabeth Bowes-Lyon, great-niece of Queen Elizabeth the Queen Mother, photographed in 1982.

LEFT: Queen Elizabeth the Queen Mother as Duchess of York. Copy of a portrait by Philip de Laszlo.

retainer knocked at the door and reminded them of the lateness of the hour and that it was nearly the Sabbath. At five minutes to midnight he returned, touched his master on the shoulder and pointed to the time. 'I care not what day of the week it is,' roared Lord Glamis. 'If we have a mind to we shall play on until Doomsday!' They played on and as the last note of midnight chimed on the castle clock the door opened silently and a cold breeze blew into the room. In the doorway stood a tall, slim figure of a man dressed in black. 'I will take your Lordship at your word,' he intoned. 'Doomsday has come for you.' The door closed but as Lord Glamis jumped up to follow the stranger, he stopped, frozen with terror. The walls were closing in, the room was growing smaller, the door was already too small for them to pass through and the window had shrunk to the size of a peephole. No one heard their terrified screams and when the old retainer returned neither he nor anyone else could ever find the room. The story is that they still sit there playing until the crack of doom.

Another room in the castle was purported to have been lost for centuries. It happened after a band of defeated Ogilvies arrived at Glamis and begged for protection after a battle in which they had just been defeated by a rival clan, the Lindsays. The lord of the castle did not want to antagonize the desperate fugitives nor his hereditary enemies the Lindsays. He invited the

men in and took them to a remote room where he assured them they would not be found. He then locked them in.

The door to the secret room remained locked for a century or more until, in Victorian times, a later Lord Glamis opened it, shone a light into the black recesses and collapsed in a dead faint. The floor was littered with a mound of skeletons with grinning skulls, some of whom still had their bony arms between their teeth indicating that starvation had caused them to eat their own flesh. The room was bricked up and its location lost but, more recently, the 16th Earl of Strathmore said he did not doubt the truth of the story.

'There are probably half a dozen rooms bricked up about this place,' he told a biographer of his family, James Wentworth Day.

Yet despite such happenings and a host of ghosts including the Grey Lady who haunts the chapel, a Tongueless Woman who has been seen running across the park or staring out of an iron-barred turret window, the Mad Earl who walks about on the roof and a little black boy who can sometimes be seen sitting outside the Queen Mother's sitting-room, Glamis Castle remains a family home for the Queen Mother's nephew Fergus, 17th Earl of Strathmore and Kinghorne, the Countess and their young family, Lord Glamis, Lady Elizabeth Bowes-Lyon and Lady Diana Bowes-Lyon.

THE CASTLE OF MEY

I found the Castle of Mey with its long history, its serene beauty and its proud setting, faced with the prospect of having no one able to occupy it. I felt a great wish to preserve, if I could, this ancient dwelling.

Queen Elizabeth, the Queen Mother,
on receiving the Freedom of Wick

A year after the death of King George VI, the Queen Mother spent a holiday with old friends, Commander and Lady Doris Vyner at their home 'The House of the Northern Gate' near Dunnet. One day they

picnicked near the most northerly castle in Britain, six miles from John o' Groats. This was Barrogill Castle, gaunt windswept and neglected, built in the sixteenth century by the Earl of Caithness and originally known

The Castle of Mey, Caithness,
the most northerly castle in Britain.

as the Castle of Mey. It was for sale but its roof was falling in, there was no heating and the garden was a wilderness. Unless a prospective purchaser suddenly materialized it seemed that demolition would be its ultimate fate. But one had. The Queen Mother fell in love with it.

Perhaps her mood was similar to Queen Victoria's when she built 'Glassalt Shiel' to try and 'get away from it all' after the death of Prince Albert. For Elizabeth, the Queen Mother, perhaps the lonely little castle promised to fulfil the same need. It is built on an isolated stretch of coastline and the views from its windows are quite breathtaking. According to the writer, James Wentworth Day, they looked out

across the racing tides of Pentland Firth to the grey-green loom of the Orkneys. The cliffs of Stroma rise

from the wine-dark sea, gold and purple in the sun. Along the shore at the foot of that brief strip of rough grass which flows from the Castle walls to the tide-line, oyster-catchers, brilliant in black, cream and scarlet, trip like ballet dancers, go scything over the waves, flinging their wild whistle to the lonely sky . . .

It is not a grand castle. No stately pile like Dunrobin, or feudal stronghold like Blair. It is small, ancient, compact and cosy. That is as cosy as you can be with all the winds of the world to beat about your ears. It sits there, as it has sat for centuries, half encircled by two little projecting woods of wind-twisted oak, ash and elm, bent awry by the sea-gales.

Caithness, where the castle stands, was a territory of the Picts until the ninth century when the Norse rulers of the Hebrides made conquests on the mainland and intermarried with the Picto-Scottish dynasty. In the fourteenth century the heiress of Orkney and Caithness, Lady Isabel, married William Sinclair, son of Sir William Sinclair who had been slain with the Black Douglas in Spain when carrying the heart of King Robert the Bruce on a crusade to the Holy Land. In 1455 their great-grandson, the last Jarl of Orkney, was granted the old family earldom of Caithness and it was he who built the beautiful Rosslyn Chapel, famous in the world of Freemasonry.

Three generations later, in 1556, George Sinclair, 4th Earl of Caithness and son-in-law of the Earl of Montrose, acquired the lands and barony of Mey from Robert Stewart, Bishop of Caithness. The Bishop had already built a great fortified store-house there at Barrogill and the Earl converted it into a castle adding living rooms above the well-protected store rooms.

The castle was built on the well-tried Scottish Z-shaped plan, suitable for defence for, like all Scottish castles, it was to have its share of feuding and fighting as evidenced by the bullet marks on the outside walls. Originally the only overt access was through the old courtyard with its arched gateway but there was also a secret escape passage to the sea.

Earl George needed a strongly fortified castle for he was as tough and ferocious as his Viking forefathers. A devoted Catholic and a Privy Councillor, he remained loyal to Mary, Queen of Scots. He was deeply implicated in the assassination of her King Consort (Henry Darnley) but nevertheless acted as foreman of the assize that acquitted Bothwell of the murder. He was then accused of instigating the poisoning of John Gordon, 11th Earl of Sutherland, known as the 'Good Earl John', and his Countess. Afterwards he carried off the new Earl of Sutherland, a fifteen-year-old boy and forced him to marry his thirty-two-year-old daughter. However when the young Earl was grown up he divorced his wife for having an affair with the Chief of the Clan Mackay.

Meanwhile Earl George carried on private wars in the north with the Mackay Chief, with Lord Oliphant and, finally with the Murrays against whom he launched an unprovoked attack in 1570. When his

eldest son, John, the kindly Master of Caithness, concluded a peace treaty with the enemy without his leave, he was so incensed he imprisoned him for seven years. He then burnt Dornoch Cathedral and murdered three Murray hostages. After his death his heart was encased in lead and placed in the kirk at Wick. However, during the Earl of Sutherland's raid there in 1588 one of Sutherland's men opened the leaden case in search of treasure, 'when the dust escaped to the winds'.

Nevertheless, Earl George's ferociousness lived on in the person of his second and favourite son, William Sinclair of Mey, to whom he had given that castle and estate. William thereupon fed his imprisoned elder brother, John, salt beef and brandy and no other liquid to slake his thirst. Not surprisingly, the kindly prisoner built up a great hatred for his brother.

One day William was taunting the imprisoned John through the bars of his cell when John leapt up in a frenzy and tried to strangle him through the bars with his chains. William managed to escape but he was so badly bruised about the throat that he died within a fortnight. His untimely death prevented him from legitimizing, 'by subsequent marriage' in the usual Scottish manner, his two sons by the exquisite lady of his choice. His murderer eventually died in great misery, still his father's prisoner, leaving a son who became Earl. Meanwhile Mey had passed to the youngest brother, George, who finished building the castle after his father's death in 1582.

Clan feuds were comparatively rare in this remote Scottish outpost and subsequent generations of Sinclairs sublimated their aggressive spirits in an extravagant standard of living and extensive gambling. At least once in the early eighteenth century the castle was seized by Sir Patrick Dunbar of Bowermadden from Sir James Sinclair in lieu of a considerable gaming debt.

It was restored to the family in 1735 in a poor state of repair by another Sir James Sinclair, Baronet of Mey. He too was a gentleman of fluctuating fortunes who enjoyed good living and in eighteen months, helped by his friends, he consumed 956 bottles of claret. Nevertheless he did his best to try and restore the castle and in the 1750s he spent £200 on repairs before he died penniless.

Inside the Castle of Mey. The castle was completely refurbished by the Queen Mother
when she rescued it from dereliction.

A sitting-room in the Castle of Mey.

A view of the Castle of Mey standing on the isolated and windswept coast of Caithness and looking over the Pentland Firth.

However, his expenditure seems to have been justified for, visiting the castle in 1762, Bishop Robert Forbes described it as:

one of the best houses in all Caithness, consisting of about eighteen fine rooms, two of which being large dining rooms or halls and one of them almost a cube.

The Bishop particularly admired the fine two-acre walled garden—still intact today—where apples, strawberries and cherries ripen in the relative warmth from the Gulf Stream flowing through Pentland Firth.

Nevertheless, the family tendency to gamble and live extravagantly continued for another thirty years until the 12th Earl of Caithness took a firm hand, paid off all the family debts, set about improving the whole estate and planted many fine trees. The seal of royal approval was implanted two generations later in 1868 when the Prince and Princess of Wales, later King Edward VII and Queen Alexandra, commemorated their visit by planting an ash and a sycamore beside the main entrance.

Their host was James Sinclair, 14th Earl of Caithness and Lord-in-Waiting to Queen Victoria. He was a Fellow of the Royal Society and a well-known scientific inventor who devised a gravitating compass which came into general use, a tape-loom which enabled a weaver to stop a single shuttle without affecting the action of the whole loom and a steam carriage for travelling on macadamized roads in which he drove from London to Mey. True to his Norse ancestry he loved the sea and cruised widely in his yacht *Francesca*. No doubt he needed this respite from his second wife, a Spanish widow who believed she was a reincarnation of Mary, Queen of Scots, whose portrait hung in the castle.

His son, the 15th Earl, died young, drunken and unmarried in 1889, willing his family home to an old Cambridge friend. So the castle left the family who had built it and lived there for more than 400 years of unbroken possession.

At first the Queen Mother's decision to save the little castle set in twenty-five acres of fields, woods, garden and lawns and restore its original name, Castle of Mey,

together with its former dignity, seemed to some people rather over-impulsive. Severe storms during the winter of 1952-3 had removed virtually all that remained of the roof and the restoration took three years at a cost of some £40,000. But in the autumn of 1955 the new owner's personal standard flew proudly from the flagstaff and a new chapter in the life of the little castle had begun. It was marked when the royal yacht *Britannia* steamed into the bay just below the castle bringing the family to disembark at the tiny harbour to greet the new owner of the Castle of Mey.

Today royal grandchildren and great-grandchildren meet and play on the long stretches of golden sand, friends are entertained and the owner has fulfilled a long-time ambition by establishing a herd of pedigree Aberdeen Angus on her 120-acre farm where she also breeds North Country Cheviot sheep. She is an expert fisherman and spends long hours standing in the chill waters of the River Thurso after salmon. The experts recognize a real craftsman in action.

Inside, this castle of pink-hued Caithness stone is a feminine castle if ever there was one. The Queen Mother's private apartments in the east tower overlook the walled garden that encloses flowering hedges dividing the area into a series of protected beds for flowers, fruit and vegetables. There is a miniature rose garden divided by paths of shells collected from the local beaches and beyond, a little conservatory to supply continuous colour inside the house and a herb garden offering every known common herb for the kitchen.

The private apartments are furnished in pastel colours and with dainty antiques—including many Sinclair family possessions restored to their original setting after coming to light in local antique shops. Victorian needlepoint chairs and Queen Anne bureaux are illuminated by Regency and Empire lamps, a carved kneeling Regency blackamoor with a polychrome flower-filled seashell on his back is a sudden reminder of the ghost of the little black boy who can sometimes be seen sitting outside the Queen Mother's sitting-room at Glamis. Perhaps he echoes a strange world of fierce legend, beauty and peace such as Elizabeth of Glamis knew in her girlhood and which, for a few weeks each year, she seeks to recapture.

An expert with a fly rod, Queen Elizabeth the Queen Mother, with her head gillie, Mr James Peart, who is ready to gaff a catch – once it is hooked and played.

PART II

PAGEANTRY AND CEREMONY

OPPOSITE: A state portrait of George IV
by Sir David Wilkie who thought
His Majesty 'looked exceedingly well in tartan'.

THE HONOURS OF SCOTLAND

We'll drink a cup to Scotland yet,
Wi a' the Honours three.

The Honours of Scotland, consisting of the Crown, the Sceptre and the Sword, are older than the regalia in the Tower of London for, after the execution of Charles I, the English regalia were destroyed by order of Parliament. The only objects saved were the Black Prince's ruby, the ampulla and spoon and Queen Elizabeth's salt cellar. Even the crown of King Alfred the Great 'of goulde wyer work sett with slight stone', as the records have it, was broken up or cast into the melting pot.

Scotland was luckier. The Scottish regalia now in the Crown Room at Edinburgh Castle certainly existed before the time of Mary, Queen of Scots, although they were not used at her austere coronation in

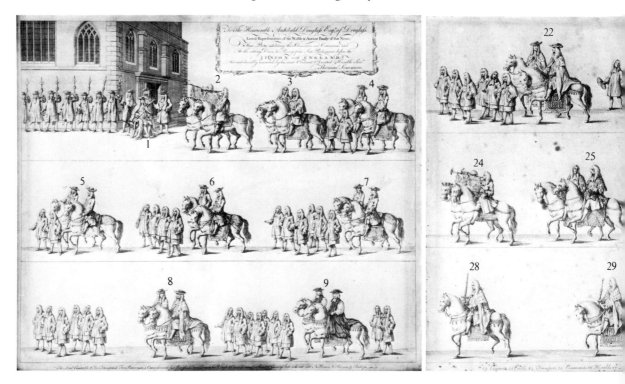

'The Solemnities, and Ceremonies used At the Sitting Down & Rising of the Scots Parliament, before the UNION with ENGLAND.'
John, 12th Earl of Erroll, is seated as Lord High Constable with his guard at the Parliament House to receive the members in the Riding of the Parliament 1685.

Key
1 The Lord Constable
2 Two Trumpets
3 Two Pursevants
4 Commissioners for Burghs
5 Commissioners for Burghs
6 Commissioners for Shires
7 Officers of State who are not Noblemen
8 Barons
9 Bishops
10 Two Macers of Privy Council

the chapel of Stirling Castle, on 9 September, 1542, when she was nine months old.

The unhappy King John Balliol was deprived of even earlier regalia by Edward I of England who took every opportunity to humiliate him. There is no mention of any substitutes until 1494 when James IV was presented with the Sceptre, along with a golden rose, by Pope Alexander VI. Thirteen years later, the Sword of State used today was presented to him by Pope Julius II, whose name is etched in gold on either side of the blade. Accompanying it was the sword belt and a consecrated hat, delivered with great solemnity in the Church of Holyrood by the papal legate and the Abbot of Dunfermline. The Mother Church was generous. This fine example of Italian craftsmanship bears two gold-filled etchings of the apostles Peter and

Paul on the blade while the papal emblems of oak leaves and acorns are heavily sculpted on the gilded silver pommel and handle. The Pope's arms are enamelled on the crimson velvet of the scabbard which is also decorated with silver-gilt ornaments.

James V, in his turn, delighted in altering and adding weight and value to the royal treasures and he ordered the Sceptre to be melted down and remodelled in its present form. It is of gilded silver, heavily engraved and surmounted by a large and a small polished crystal globe with a Scottish pearl fixed to the top of the small one. The two globes surmount the handle which is flanked by three dolphins protecting small figures of the Virgin Mary holding the Saviour, St James holding an open book and St Andrew carrying a cross.

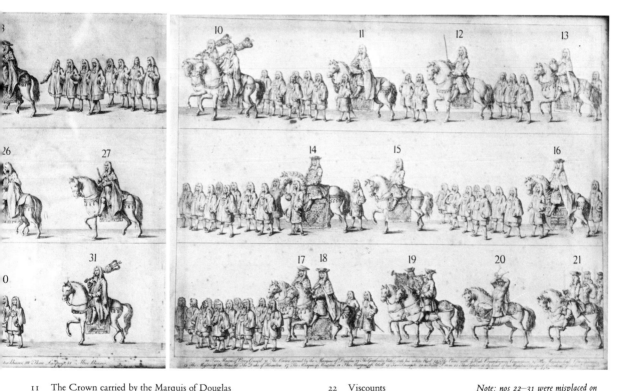

11	The Crown carried by the Marquis of Douglas	22	Viscounts
12	The Gentleman Usher with his white Rod	23	Earls
13	The Purse with ye High Commissioners Commission	24	Trumpets
14	His Majesties high Commissioner	25	Pursevants
15	The Master of the Horse	26	Heralds
16	The Duke of Hamilton	27	Lord Lyon
17	The Marquis of Montrose	28	Sword Bearer
18	The Marquis of Atholl	29	Scepter Bearer
19	Two Trumpets	30	Three Laqueys
20	a Kettle Drum	31	Mace Bearer
21	The Captain at the head of his Majesties Troops of Guards which finishes ye Cavalcade		

Note: nos 22–31 were misplaced on the original engraving, and are correctly placed here between nos 9 and 10: i.e. Viscounts directly after Bishops.

The Honours of Scotland, the Sceptre, the Crown and the Sword with the other crown jewels.

As for the Crown, the circlet of gold with which Robert the Bruce was crowned in 1306 and which he is said to have worn round his helmet at the Battle of Bannockburn, is thought to form the foundation. It was apparently arched over in 1540 when James V commissioned an Edinburgh goldsmith, John Mosman, to refashion it, using some of the new gold found in Scottish mines.

This is the oldest crown in the British regalia and its splendour is dazzling. It is ablaze with a myriad of magnificent jewels including fiery carbuncles, glowing jacinths, glittering rock crystals, topazes and amethysts set in gold and pearls and sparkling with diamonds. Above the original gold circlet, jewelled as Bruce would not have recognized it, four golden arches rise to enclose a crimson velvet bonnet. Where the arches meet, at the summit of the crown, is a blue enamel celestial globe ornamented with gilt stars—a symbol of sovereignty, surmounted by the non-secular symbol of a

black and gold enamel cross studded with amethysts and pearls.

The Honours of Scotland were not only carried at coronations but also at the State Opening of Parliament known as the Riding of the Parliament. The peers, bearing and attending them, wore State Robes—known in England as Coronation Robes. However, since the Scottish Parliament came to an end in 1707 the Honours of Scotland have only been carried in public on two occasions: for George IV in 1822 and for the present Queen on her accessional visit to her Scottish capital in 1953. In each case they were borne in state procession from the Palace of Holyroodhouse to St Giles' Cathedral.

The Sceptre is carried by the Premier Earl 'upon the place'. In 1953 this was Lord Crawford. 'The Ceremonies of the Sword' belong to the Lord High Constable but, otherwise, the sword is borne by the holder of the second earldom 'upon the place'. In 1953 the right belonged to the Countess of Erroll, both as Constable and as holding the second earldom in precedence. The Earl of Home carried the Sword as her deputy.

From the 1400s the right of bearing the Crown on state occasions and of crowning the king was vested in the Red Douglas, Earls of Angus as Lords of Abernethy, and it was also claimed by the Earls of Argyll by virtue of a descent from the Earls of Fife. The right is now invested in the Duke of Hamilton as Earl of Angus and Lord Abernethy whose ancestors bore the Crown in 1822 and 1953.

The story of how the Honours, symbols of Scottish independence and royal status, survived throughout Cromwell's invasion is a tale of courage and determination. During the sixteenth and seventeenth centuries they were kept in Edinburgh Castle and brought out only for the Riding of the Parliament and coronations such as those of the infant James VI at Stirling and Charles I at Holyroodhouse. They were also seen at the impromptu coronation of Charles II at Scone in 1650. Afterwards, for greater safety, they were stored in Dunottar Castle, coastal stronghold of the Earl Marischal of Scotland. There, just before the castle fell to Cromwell's forces, they escaped capture only through the determination and courage of three innocent-looking ladies; Mrs George Ogilvy of Barras, the Governor's wife, Mrs Christian Granger, the wife of the Minister of the neighbouring parish of Kinneff, and the servant girl who worked for Mrs Granger.

The girl was a familiar figure to the besieging troops for she often walked along the cliff-side near the castle, gathering edible seaweed. One day the Governor's wife managed to secrete the Honours of Scotland under a layer of seaweed in the girl's basket. They were carried back to the manse and hidden at the bottom of a bed until the Minister had an opportunity to bury them safely under the floor of Kinneff Church.

When Dunottar Castle fell in 1652, Cromwell's invaders found the regalia was missing and they tortured the Governor and his wife to try and make them confess what had happened to it. Mrs Ogilvy eventually died from the fearful treatment but, on her death-bed, she made her husband promise never to reveal the secret.

The regalia lay in the church for nine years until it could be returned to Charles II. It was then returned to Edinburgh Castle and produced during sittings of the Scottish Parliament. When Parliament was dissolved in 1707 on the Act of Union, a pledge was made that the regalia should always remain on Scottish soil. It was locked in an oak chest which was left bolted inside the Crown Room of Edinburgh Castle where it remained for more than a century.

Then, suddenly, rumours began to circulate. No one had seen the regalia and it was feared that, after all, it had been illegally smuggled into England. Eventually, the Crown Room was opened and the chest was revealed smothered in about six inches of dust. Moreover no one knew where the keys were and it required a Royal Warrant before the chest could be broken open.

Eventually, the writer Walter Scott, who had become a valued friend of the Prince Regent (afterwards George IV), persuaded him to issue a warrant to him and to the Scottish Officers of State, to open the chest. Scott's description of the scene in the Crown Room on 4 February, 1819, when the chest was broken open, is as dramatic as anything in one of his novels:

> The blows of the hammer echoed with a deep an hollow sound . . . even those whose expectations had been most sanguine felt at the moment the probability of disappointment. . . . The joy was therefore extreme when, the ponderous lid of the chest being forced open, at the expense of some time and labour, the Regalia was discovered lying at the bottom covered with linen cloths, exactly as they had been left in the year 1707. . . . The discovery was instantly announced by running up the royal standard above the Castle, to the shouts of the garrison and the multitude assembled on Castle Hill.

Since that day the Honours of Scotland have been available for public inspection in Edinburgh Castle, apart from periods during World Wars I and II when they were, yet again, removed to a secret place for safety. Ever since, they are brought out, with due ceremony, on only very special royal occasions. However, the Sword of State also appears at Thistle Services when it is borne by a Knight of the Order of the Thistle before the Queen.

THE ROYAL COMPANY OF ARCHERS

Draw in your arrow ere you take your aim,
Hold close your eye and fixt your bow and arme;
In aiming alter not your hands, but move
Your whole waist round; slow shooting best doth
    prove.

By a seventeenth-century member of the Archers,
Thomas Kincaid

On state and certain other public occasions in Scotland the Queen is guarded by a stalwart body of men wearing braided green doublets and Kilmarnock bonnets decorated with eagles' feathers. Their unlikely weapons, which can be devastatingly effective, are bows and arrows. They also wear 'Roman' type swords. The men are picked from the Royal Company of Archers a 400-strong élite band, the legatees of a tradition established by their predecessors who are said to have surrounded James IV when he fell at the Battle of Flodden. The tale goes that his body was found buried under his dead archers who had stood firm around him and had fought to the end even after he had been slain.

Some hundred years previously archery had been especially encouraged in Scotland when James I, realizing that Scotland might be short of skilled defenders in time of attack, commanded that 'futeball and golfe be utterly cryed down' and, on fear of a fine, all men and boys between the ages of twelve and fifty were ordered to take part in shoots at the parish butts four times a year. Moreover members of Scottish noble families were particularly enthusiastic and provided an exclusive band known as the Scottish Archer Guard of the Kings of France, an élite body of Scotsmen formed in the 1400s, sworn to protect the Sovereign in times of danger. In Scotland nobles decided to emulate their kinsmen abroad.

In 1676, after the restoration of King Charles II to the throne, the Company of Archers was formally constituted by the influential nobility and gentlemen to encourage the 'Noble and Useful Recreation of Archery, for many years much neglected'. At the same time the foundation stone of Archers' Hall in Edinburgh was laid. The hall, rebuilt in 1899 on a more splendid scale, is still the Company's headquarters.

In 1703, under a charter from Queen Anne, all rights and privileges were confirmed and new ones conferred in return for the *reddendo*—or due gift of a pair of barbed arrows*—to the Crown.

The Company became increasingly exclusive. For the first hundred years of its existence members were elected by a council but from 1775 a secret ballot was introduced and a single objection was sufficient to exclude a candidate for life. However, in time, members from the nobility and landed gentry were joined by distinguished representatives of the Arts, the Law and other learned professions. Robert Burns, Sir Walter Scott and the painter Sir Henry Raeburn were members and also Dr Nathaniel Spens, a President of the Royal College of Physicians. He was a keen shot until he was over eighty and another of his claims to fame was that he was the first person to carry an umbrella in Edinburgh, 'that useful article having been unknown in Scotland until the second half of the eighteenth century'.

The first time the Archers attended the Sovereign as an official bodyguard was on George IV's visit to

*In technical terms three arrows constitute a pair.

The Royal Company of Archers marching out of the Palace of Holyroodhouse.
Oil painting by W.S. Cumming, 1886.

Queen Elizabeth with her Scottish Body Guard, the Royal Company of Archers.

Edinburgh in 1822 when their duties were similar to those undertaken by the Honourable Corps of Gentlemen-at-Arms in London. A unique part of their ceremonial is that when presenting arms or giving a royal salute they thrust out their bows with their left hand while with their right they touch their broad eagle-plumed bonnet.

The king was intoxicated by the unexpected warmth of his Scottish welcome and showered honours on the Royal Company, authorizing them to be known also as the King's Body Guard for Scotland. Its head, the Captain-General, was given a Gold Stick entitling him, as part of the Royal Household, to take part in Coronation ceremonies, standing just behind a Gold Stick of England. One of the Royal Company's proudest moments was when they attended King George V and Queen Mary at the Coronation Durbar at Delhi in 1911—the first time they had guarded the Sovereign outside Scotland.

Apart from their ceremonial duties the Royal Company maintains a high standard of bowmanship through regular practice and instruction at the butts in the grounds of Archers' Hall. They compete in international prize shoots and competitions and, on their own ground, have met exciting challenges from a team of Red Indians who celebrated their victory with a wild war dance, and a Turk who broke all records by shooting 415 yards against the wind and 463 yards with it. Nowadays the Archers' principal competitors are the Woodmen of Arden from Sherwood Forest against whom they compete annually.

However, there have been moments of inconsistency in their bowmanship. In 1791 two members of the Company decided to settle their quarrel in a duel with bows and arrows. At dawn one October, accompanied by their supporters, they made their way to the meadows. The surgeon opened his bag and prepared to tend the wounded or dying. Coffee was ordered for the victor.

Three times the bows from the highly skilled archers twanged and their arrows whistled through the air—completely wide of their marks. The duellists stared angrily at each other and the order for coffee for one was changed to coffee for two.

These and other stories are recounted when the

Royal Company of Archers, wearing mess uniform of green tail coats, dine in Archers' Hall under the magnificent crystal chandelier copied from one hanging in the dining-room of a château once occupied by the Emperor Napoleon. Round the walls are fine portraits of distinguished Archers. After the meal the music of an old march of uncertain origin strikes up and the Company drink the first toast—sitting down—to 'the Mark'. Then, as one man, they rise for the loyal toast of 'the Queen'.

Yet despite their loyalty to tradition they are the first to realize the difficulty of maintaining an impeccable standard of discipline and a warlike spirit in peacetime when a full turn-out is required mainly for Royal Garden Parties, Thistle Services and state occasions. One of their members expressed this problem in a refreshingly frivolous composition called

LINES WRITTEN IN CONTEMPLATION OF THE KING'S BODYGUARD FOR SCOTLAND

Between the Palace and the Hill
Behold the ranks of archers stand!
They are not standing straight or still
And yet the spectacle is grand.

Upon their bosoms, row by row,
Medals acquired in warfare shine!
Look! there's a lad who fought the foe
(Six clasps) in 1889.

And there are other medals too
Won from the battle's strife afar,
This man's a Fellow of the Zoo
And that's an OBE (with bar).

The Adjutant has called out 'Shun!'
What do they care? 'It's only Cis,'*
And through the serried ranks there run
Fragments of dialogue like this;

'Have you got heather-beetle still?'
'This year the plover's eggs were late.'
'What do you think of Herbert's Bill?'
'My God! I've dropped my dental plate!'

But yet the Monarch proudly knows
In gazing on this noble Corps
That he is guarded by those bows
Which few can hold and fewer draw.

*Colonel 'Cis' Dalrymple Hamilton, then Adjutant.

Prince George, later George III, (second from the right), wears the uniform of the Royal Company of Archers
in this painting of the children of Frederick, Prince of Wales,
by Barthélemy du Pan.

Edward VII, attended by the Royal Company of Archers, holds his first levée at the Palace of Holyroodhouse.
Painting by Messrs Dickinson.

THE ORDER OF THE THISTLE

This most ancient order of chivalry, a kind of Caledonian equivalent to the Order of the Garter, is the unfettered gift of the Sovereign. It is said to have been founded by James V in 1540 and dedicated to St Andrew, the patron saint of Scotland, and was revived by James VII in 1687. It then consisted of the Sovereign and eight Knight Companions, but it fell into abeyance during the Revolution of 1688 when James VII of Scotland and II of England was ousted from his thrones by his eldest daughter Mary and her husband the Dutch prince William of Orange.

In 1703 the order was revived by Queen Anne who ordained it should consist of the Sovereign and twelve Knight Companions, a number increased by statute to sixteen in 1827.

The Officers are the Dean, the Secretary (the Lord Lyon King of Arms), the Royal Heralds and Pursuivants and the Gentleman Usher of the Green Rod. Services take place in the tiny Thistle Chapel erected outside the south-east corner of St Giles' Cathedral, Edinburgh which can be closed to the general public when the Knights meet in solemn conclave.

Its miniature Gothic splendour makes it one of the most beautiful places of worship in the world. It was designed in the twentieth century by Robert S. Lorimer, architect of the Scottish War Memorial at Edinburgh Castle and created by a group of artistic craftsmen who worked together in the spirit of the builders of mediaeval churches. Building began in the reign of Edward VII on a bequest of £40,000 from a former Knight of the Thistle, the Earl of Leven and Melville who died in 1906. However, the chapel was not ready to be opened and dedicated until 1911, a year after the King's death.

The tiny chapel is just 38 feet long, 8 feet wide and 48 feet high to the apex of its multi-coloured vaulted roof. High among the elaborate ribs and bosses, angels carry shields of Knights of the Order. The windows are set at a height of 20 feet from the ground in the grey stone walls and eight of them carry, in coloured glass, the names of a pair of knights with their armorial bearings. The east window, the royal window, shows the blue-mantled St Andrew with his fishing net and boat, beside the Sea of Galilee. Above him are two angels with Cross and Crown and below, the Lion of Scotland crowned and surrounded by a wreath of the Order of the Thistle and the motto 'Nemo me impune lacessit' ('No one harms me with impunity' or, loosely translated, it means 'Ye Maunna stamp on the Scots thistle'). On either side of the chapel are the Knights' stalls with their crested helmets above them, and on the back of each stall, the armorial stall plates of present and past Knights, enamelled in colour.

King George V conferred the Order on his son, the future King George VI, on his wedding day. He, in turn, made his wife, Queen Elizabeth, a Lady of the Order, and thirty years later the Queen, during her Coronation visit to Scotland in 1953, installed the Duke of Edinburgh. Nine years later there was a double installation for King Olaf V of Norway and the Earl of Home (later Sir Alec Douglas-Home, Prime Minister).

At the ceremony the Queen, in the robes of the Order, a flowing dark green velvet mantle lined with white taffeta and a black velvet hat with a white plume, looks as magnificent as she does in the Garter cloak portrait in which Annigoni captured, for all time, the spirit of Majesty. About her shoulders is the Collar of the Order formed of thistles for the Scots, alternating with sprigs of rue for the Picts.

The mystique of monarchy was never more apparent than in that tiny chapel during the Royal Jubilee

OPPOSITE: Queen Elizabeth in the
Robes of the Order of the Thistle.
Painting by Sir William Hutchinson.

visit to Scotland when the Queen installed her eldest son as a Knight of the Thistle. Conducted by the Lord Lyon King of Arms to one of the vacant stalls, Prince Charles swore:

I shall never bear treason about in my heart against our Sovereign Lady the Queen, but shall discover the same to her. So defend me God.

His words were based on the oath of fealty as introduced into Scotland by the Normans about the time of King David I.

THE ROYAL HOUSEHOLD IN SCOTLAND

When Queen Elizabeth visits her Scottish capital and stays at the Palace of Holyroodhouse or when she is in other parts of Scotland for official duties she is attended by appropriate members of her Household in Scotland. Excluding a large number of chaplains and medical men the Royal Household in Scotland numbers about a couple of dozen. Several of the positions held are hereditary ones and most are either unpaid or carry only a nominal salary. Chief among them are:

THE LORD HIGH CONSTABLE

The Earl of Erroll, 24th Earl, Merlin Sereld Victor Gilbert Hay, Chief of the Hays, 28th hereditary holder of this office. Born 1948. He was senior colleague of the Earl Marischal of Scotland (forfeited as a Jacobite in 1715), just as the Lord High Constable of England (abolished by Henry VIII except for coronations) is senior colleague of the Earl Marshal of England—from which office developed the modern British title of Field Marshal.

The office was given in 1306 by King Robert the Bruce to his companion in arms, Sir Gilbert Hay, 5th Lord of Erroll, and made hereditary in 1314 after the Battle of Bannockburn. Lords High Constable were killed in battle against the English at Nevill's Cross in 1346 and at Flodden in 1513. He is responsible, in principle, for safe-guarding the Sovereign in Scotland, especially on public occasions, and therefore takes precedence over every hereditary title in Scotland after the Blood Royal. He has jurisdiction, in principle, over all matters of assault and riot 'within the Verge of the Court' (i.e. a certain distance from the Sovereign's person); today this is normally maintained by the Earl granting a commission to the Bailie of Holyrood to act as Constable Depute there. He attends the Sovereign or her Lord High Commissioner, and carries a gold-tipped silver baton.

THE HEREDITARY MASTER OF THE HOUSEHOLD

The Duke of Argyll, 12th Duke, Ian Campbell, Chief of Clan Campbell. Born 1937. He ranks immediately after the Lord High Constable. The office of Master of the Household was given in 1494 by King James IV to Archibald, 2nd Earl of Argyll and Clan Chief, who was killed with the King at the Battle of Flodden. His son, Colin, succeeded him immediately as Master of the Household to the new boy-King, James V. The position was made hereditary in 1528 when it was held by the 3rd Earl. The holder was originally responsible, in principle, for all matters 'below stairs' which formerly included making arrangements for state banquets. Today's duties—like those of the Lord High Constable—involve attending the Queen or her Lord High Commissioners on state and certain other important public occasions. He carries a red velvet baton embellished in gold.

THE LORD LYON KING OF ARMS

Malcolm Innes of Edingight, CVO. Born 1938. He is the Monarch's 'Supreme Officer of Honour' in Scotland, responsible for the preparation, conduct and record of state, royal and public ceremonial. In England this responsibility is shared between the Earl Marshal and other departments. The office first appeared in the 1300s, evidently as successor to the royal sennachies (genealogists and transmitters of family lore) of Celtic times, as guardians and preservers of the royal pedigree and family records for each coronation.

No grant of arms is effective except when made by him. From 1672 he has administered Lyon Register which authenticates and records coats of arms, and in his ministerial capacity, as king-substitute and a Judge of the Realm the Lord Lyon grants and records through Lyon Court new arms to suitable applicants. In Lyon Court the Lord Lyon decides cases of disputed Chiefship and settles legal disputes about arms' ownerships. The office is more important today than for more than three centuries because of the world-wide growth of clan societies. The boom in Scots heraldry is indicated by the fact that sixteen slim volumes of the Lyon Register recorded all the coats of arms granted until 1903. Since then forty-one thick volumes have already been filled.

The Lord Lyon wears the royal tabard, the Queen's most sacrosanct and personal coat, indicating that he is inviolable and the voice of his proclamation is the voice of the Sovereign. Under him are six of Her Majesty's officers of Arms; the heralds, Albany, Islay and Marchmont and the pursuivants, Carrick, Unicorn and one other, formally in daily attendance at the palace, who perform many ceremonial duties on state and other public occasions. They also have statutory duties in connection with Scottish heraldry and those who wish to practise may be consulted about it and about genealogy in a professional capacity like an advocate or

The Lord Lyon King of Arms,
Malcolm Innes of Edingight, CVO,
wearing the royal tabard of velvet embroidered in gold
thread, the Queen's most sacrosanct and personal coat.

law agent. They may appear for members of the public before the Lyon Court, other nobiliary courts and before the English Court of Chivalry. Some are members of the Scots Bar. They wear a special variety of uniform of the Royal Household and over it Her Majesty's tabard of silk or damask and gold.

THE HEREDITARY BEARER OF THE ROYAL BANNER OF SCOTLAND

The Earl of Dundee, 11th Earl, Henry James Scrymgeour, PC, LLD, JP, DL, Chief of the Scrymgeours. Born 1902. In the reign of Alexander III, Sir Alexander Scrymgeour, then ancestor of the family, was already bearer of the Royal Banner which he carried under Wallace and Bruce in the Wars of Independence against England until he was captured and hanged by the English in 1306. King Robert the Bruce confirmed that the offices of Royal Banner Bearer and Constable of Dundee were hereditary in his family. The first Earl of Dundee was created in 1660. Today the Royal Banner Bearer's duties include parading with the Royal Banner—the lyon rampant—annually at the opening of the General Assembly of the Church of Scotland in Edinburgh, at state visits to Edinburgh, at certain other royal occasions in Scotland and Coronations in Westminster Abbey.

THE HEREDITARY BEARER OF THE SALTIRE (ST ANDREW'S FLAG)

The Earl of Lauderdale, 17th Earl, Patrick Francis Maitland. Born 1911. Since 1790 the family had been rival claimants with the Scrymgeours for the honour of carrying the Royal Banner or Standard of Scotland. The matter was resolved in favour of the Scrymgeours in 1901. Afterwards, in an amicable settlement, the 15th Earl of Lauderdale rematriculated his arms and was allowed to bear the St Andrew's flag on ceremonial occasions alongside the Earl of Dundee bearing the Royal Banner. The first time both flag and banner were seen together was at the Queen's Coronation Progress through Edinburgh in 1953. The Hereditary Bearer of the Saltire wears a specially designed officer's uniform, a many-buttoned tail-coat as worn at the time of William IV's progress through Edinburgh. Buttons bear the Lauderdale crest.

HEREDITARY KEEPERS

THE PALACE OF HOLYROODHOUSE The Duke of Hamilton and Brandon. 15th Duke. Angus Alan Douglas Hamilton, Premier Duke of Scotland. Born 1938. He is the most important of the Hereditary Keepers because it is at the royal Palace of Holyroodhouse that the Queen and the Lord High Commissioner hold their ceremonial courts. The office was bestowed in 1646 on the 1st Duke. He welcomes the Queen to the palace and maintains order through his blue-coated High Constables of Holyrood, their top hats turned up with black cocks' plumes, who are answerable to his *Bailie of Holyrood*, Ivor Guild, WS, who presides over the Abbey Court of Holyrood and over the High Constables of Holyroodhouse and their Guard of Honour mounted on the Sovereign. The Bailie is responsible in principle for maintaining law and order under the Hereditary Keeper. When the Sovereign is present the Bailie of Holyrood also functions on a separate commission as Constable Depute of Holyroodhouse for the Lord High Constable.

The Hereditary Keeper of the Palace of Holyroodhouse:
the 15th Duke of Hamilton and Brandon,
Angus Alan Douglas Hamilton, Premier Duke of Scotland.

THE PALACE OF FALKLAND Ninian John Crichton-Stuart of Falkland. Born 1957. His late father, Major Michael Crichton-Stuart, MC, appointed the National Trust for Scotland to be Deputy Keeper and made over to the Trust a generous endowment for future maintenance of the palace and gardens. Since then the Keeper's duties (as Guardian on behalf of the Trust) have been extended to coping with 53,000 visitors in six months in addition to receiving many VIPs.

STIRLING CASTLE The Earl of Mar and Kellie, 15th Earl, John Francis Hervey Erskine, Chief of the Erskines. Born 1921. The office dates from the 1500s when his ancestors, the Lords Erskine, and later Earls of Mar, were the guardians and foster parents of heirs to the throne and of child sovereigns: the future James V, Mary, Queen of Scots, and the young King James VI of Scotland. Stirling Castle was especially reserved for their protection in childhood. Following the 1715 Rising against the Hanoverian successor to Queen Anne, the 6th Earl of Mar was attainted. The office was restored to the 14th Earl of Mar and Kellie by George V in 1923 and the present Keeper succeeded on the Earl's death in 1955. There are no written duties but the Keeper considers it obligatory to greet members of the Royal Family or foreign ambassadors who visit the castle, officially or privately. When the Queen visits, the Keeper stands on the drawbridge and offers the key of the castle as a token of allegiance. He also attends military functions, gun salutes on royal anniversaries and other ceremonial occasions. He has no robes but wears Scots Guards uniform or the kilt.

DUNSTAFFNAGE CASTLE The Duke of Argyll. This castle is held for the Duke as Keeper by a Campbell Chieftain who is the Hereditary Captain of Dunstaffnage.

EDINBURGH CASTLE This office is nowadays always held as Governor by the General Officer Commanding Scotland.

DUNBARTON CASTLE Brigadier A. S. Pearson, CB, DSO(4), OBE, MC, TD. Born 1915.

DUNCONNEL CASTLE Brigadier Sir Fitzroy Maclean of Dunconnel, 1st Baronet, CBE. Born 1911. The Macleans were confirmed as Hereditary Keepers of Dunconnel in the Isles of the Sea in 1495 but deprived of it in 1691 after the Whig Revolution. The Keepership was recovered by Sir Fitzroy, descendant of the 11th Hereditary Keeper in 1980 when he was duly recognized as such by the Lord Lyon.

ROTHESAY CASTLE The Marquis of Bute, 6th Marquis, John Crichton-Stuart. Born 1933. Ninian Stewart, Hereditary Sheriff of Bute, was also made Hereditary Keeper of Rothesay Castle by King James IV in 1498. The family became Earls of Bute in 1703 and Marquises in 1796.

HERALDS AND PURSUIVANTS OF SCOTLAND

ALBANY HERALD Sir Iain Moncreiffe of that Ilk, Bt, CVO, QC, DL.

ISLAY HERALD AND LYON CLERK John Pottinger, DA (Don Pottinger, author and artist).

MARCHMONT HERALD Major David Maitland-Titterton, TD.

CARRICK PURSUIVANT John Spens, RD, WS.

UNICORN PURSUIVANT Sir Crispin Agnew of Lochnaw, Bt.

Unlike the English royal officers-of-arms (who were formed into a separate corporation or College of Arms by Richard III), the Scottish heralds and pursuivants remained in the Scottish Royal Household although they are sometimes conveniently referred to as Lyon Court, where they also have a function. They attend the Sovereign or the Lord High Commissioner on ceremonial occasions.

THE CAPTAIN-GENERAL OF THE QUEEN'S BODY GUARD FOR SCOTLAND. (ROYAL COMPANY OF ARCHERS) AND GOLD STICK FOR SCOTLAND

The Earl of Stair, 13th Earl. Sir John Aymer Dalrymple, KCVO, MBE. Born 1906. He commands the Royal Body Guard on ceremonial occasions.

THE DEAN OF THE ORDER OF THE THISTLE

The Very Reverend Professor John McIntyre, DD, DLitt. Born 1916. He conducts the Service of Installation of new Knights of the Thistle at which the Sovereign is present, held in the Thistle Chapel in St Giles' Cathedral. He officiates at a service on the first Sunday after St Andrew's day each year in the Thistle Chapel, consisting of prayers, readings and self-dedication on the part of the Knights.

THE DEAN OF THE CHAPEL ROYAL

The Very Reverend Professor R. A. S. Barbour MC. Born 1921. This is the oldest non-episcopal ecclesiastical office in Scotland and was created when the Chapel Royal was founded by King Alexander I at Stirling in 1120. In 1617 James VI transferred the Chapel Royal to the Palace of Holyroodhouse. Since the destruction of the Abbey Church there in 1688 the Dean has no building in which to officiate but he accompanies the reigning monarch in Scotland as her Senior Chaplain or her Lord High Commissioner at the annual meetings of the General Assembly of the Church of Scotland.

THE HISTORIOGRAPHER

Professor Gordon Donaldson, MA, PhD, FBA, FRSE, DLitt. Born 1913. This office was originally a sign of patronage conferred on distinguished historians. In the eighteenth century the annual salary was about £300, but the salary came to an end in 1940. The present holder of this honorary office has said, 'If the Scottish Office wanted information I would be willing to help.'

THE PAINTER AND LIMNER

David Donaldson, Royal Scottish Academician. Member of the Royal Society of Portrait Painters, LLD. Born 1916. This is an honorary office with no official duties. The office was originally established by Queen Anne in 1703 when she commissioned George Ogilvie (a nephew of Lord Banff) 'during all the days of his life' at a salary of £100. He was appointed for 'drawing pictures of our person or our successors or other of our royal family, for the decorment of our houses and palaces, and for painting our said houses and palaces, and for doeing all other things pertaining to the said airt'. Possibly the post was a concealed form of charity as Ogilvie was deaf and dumb and his family had suffered for its loyalty to the Stuarts.

In 1823 when Sir David Wilkie was appointed in the time of George IV the salary was increased to £300 but in 1933, when Sir David Young Cameron accepted the honour, the salary was abolished.

THE ASTRONOMER

Professor Malcolm Longair, PhD, FRSE 1981. Born 1941. Astronomy was taught at the University of Edinburgh in 1607 and in 1776 the foundation stone of the first Edinburgh Observatory was laid. The Astronomical Institution of Edinburgh, the earliest British Society devoted entirely to astronomy, was founded at the end of the eighteenth century. In 1818 a new observatory was erected near the old one and equipped with excellent instruments. King George IV, on his visit to Scotland in 1822, raised it to Royal status. Twelve years later the Regius Chair of Astronomy, established at the University in 1786, was linked with the Royal Observatory whose Director was also appointed to the Regius Professorship with the title of Her Majesty's Astronomer Royal for Scotland. In 1896 a new Royal Observatory was built on the city outskirts through the generosity of the 26th Earl of Crawford. It remains unique among British astronomical institutions in combining a Government Research Establishment and a University Department. The Astronomer to the Royal Household in Scotland holds no official duties as such.

THE BRAEMAR GATHERINGS

The clans start to gather on Braemar days before the games begin—as they have done for centuries, for the history of the Braemar Gatherings which have come to be an integral part of the Royal Family's autumn holiday on Deeside goes back nearly a thousand years.

In the eleventh century King Malcolm III summoned the clans to meet at the Braes of Mar, a centre for drove roads and tracks which lead out through the hills

ABOVE: The Gathering of the Highland Clans at Braemar Castle in 1864
in the presence of the Prince and Princess of Wales.
The leading champion was the legendary
Donald Dinnie from Aboyne.
Engraving from a sketch by Colebrooke Stockdale.

RIGHT: Queen Elizabeth the Queen Mother with the Prince and Princess of Wales
at the Braemar Gathering of 1982.

in all directions, so that he might select by competition 'his hardiest soldiers and his fleetest messengers'. Six hundred or so years later at Braemar, John ('Bobbing John') Erskine, the then Earl of Mar, called a gathering in 1715 to raise the standard for the exiled Jacobite 'king over the water', an ill-fated venture which ended at the Battle of Sheriffmuir.

A century later people met at Braemar for a very different purpose. Under the aegis of the Braemar Wright's Friendly Society, meetings were held every quarter for the purpose of collecting subscriptions to help the sick and the old, the widows and the orphans. It was an early and very worthy experiment in social insurance and one of its earliest welfare services was the wholesale purchase of oatmeal from surrounding mills and its resale to members at reasonable prices. In 1826 the society became the Braemar Highland Society whose interests extended to preserving the kilt, the language and the culture of Scotland and to promoting sport. The original name was commemorated in 'the Wright's Walk' when a procession, headed by pipers, made its way to a select spot where piping, dancing and athletics took place.

The society's royal associations began in 1848 when Queen Victoria attended the Gathering at Invercauld, home of the Farquharsons. In front of the house

Queen Victoria's tent at the Highland Games at Balmoral in 1899.
From left to right: Beatrice, Princess Henry of Battenberg (seated
far left); Victoria Mary, Duchess of York; Louise, Duchess of Fife;
Louise Margaret, Duchess of Connaught; Prince Arthur of Connaught;
Princess Patricia of Connaught and Princess Margaret of Connaught.

clansmen piped, danced, tossed the caber and putted river stones to the delight of the Queen, Prince Albert and members of the Court. Later the Queen became a Royal Patron of the Society and a generous contributor to its funds. All her life she remained keenly interested in the Gatherings which were held at Braemar Castle, Balmoral and Old Mar Lodge as well as Invercauld House.

In 1850, the year that Queen Victoria's mother, the Duchess of Kent, first visited Scotland, the Gathering was held at Braemar Castle for the second year running. The Queen was there soon after lunch, with her children and her mother and afterwards, wrote in her *Journal*:

There were the usual games of 'putting the stone', 'throwing the hammer' and 'caber', and racing up the hill of Craig Cheunnich, which was accomplished in less than six minutes and a half; and we were all much pleased to see our gillie Duncan, who is an active, good-looking young man, win. He was far before the others the whole way. It is a fearful exertion. Mr Farquharson brought him up to me afterwards. Eighteen or nineteen started, and it looked very pretty to see them run off in their different coloured kilts, with their white shirts (the jackets or doublets they take off for all the games), and scramble up through the wood, emerging gradually at the edge of it, and climbing the hill.

After this we went into the castle, and saw some dancing; the prettiest was a reel by Mr

The Duke and Duchess of York,
(later King George VI and Queen Elizabeth), watching the Braemar Games
in 1929.

Farquharson's children and some other children. . . . The twelve children were all there, including the baby, who is two years old.

Unfortunately the race up the hill of Craig Cheunnich had been too strenuous for many of the competitors who spat blood as a result of their exertions and the winner, the gillie Duncan, never fully recovered from the strain although he was made a keeper in the following year.

In those days the Gatherings, as small and strictly local functions, were truly rallies of the clans—the clansmen walking tirelessly through the night to meet their traditional rivals in friendly combat. But from 1906 when the event found a permanent home on a 12-acre site presented by the 1st Duke of Fife, with the coming of the bus and motor car the Gathering became a Highland Show, widely reported and attracting professional competitors and sightseers from all over the world. Every autumn they see successive Gatherings rise to acclaim the reigning Monarch as their Chief and although every year new records are established for the old sports, no one has yet exceeded the record of the legendary Donald Dinnie who, in 1860, joined the society at the age of twenty-three and in the next sixteen years won 11,000 prizes, including 2000 for throwing the hammer, as well as prizes for running, jumping and dancing.

PART III

ROYAL VISITS TO SCOTLAND

KING GEORGE IV

Auld Reekie in her rokelay grey
Thought never to have seen the day!
He's been a weary time away—
But, Carle, now the King's come!

From Sir Walter Scott's ballad in thirty-nine quatrains,
distributed as a broadsheet for the royal visit.

For nearly 200 years since Charles II's unhappy visit to Scotland, no reigning monarch had set foot in that country. Suddenly, in August 1822, King George IV, the personally and politically unpopular ruler, on the advice of his ministers rather reluctantly agreed to go. To his own and everyone else's surprise, he burst upon the Scottish scene with an impact that has never been forgotten. No one could have foreseen the dramatic effect of that fortnight of 'royal turmoil' masterminded by the dramatic romantic writer Sir Walter Scott. From that time relations between England and Scotland never looked back.

There was little time to make preparations. 'Coming *suddenly* upon us . . . thus we shall be saved from premeditated absurdities,' Scott remarked, consoling himself during a month's plan-making when he hardly slept. He arranged a non-stop round of courts and levées, a military review and a state procession, balls and banquets punctuated with incidents like the presentation of a pair of Shetland hens to the portly monarch by the magistrates of Lerwick.

The ambitious programme, by its sheer exuberance, opened the frontier for future royal visits, created a new recognition of Highland culture and tradition and a revival in Highland dress which since the Battle of Culloden had been forbidden in a serious attempt to break up the clan system for ever, so that, as military units, they would never again menace the peace of the state. The act forbidding the wearing of tartan had been repealed in 1782 but George IV's visit resulted in a rash of authentic tartans that had not been seen for nearly eighty years and would never again be repressed. They

costumed a fortnight's dramatic performance, produced by Scott and starring the sixty-year-old monarch—an inspired combination—and the whole entertainment, for all its lack of rehearsal, could not have been bettered.

The two men had first met two years previously when Scott, already a literary lion, visiting London, was invited by the Prince Regent (the future George IV), to 'a snug little dinner' at Carlton House. The Prince was a great admirer of Scott's work. Despite his bloated, dissipated appearance and his odious behaviour to his wife, he was a person of taste, a connoisseur of art and architecture, a lover of music and literature and he had a great zest for life. He immediately called his guest of honour 'Walter' and invited him to use his fine library. There they had a long and interesting discussion about Scotland.

Later, at an even more select dinner party, the Prince sang songs, told stories and continued affectionately to call Scott by his first name. A fellow guest, John Croker, Secretary of the Admiralty, described the Prince and the writer as 'the two most brilliant storytellers . . . I have ever happened to meet'.

Afterwards, the Prince sent Scott a gold snuff-box set in jewels with a medallion of the donor's head on the lid, as a token 'of the high opinion His Royal Highness entertains of your genius and merit'. He endorsed his opinion two years later, on his accession to the throne when, as King George IV, he created Walter Scott a Baronet. He also commissioned the fashionable portrait painter, Sir Thomas Lawrence, to paint Scott's portrait first in the series of great figures in literature and science, the most distinguished men of the age, to hang in the great gallery being built at Windsor Castle.

As soon as the royal visit to Scotland was settled, the Lord Provost of Edinburgh begged Scott to help him to make the arrangements and the writer suddenly found himself virtually in charge. He was a fortunate choice for he applied his colourful literary imagination, his boundless energy and love of Scotland to devising a fortnight's non-stop pageantry fit for a king.

He urged the clan chiefs to bring 'half-a-dozen or half-a-score' of clansmen to Edinburgh and attached a long list of the dress and accoutrements a Highlander 'of decided respectability' should wear when waiting on the King. On the King's part, two complete Highland outfits were tailored in the royal tartan — kilt, plaid and bonnet and tartan coat, to accommodate his 20-stone figure. They looked slightly incongruous worn with flesh-coloured tights, but they conveyed their message.

The clan chiefs responded enthusiastically to Scott's invitation although fine points of etiquette needed to be adjusted regarding matters of precedence for they based their angry claims on the positions they believed their clans had held at Bannockburn. Eventually, the order was decided by lot.

Every trade, craft, profession and public body was determined to be represented. Poets and painters converged on the city, including George Crabbe who was provided by Scott with a bedside lamp and table in case poetic inspiration struck him in the night, and Turner who painted *The March of the Clans* against the tremendous backdrop of Edinburgh Castle.

ABOVE: A caricature showing King George IV and Sir William Curtis, Lord Mayor of London (and a sea-biscuit manufacturer from Wapping), wearing identical Highland dress. Apparently, neither could refrain from smiling when they met.

PREVIOUS PAGES: Turner's painting of *The March of the Clans* against the tremendous backdrop of Edinburgh Castle. The painter came to the city during George IV's memorable visit in 1822.

It was a magic moment for Scott, just four years after he had been instrumental in rediscovering the Honours of Scotland in a locked chest in Edinburgh Castle, formally to apply for a warrant to remove them to Holyroodhouse so they could play a prominent part in the ceremony. For good measure, from his own private armoury, he lent the magnificent sword given by Charles I to the great Marquis of Montrose. He thought it would look well carried in procession by the Knight Marischal.

On 14 August, two days overdue, the *Royal George*, bringing the royal party, anchored at Leith Roads and Scott was welcomed aboard by the King, most heartily. A bottle of Glenlivet whisky was called for by the King to drink his guest's health. Scott drained his glass and, with a courteous gesture, begged the one just touched by the royal lips as a keepsake and tucked it carefully away in the skirt pocket of his overcoat. He then presented the King with a silver St Andrew's cross set with pearls and cairngorms and engraved with the motto 'Righ Albain gu brath', ('Long life to the King of Scotland'), sent by a band of loyal 'Sisters of the Silver Cross'.

The mood well set, Scott departed. He hurried home in excitement, rushed into the drawing-room and, forgetting about the glass in his overcoat pocket, threw himself gratefully into a chair. He immediately leapt up with a yell, clutching his backside. The historic glass was smashed to smithereens and Scott's scar was his only tangible keepsake of the entire royal visit.

The next day the sun shone as the royal procession wound its way through the densely packed route between Leith and Holyroodhouse. A line of open carriages bore Scott and the civic dignitaries culminating in White Rod, the Lord Lyon Depute, the Lord High Constable and, finally the royal carriage and six. Preceeding and flanking it marched trumpeters, yeoman, kilted Highlanders and Grenadiers followed by Dragoons, cavalry, Scots Greys, mounted heralds and grooms. For the first time the Royal Company of Archers attended a sovereign as an official bodyguard. Scott, a member of the Company, had helped to design a more elaborate uniform for them than their familiar field dress. However, the mediaeval neck-ruff and

gauntlet glove he suggested proved most impracticable for archery and were soon abandoned.

Seldom had the unpopular Monarch received such a welcome. When he saw the huge crowds packed into Prince's Street waiting to greet him, he rose in his carriage and then fell back and burst into tears.

The royal party stayed at Dalkeith Palace, remodelled by Sir John Vanbrugh little more than a century before. Their host was the boy-Duke of Buccleuch, Henry Scott. Every night at dinner he made a point of keeping the King informed of the names of the tunes played by the Highland piper in an adjoining room. Suddenly, Scott recognized only too well the name of a familiar tune and shuddered at the possible effect it might have on the unhappily married King.

> 'What are they playing now?' the King asked his host.
> 'The old song—"My wife is come back again",' the innocent youngster replied.
> 'Oh! Then I'm off,' the King said, rising but laughing with unusual good humour.

Holyroodhouse was opened up for glittering levées and courts. It was the first time a monarch had been there since James II of England visited it as Duke of York. The once handsome George IV participated with a will in all the arrangements. One bewildered old laird attending a levée and quite unfamiliar with court etiquette, was told to bow deeply to His Majesty and pass on. Blind with terror, he kept repeating his bows without noticing that the King was graciously extending his hand. Lord Erroll, in a loud whisper, exhorted him to 'Kiss hands, kiss hands!' The old man, still bowing and retreating backwards, blew kisses alternately from each hand in an effusive affectionate farewell, much to the King's enjoyment.

One of the highlights was the procession from Holyroodhouse to the castle when the Honours of Scotland were carried before the King in full public view. There were soldiers in scarlet, sailors in navy, archers in Lincoln green and three hundred clansmen bearing heads of deer high on poles as gifts. The guns on Arthur's Seat boomed out their welcome.

'Never King was better received by his people.

Never King felt it more,' George IV told Scott and, again, there were tears in his eyes.

Parliament House was hung with tapestries for a banquet at which the King proposed a toast to 'the Chieftains and Clans of Scotland', whereupon Sir Evan MacGregor of MacGregor replied with 'The Chief of Chiefs—the King'.

In the second week of the visit there was a presentation of a masque called *Royal Jubilee* and at the theatre, another highlight of the visit was a performance of Scott's own tartan drama *Rob Roy*. Finally to Scott's delight, the King knighted his old friend, Adam Ferguson, Deputy Keeper of the Regalia, and also the artist Henry Raeburn, a distinguished member of the Royal Company of Archers, and representative of fine arts in Scotland.

For Scott himself reward enough was an extremely appreciative message of gratitude and the knowledge that he had helped to make history as well as record it by bringing the Highlands into the mainstream of Scottish life through the rebirth of the pageantry of monarchy. Meanwhile, even before the visit ended, through sheer exhaustion, he had broken out in violent and painful skin eruptions which lasted until October.

QUEEN VICTORIA

THE TRAVELLER

The opening of the Royal Deeside Railway in the mid-nineteenth century made Queen Victoria's bi-annual visits to Balmoral more simple and comfortable than the long voyage by steamer and she took an active interest in working out details of the journeys well in advance.

She stipulated that the speed of her special train should be limited to thirty-five miles an hour by day and twenty-five by night and, as she suffered from the heat, a bucket of ice was placed under her bed on warm nights.

The evening of 6 June, 1889, was particularly sultry when the Queen and her party set off from Windsor to Balmoral and, for the first time, the Queen was to share her sleeping apartment with someone other than one of her daughters. This curious privilege was given to her granddaughter, Princess Victoria of Prussia, who described the 18½-hour journey in a letter to her mother. She wrote:

The day had been frightfully hot at Windsor and when we left the heat was still very oppressive. Poor Grandmama felt very uncomfortable and dreaded the night. After Leamington, where we had some tea, I 'turned in', and a lovely soft bed it was too—one quite forgot that one was really in a train. I never saw anything so perfect in arrangement and comfort. Of course you know the carriage well—I *do* wish you had one like it. I was just dozing off, when Grandmama came to bed—and *how* it reminded me of you, my Mother. She looked so clean and dear—all in white—and it took some time before she was settled—the shawls, and cushions—then the lamps to put out—then again, it felt too hot—then not warm enough, and in the night—Annie was called many a time—to bring her something to drink etc. Oh! it did remind me so of our travels. Well finally we had some sleep, and in the morning I dressed first, so as to make room—and then we soon reached Perth, where the same breakfast awaited us, as you and I enjoyed, some years ago.

The country looked lovely as we travelled on—everything quite springlike—the lilac just coming out and the hills bathed in richest tints. The drive from the station to the castle, is also long, but so pretty. We found a delicious luncheon awaiting us on our arrival and then I took a walk with Ethel . . . as the things had not come and went to the 'Merchants' and bought some nice trifles.

The train often made a lengthy stop at Leamington which gave rise to several rumours, one being that, in the early hours, the Queen had a rendezvous there with an illegitimate royal relative, the identity of whom was kept a close secret. The simple truth was that she had an arrangement with the buffet there to provide her party with cups of tea.

Her guests revelled in the unfamiliar novelty of the train journey and Empress Eugénie of the French once asked, with her tongue in her cheek, if the ladies should undress and wear their nightdresses. On being assured that this was the correct procedure, she replied that if there were an accident, it would be most embarrassing for a near-naked Empress to be found on the railway line.

The railway brought about a change in Queen Victoria's Balmoral holidays. As a widow of advancing years she no longer wished to ride out on excursions, but the train allowed her to travel much further afield, with the result that she sometimes accepted invitations to stay at the big houses of friends. These visits were planned with great care a long way ahead and sometimes the royal party was so large that her hosts preferred to vacate their home altogether for the duration of the visit and lend it to the Queen, meanwhile finding alternative accommodation for themselves nearby.

An insight into the preparations involved in entertaining royalty in those days is given in letters belonging to the family of one of Queen Victoria's hosts, Steuart Macnaghten (later Sir Steuart) who had suggested to the widowed Queen that she might like to visit their estate of Invertrossachs, overlooking Loch Vennachar. The Queen had long wished to explore the Trossachs, that lovely glen extending from Loch Achray to Loch Katrine, immortalized by Sir Walter Scott in *The Lady of the Lake* and *Rob Roy*.

The first intimation Lady Emily Macnaghten, the daughter of the Countess of Antrim, had that her husband's invitation had been accepted, came indirectly through her niece, Lady Helen MacGregor of MacGregor who lived nearby at Lochearnhead. Lady Helen had received a letter from her friend, the Dowager Duchess of Atholl, a favourite Lady of the Bedchamber, which read:

Balmoral,
Ballater,

May 24th, 1896.

My Dear Helen,

I ought to have written to you some days sooner, but you know what a bad correspondent I am.

I do not remember which day it was last week, but one day the Queen introduced the subject of Invertrossachs, and said how kind she considered it of Mr Macnaghten and Lady Emily to *wish* to lend it to her. Your Aunt told the Queen that was their wish, as she could not see *how* the *rent* would ever be decided. The Queen desired that Her thanks might be expressed and I said I would write and do so through you.

Her Majesty is delighted with the situation of Invertrossachs—the only difficulty is about the accommodation. But *I* feel sure *that* will be sufficient—the amount of Bedrooms I mean for all Her Majesty's necessary attendants. The Queen however proposes to send a Person (who knows *all* the requirements) one day this week to see the house and report upon it, and this I think by far the most satisfactory plan because if *he* says it *will* do, it will do . . .

Interrupted so often—and now to dinner—Forgive me!

Very affectionately,
A. Athole

The 'Person', Mr J. J. Kanné, Director of Continental Journeys and accustomed to organizing the royal expeditions to Germany, France and Switzerland, duly arrived, inspected and reported back favourably concerning the proposed ten-day visit. His chief difficulty in arranging a visit to such a comparatively small house was the Queen's habit of insisting at the last moment on including people in the party for whom no accommodation had been arranged.

Lady Emily had three months to prepare but was warned that no mention must be made of the royal visit. With friends she had to find excuses why her home was being spring-cleaned from front door to attics and the local shopkeepers were curious to know why new carpets had been ordered for the whole house. But carpets got hard treatment in Scotland, hammered by heavy shooting boots and used as towels by wet dogs.

Even the name of the house, Drunkie, was changed to Invertrossachs House which was thought more appropriate for the occasion.

The Macnaghtens arranged other accommodation for themselves and waited for further instructions. On 24 August Mr Kanné wrote saying he was 'now able to give positive information about Her Majesty's intended visit to your Country Seat'. He wrote:

The Queen will leave this on Wednesday, September the first and reach Invertrossachs the same day . . .
I subjoin an approximate list of Her Majesty's Suite and Personnel.

	Her Majesty
	Two Princesses (Louise and Beatrice)
5	Lady Churchill
	Colonel Ponsonby
	Four Female attendants
6	Viz. Dressers and Maid and one House, one Kitchen Maid
2	Two Cooks
3	Three Footmen
4	Stablemen
1	Her Majesty's personal Servant (Mr Brown)
1	and myself
22	

I expect to be at Callander on the 25th or 26th and will consequently have plenty of time to make all necessary arrangements.

I have taken the liberty to have directed a number of packages to your care and, in order to avoid undesirable curiosity or excitement I will, on my arrival, state that some of the junior members of Her Majesty's family will occupy your house for a short time. This measure, I think, will be better than to entirely contradict or deny the arrival of the Royal Family.

Her Majesty will send one or two Carriages and four ponies. You will perhaps permit me to repeat to you Her Majesty's private observation to me. The Queen said 'She hoped you would not go to any unnecessary expense in regard to new Carpets or new furniture etc'. . . .

It was too late for the carpets. They lay unsullied, in every room and corridor.

At that point the imperturbable Mr Kanné fell ill and the responsibility for the visit was taken over by Colonel Ponsonby (later Sir Henry Ponsonby, Private Secretary to the Queen). He was equally accustomed to coping with royal crises. Letters arrived from him daily:

I should feel obliged if you would kindly order. . . .

Four horses should be ready to take the Queen from Callander to your house at 3 o'clock on Wednesday next, the 1st September. The Carriage will go on Tuesday.

Perhaps you will kindly explain to the Station Master that I trust he will have no crowd of people in the Station, and that no one (except yourselves) are expected to meet the Queen.

There should be no Guard of Honour at all anywhere as Her Majesty wishes to travel quite privately. . . .

There had better be no question of a flag on your house while the Queen is there. . . .

On the day before the expected arrival the Macnaghtens vacated their home. Lady Emily made her final inspection, checking the flower arrangements and the hang of the curtains, and gave last-minute instructions to the under-housemaid who was staying as liaison officer to the royal servants.

On her arrival at the house the following tea-time, the Queen immediately inspected her quarters, memorizing the lay-out of the rooms until she knew where everyone in the party slept.

'They have put down new carpets everywhere,' she wrote in her *Journal* the next day.

Colonel Ponsonby was quick to reassure the exiled owners:

'The Queen appeared delighted with the place as soon as she arrived,' he wrote. 'The Queen has been admiring your chintzes. . . .'

His only complaint was of the roughness of the waters of Loch Vennachar where he had been drenched by

Queen Victoria and her family land at Aberdeen in 1849,
some eighteen years before the Royal Deeside Railway track
reached Ballater and made the journey to Balmoral much easier.
Aquatint by J. Harris after E. Cleland.

the waves when following the Queen's party in a small boat and the Royals had been convulsed with laughter.

There followed day-long expeditions in which the Queen delighted. The party travelled by carriage or ponies, was rowed across the small lochs and took the steamers on Katrine and Lomond. They explored old churches and places of historic interest and visits to a few local people were also included.

Colonel Ponsonby's constant concern was that the water supply for the house depended on rainwater but that summer there had been a long drought and the tanks were empty. Fortunately the Queen was not a

believer in the frequent immersion of the human body in hot water but, after a long day's outing, an adequate supply had to be available. There were also more than twenty bedroom jugs to be kept full and a constant demand for washing-up water.

Weatherwise, the Colonel was in a dilemma. If it rained, his problems over the water would be solved, but a greater problem would then present itself. The Queen might be confined to the house and robbed of the expeditions she loved. From experience the Colonel knew that she was then liable to become both testy and demanding. So he forebore to pray for rain

Queen Victoria's watercolour sketches of Ardverikie Lodge on
Loch Laggan and the view when she stayed there with the
Marquis and Marchioness of Abercorn in 1847.

and arranged for the watercart to make frequent journeys to the pollution-free loch.

One day the two Princesses decided to discover how 'the other half' lived and, accompanied by Lady Churchill, they set off for Brig of Turk to visit the poor widow Macfarlane. Later Mrs Macfarlane described the meeting to Lady Emily:

I was bilin' and washing and they cam up and askit me what I was doin', and to tell ye the truth I thocht they were servants, and I was raal short wi' them for spearin' sae mony questions. Had they been ridin' I wad hae kent wha they were, but they came donnering doon the road clacking aboot the hens . . .

The auldest ane askit me . . . 'What do you get for your breakfast?' 'I get parrit mild and whiles tea when I rise, and a wheen tatties and mild and the like o' that.' 'And do ye get a bit steak ana?' 'Eh! Na. Poor folks like us canna wun at that.' 'Weel,' says she, 'the Queen bade us come and see your cottage.'

'Ye'll be the Queen's servants,' quo' I. (They were that plain, I couldna think they were the Queen's dochters—they had na a ring on ane of their hans, or a bit gowd in their lugs) 'Nae,' says she, 'we're the Queen's dochters.' 'Ye're no very like it,' quo' I. Then the big lady, that I thocht was the ladysmaid, telt me this was the Queen's second youngest dochter. 'Weel,' says I, 'ye min just excuse me, for I didna ken.'

. . . Sae then thet gied me goodbye and steppit wast I had a wheen claes hingin' dryin'. And the lassie keekit oot, and said the three ladies wast there were countin' oot siller. 'Whist, lassie,' quo' I, 'that's the two Queens—they'll surely be no comin' in here again.' And wi that, in they came and gaed me jist a pund o' siller, and said 'That's for keeping your hoose sae clean.'

On the last day of the visit the Queen wrote to her hostess:

Dear Lady Emily,

I cannot leave this charming spot without expressing to you and Mr. Macnaghten my very warmest thanks for your kindly allowing me to spend some days here, thereby enabling me to visit with ease and privacy the splendid scenery of this romantic and lovely neighbourhood.

My daughters and I have greatly enjoyed our stay here and we shall ever retain the most pleasant recollections of the comfortable House of Invertrossachs and of beautiful Loch Vennachar.

Pray accept the accompanying bracelet in remembrance of this occasion, as well as an illustrated Copy of my book (*Leaves from the Journal of Our Life in the Highlands*) and some prints of ourselves, which I hope will find a place in this House.

Again thanking you and Mr. Macnaghten,
Believe me,
dear Lady Emily,
Yours sincerely,
Victoria R.

There was also a present of a bracelet for Lady Emily's under-housemaid who had stayed on to help the royal servants.

The system whereby the family vacated their home when Queen Victoria came to stay seemed to work better, unless the house was a large one, than when they remained in residence. At any rate this might be judged from an earlier royal visit to the Marquis and Marchioness of Abercorn at Ardverikie on Loch Laggan.

The arrival of the Queen and the Prince Consort with two of their children and staff stretched the accommodation of the small house to the limit and the four eldest Abercorn children, two boys and two girls, were moved from their comfortable nursery to cramped quarters in the home farm to make room for the royal children. This upset four-year-old Claud considerably.

When Lady Abercorn presented her children to the Queen, the girls in their best frocks, the boys in kilts, the three eldest behaved impeccably. Claud, however, remembering his expulsion from his nursery, refused to bow. Instead, he stood on his head and displayed his half-nakedness to the assembled company. It was a trick of which he was very proud and only with difficulty could he be forced back onto his feet. The Queen was not amused.

The young culprit was taken away and lectured and, after saying he was sorry, he was again taken to the Queen. He promptly stood on his head once more and for the rest of the royal visit the youngest son of the house was in disgrace.

Forty years later, as Lord Claud Hamilton, the stubborn young man became ADC to the Queen.

QUEEN VICTORIA AT THE 'WET REVIEW'

Of all Queen Victoria's visits to Scotland the one she made to Edinburgh on 25 August, 1881, for the purpose of holding a great review of Volunteers in Queen's Park, was most memorable in terms of the weather. Known as 'the Wet Review', it gives a vivid insight into royal stoicism.

The Queen and her party were due to start from Holyroodhouse at a quarter to four but after lunch the rain increased and there was a perfect sea of umbrellas. Writing in her *Journal*, the 62-year-old Queen noted:

The sky became white and grey, with mist in the distance, and the ground where the march past was to take place, which could be seen from the windows, and which had partially recovered from yesterday's rain, became like a lake of muddy water, too distressing.

The Queen, with her youngest daughter, Princess Beatrice, and her future daughter-in-law, the Grand Duchess Marie of Russia, future wife of her second son, Prince Alfred, set off in an open landau and four with the gentlemen riding alongside. She wrote:

There was nothing for it, but to start with waterproofs and umbrellas . . . The marching past then began, in a sea of mud, most despairing to witness. There were 40,000 men, and such fine ones . . . Once or twice it seemed as though the rain were going to cease, but only to come down again with renewed force. Pitilessly it came down, drifted by a high wind, on all those poor men, who nevertheless continued marching steadily along, with patient and gallant endurance. . . .
At 6 we got back, coming in through the garden, and scrambled into the house by a lower passage,

Queen Victoria attends the 'Wet Review' at Edinburgh in
1881. From a painting by William Simpson.

close to the kitchen, everyone soaked, but I only partially so, down the side from which the wind came, and while I sat in a pool of water. I had to change many under-garments. After, with great difficulty, getting a fire lit, I ran down to look after Beatrice and Marie, the latter wet through to the skin, the rain having penetrated through her waterproof. She had to have some clothes lent her, till hers could be dried. Beatrice got less wet, but I was more anxious about her, as she had a bad sore throat, and had not felt at all well this morning. I went also to see after Arthur, [Duke of Connaught], who had been quite wet through, and his nice new General's uniform quite spoilt by the green of the ribbon of the Thistle coming off on his tunic.

Queen Victoria was also very concerned about the effect of the rain on her bodyguard, the Royal Company of Archers, who had been commanded to furnish 'A Guard of Honour of the Royal Standard'. One of the oldest of the 141 was John Wilkie of Foulden who had been on duty for King George IV's visit of 1822 and many of the Company had to return to distant parts of Scotland directly after the Review.

In those days the Royal Company of Archers were not provided with overcoats or capes and the Marquis of Lothian, recalled the Queen's concern on seeing that their Captain-General, the Duke of Buccleuch, had no protection from the rain. He wrote:

Her Majesty . . . summoned the Duke of Connaught, who was mounted at the side of her carriage, and told him to tell the Duke to put on his greatcoat.

The Duke of Connaught obeyed, but brought back a message that His Grace could not think of thus protecting himself in Her Majesty's presence.

On hearing this Her Majesty said to His Royal Highness:

'Ride over and tell the Duke that I *command* him to put on his greatcoat.'

The Duke of Connaught delivered the second message to the Captain-General, who said 'To tell you the truth, Sir, we do not possess greatcoats; but I did not like to confess this when you first made known Her Majesty's kind wish to me.'

The Duke galloped back to the Royal Carriage and explained matters to the Queen who, without further comment, turned in her seat and asked one of the kilted attendants sitting behind her to give her her brown Shetland shawl. When the article was handed to her, the Queen held it out to the Duke of Connaught and said 'Take this to the Duke and tell him to wrap it round his shoulders at once!'

'History,' Lord Lothian added, with obvious regret, 'Does not relate what the Captain-General did on receipt of the shawl.'

KING EDWARD VII

The country of Scotland, like his mother Queen Victoria, was not always sympathetic to Prince Albert Edward, later Edward VII. The fact that, on his accession, he chose to be known as Edward 'the Seventh' gave deep offence, unwittingly no doubt, to many of his Scottish subjects. He was, in fact, the first of that name to rule over Great Britain and the United Kingdom and the previous six Kings Edward of England were not Kings of Scotland at all.

His initiation into Scottish life was equally disap-pointing. He accompanied his parents on their autumn trip to Balmoral and looked forward to climbing and exploring the hills, but he was told that for him and his tutor there would be no break with school-room routine. Lessons would continue every weekday, including Saturday. All through his boyhood his father imposed great educational pressures on him.

When he was seventeen, his father decided that he should spend three months before he went up to Oxford at the Palace of Holyroodhouse and take a preliminary course in applied science in Edinburgh under Dr Lyon Playfair, Professor of Chemistry at Cambridge University. The Professor had helped the Prince Consort with the 1851 Exhibition and one day he decided to test his new pupil's courage allied to his scientific knowledge.

Master and pupil were standing over a cauldron containing lead boiling at white heat.

'Has your Highness any faith in Science?' Playfair asked.

'Certainly,' replied the Prince.

Playfair then washed the Prince's hand thoroughly with ammonia and invited him to place it in the boiling metal and ladle out a portion.

The Prince: 'Do you tell me to do this?'

Playfair: 'I do.'

The Prince immediately put his hand into the cauldron and ladled out some of the boiling metal. He suffered no injury but the experiment had certainly proved he had a stout nerve.

The Prince of Wales liked Playfair and never entirely forgot his lectures on the composition of certain metals. However, during his stay in Edinburgh he resented not being allowed to shoot in the neighbourhood. Instead he was forced by his parents to give solemn dinners to the leading citizens in the Scottish capital. The Queen wrote suggesting he might be able to hold his own better if he learnt to part his hair in a less 'effiminate and girlish way' and if he would give up wearing slippers and *loose* long jackets which she characterized as 'slang'.

However, at this stage the public were beginning to sympathize with him, according to some verses which appeared in *Punch* entitled 'A Prince at High Pressure', which began:

Thou dear little Wales, sure the saddest of tales
Is the tale of the studies with which they are
    cramming thee . . .

Edward VII, when Prince of Wales, leading a torchlight dance at Mar Lodge,
the home of his sister Princess Louise, Duchess of Argyll.
October 1880.

Edward VII and his guests
in the Highlands.

Nevertheless, no amount of cramming seemed to impair his amazing capacity for good living for long.

Five years after his marriage to Princess Alexandra the young couple made a tour of Scotland which included a visit to the Castle of Mey, then called Barrogill. As usual the Prince travelled with a huge convoy which accommodated his enormous suite consisting of a valet to cope with some forty suits and uniforms and twenty pairs of boots and shoes necessary for a stay of more than a week, a sergeant footman, a brusher, two equerries who needed a valet apiece, two secretaries, two drivers and an Arab boy to prepare the coffee just the way he liked it. If shooting were contemplated there would be two loaders for the Prince and one for each of the equerries. There would be a staff of six for the Princess, including a hairdresser, ladies-in-waiting and personal servants.

In this most northern part of Scotland the local people had never seen royalty before and, knowing the Prince of Wales's reputation with the fair sex came to the conclusion that most of the elegant ladies in the party were his concubines.

Despite his love of good-living when, on his accession, Edward VII inherited Balmoral, he at once took strong measures to curb the drinking that went on there. Sir Frederick Ponsonby, a frequent guest recalled that in Queen Victoria's reign whenever anyone went out stalking, a whole bottle of whisky was given out, and whatever the guest did not drink became the perquisite of the stalker. He said:

Edward VII at a deer drive in Mar Forest, from the *Illustrated London News*, 16 October, 1880

It was quite a common thing for a stalker to come to the Castle and drink off a glass of neat whisky before he started. Of course if he went out stalking no harm was done, but when the weather was impossible and the mist came down he retired to his house and started the day slightly intoxicated.

I was really very sorry for one of the stalkers, a splendid-looking man with a white beard of the name of Cameron. A deer drive was ordered and all the stalkers and gillies turned out, but the weather made everything impossible . . . so the drive was cancelled. No sooner had all the men been sent back to their houses than the sun came out and it cleared up completely. The King therefore said he would have luncheon on the hill and the deer drive would take place afterwards. Cameron, who lived some way off, feeling sure that he would not be wanted,

had commenced drinking, when a messenger arrived summoning him. Had it been later in the day he would have been too drunk to obey the summons, but as it was he was only rather drunk. He turned up for luncheon and instead of keeping out of sight he insisted on going up to the King and talking. Of course His Majesty saw he was drunk although he could just walk . . . dismissed he was, without a pension. This was making an example with a vengeance, and it was said that the stalkers and gillies were partly resentful at a man with thirty years service being sacked, and partly frightened lest the same thing should happen to them. . . . But the King told me confidentially that when the affair had blown over he would see Cameron was given a pension on the understanding that he did not return to Balmoral.

The curtailment of the stupendous amount of whisky consumed at Balmoral in Queen Victoria's time coincided, for the time being, with the end of the truly Scottish home Victoria had created. The gillies were less like friends and were merely servants and the Sovereign's country house in the Highlands became a part of the social roundabout for the King and his Court.

Certainly Edward VII made it a much freer place and most of his guests found their visits more enjoyable. Card games and the occasional cinema show were introduced and Winston Churchill, who stayed there as a 27-year-old MP, told his mother how 'pleasant and easy-going' it all was.

Although the atmosphere was different, however, the decor remained largely unchanged. Queen Alexandra insisted that her mother-in-law's favourite home must be kept just as she had left it, — with the exception of the drawing-room with its tartan carpets and curtains which Queen Alexandra had found very oppressive. Her husband, on his part, ordered the immediate destruction or removal of all statues and other memories of Queen Victoria's favourite Highland servant, John Brown.

PRINCE ALBERT VICTOR, DUKE OF CLARENCE

'Prince Eddy', as Queen Victoria's eldest grandson, the Duke of Clarence, was known, fell in and out of love from his early twenties with a speed that caused a good deal of anxiety to the relatives of this heir to the throne. One of his early passions was for his cousin, Princess Alix of Hesse, sixth child of Queen Victoria's daughter, Princess Alice, and the Grand Duke of Hesse, but she turned him down. One month later he was in love with the tall, distinguished-looking Princess Hélène of Orleans, a daughter of the Comte de Paris, the Pretender to the French throne. As far as Queen Victoria was concerned the marriage was 'impossible' because the nineteen-year-old Princess was a Roman Catholic.

Prince Eddy had been mildly flirting with her for three years during which time she had fallen passionately, hopelessly and silently in love with him. Such loyalty endeared the girl to Eddy's mother Alexandra, the Princess of Wales, and she encouraged her son to persuade the Princess to change her religion and marry him. She then arranged for her daughter, Princess Louise, Duchess of Fife, to invite the young couple to stay at her Scottish home, Mar Lodge, twelve miles from Balmoral. It was August 1890 and the

Prince Albert Victor, Duke of Clarence, the eldest son of Edward VII.

Alice, Princess Louis of Hesse,
Prince Eddy's aunt (seated)
and the Duchess of Roxburghe, 1865.

Prince of Wales was safely out of the country while all the intrigue was going on.

At Mar Lodge, a shapeless old shooting lodge set among the purple heather and silver birch trees, Eddy proposed and was accepted. The next step was to obtain the Queen's blessing. Here again the Princess of Wales made her plans, lending weight to a poem of the time published by Henry Labouchere in which all the Royal Family, including the Queen, were castigated except Alexandra. Of her it read:

Your every word, your every glance
Is able to the land entrance.
Your will we willingly make law
Whenever you express it.
You have magnetic influence,
Though little you may guess it.
None can *your* potent charm resist—
You are the subtlest hypnotist.

In her son's interest Alexandra moved subtly and swiftly.

ABOVE: Princess Victoria, sister of Prince Eddy, with Princess Hélène, the Duchess of Aosta.

LEFT: Prince Albert Victor, Duke of Clarence, known as 'Prince Eddy', in 1891, the year before his death.

Queen Victoria had just arrived at Balmoral for her autumn holiday and, being delighted to be back at Deeside, was at her most amiable. Alexandra decided to take advantage of her mother-in-law's affable mood.

Early one morning she bundled Eddy and Hélène off in a carriage with a picnic lunch, to Balmoral. The Queen was working on state papers in the hut on the castle lawn when the couple arrived and surprised her. She loved surprises and was incurably romantic.

When Eddy stood before her and professed his love she was reminded of how Albert had confessed his feelings to her half a century ago and gave her blessing to the romance.

'You can imagine what a thing to go through,' the suitor told his younger brother George. '. . . I naturally expected Grandma would be furious at the idea, and say it was quite impossible etc. But instead of that she was very nice about it and promised to help us as much as possible, which she is now doing. . . .I believe what pleased her most was my taking Hélène into her, and saying we had arranged it entirely between ourselves without consulting our parents first. This as you know, was not quite true but she believed it all and was quite pleased. Hélène however had said nothing as yet to her parents which was the worst to come for her poor girl.'

However, the affair ended sadly for both of them for Hélène's father refused to agree to the match, nor would the British statesmen. The Pope also refused to give his permission when Hélène went to Rome to plead with him. At one stage Prince Eddy said he would willingly abdicate his rights to succession. But by the spring the whole affair was over.

Whenever Queen Victoria saw her grandson he was on his best behaviour and she feared it would be years before he recovered from his 'broken heart'. But he was more resilient. In June he was writing love letters again, this time to the beautiful Lady Sybil St Clair Erskine and continued to do so until the eve of his engagement to the somewhat hesitant Princess May of Teck.

Princess May had liked and respected Princess Hélène, who afterwards became the Duchess of Aosta. Perhaps, in moments of her own private misgivings about her impending marriage, she regretted that the romance between her fiancé and Princess Hélène had been broken. Long afterwards, on her instructions, it was commemorated at Windsor Castle by a bead wreath on the Duke of Clarence's ornate tomb in the annexe to St George's Chapel. It bore just one word — 'Hélène'.

KING GEORGE V

Sandringham in Norfolk was to King George V the home that Balmoral was to Queen Victoria but, nevertheless, Balmoral also became his dearly loved holiday home. He grew to love it as a boy because it was his grandparent's holiday home and later he sometimes went there for the spring fishing as well as for the regular autumn holiday.

For his bride Balmoral had different associations. Princess May and her brother Prince Adolphus of Teck were summoned there by Queen Victoria one cold November because the Queen wished to get to know the Princess better to see if she would make a suitable bride for her grandson, 'Prince Eddy', the Duke of Clarence. In this respect the ten-day visit proved a great success and the young couple became engaged one month later, at the end of 1891. Six weeks later the Prince was dead from influenza and pneumonia and, within eighteen months, Princess May had married his younger brother Prince George, Duke of York. From then on regular visits to Scotland were part of her autumn programme.

At first the weather and the invitations to stay with Queen Victoria, where she was subjected to the monarch's personal system of cross-examination, made the Scottish visits something of a trial.

I like Balmoral for about a fortnight, [she wrote to her husband in 1895] but I honestly think that longer than that is rather an ordeal as the everlasting questions and the carefulness of ones replies is extremely fatiguing in the long run. However as she kindly asks us to stay I suppose we had better do so.

The Scottish holidays became less of an ordeal after the death of Queen Victoria when Princess May became the Princess of Wales. King Edward and Queen Alexandra moved to Balmoral and the Prince and Princess of Wales took over Abergeldie. Year by year its new mistress succeeded in making the little fortress more comfortable with new carpets, wallpapers and heating. She still had to learn to come to terms with the weather. 'It really is not so bad when the weather is

George V in the Highlands in 1889 with
Sir Christopher Teesdale.

The three eldest children of the Duke and Duchess of York
(later George V and Queen Mary), at Balmoral *c.* 1899.
From left to right: Prince Edward (later King Edward VIII),
Prince Albert (later King George VI) and Princess Mary.

fine,' she wrote to her aunt in 1909, 'but in bad weather, oh!!!' However, on the rare fine days she gradually succumbed to the family tradition of arrang, ing picnics and excursions.

Balmoral, when as Queen Mary she eventually succeeded to it, no longer filled her with misgivings. She had none of Queen Alexandra's reservations and immediately had all the dark marmalade,coloured paint stripped from the panelling and other woodwork so that the whole house seemed lighter. She then dispensed traditional hospitality every September to certain chosen statesmen, to the Archbishop of Canter, bury, Dr Cosmo Lang, and to old friends including King George's old tutor, Canon Dalton, and Sister Agnes Keyser, founder and matron of King Edward VII's Hospital for Officers in London. Her speciality there was patients from the Household Cavalry and the Brigade of Guards and, according to Sir Harold Nicolson, 'Sister Agnes' could be relied upon to enliven the Balmoral conversation by repeating, not always with useful results, the talk of the town.

Meanwhile, King George, a knowledgeable Highland landowner, spent most of his time in Scotland out on the heights and in the woods and valleys he knew and loved as well as did most of the locals. He needed no guide on the hills and many of his friends were the people who had been the tyrants of his youth. There was Donald Stewart who taught him to shoot grouse, David Rose the stalker, who was also an expert at dancing the reel, and Meysie Anderson who kept the fishing lodge at the head of Loch Muick and who was not slow to show her displeasure if the King failed to do justice to the splendid teas she prepared.

One fact that endeared him to all of them was his extraordinary memory for detail which enabled him to pick up a point of discussion after perhaps a year's interval.

He often walked about unattended and he knew his tenants and their families personally and, here again, showed his uncanny memory for remembering int, imate details of their lives. Sometimes he stopped the children on their way home from school, took their books from them and questioned them about their work. He might tease them if their answers were unsatisfactory, showing rather more indulgence, it seemed, than he did with his own sons.

In his prime, George V preferred stalking to grouse shooting and, even on the first day of the season, would prove a match for anyone. He could walk for ever and always seemed to be in condition, even when a long crawl after quarry was involved. During most of his stalking career he used his first rifle (a cordite hammered one), made for him in India, with which he was as quick and sure as with a gun. Abercrombie, the head stalker, recalled seeing him bring off marvellous standing shots at moving deer.

However, he was never the same man, either physically or as an efficient shot, after his accident in France during World War I. It happened when he was inspecting a Wing of the Royal Flying Corps and his horse took fright at the cheering. It reared and fell back on top of him, fracturing his pelvis, and it was more than two months before he was out with a gun again.

The Duke and Duchess of York with their children at Abergeldie in 1906.
Front row, from left to right: Princess Mary (later the Princess Royal), Prince Henry (later the Duke of Gloucester),
Prince George (later the Duke of Kent), Prince Edward (later the Duke of Windsor) and Prince Albert (later George VI).
Back row: the Duke and Duchess of York with Prince John.

King George V and Queen Mary at Balmoral with Princess Mary.

King George V and Queen Mary driving back to Balmoral with
Princess Elizabeth after attending church at Crathie.

Gradually, however, some of his old skill returned and one day, towards the end of his life, Abercrombie reported that two stags had got through the deer fence and were in a wood inside the grounds. The King and a friend went out to look for them. The woods were driven and the stags broke out together about two hundred yards from the King affording him right and left galloping shots. He killed both.

In those last stalking years Queen Mary sometimes gave private instructions to Abercrombie to take special care of the King and try and prevent him from getting over-tired.

One day, stalking with Archbishop Lang and the stalker Grant who was a real old 'candid friend', the King rested his rifle on Grant's shoulder for a fairly easy shot. He missed and the whole herd galloped away.

'Take this damned rifle away. Never let me see it again,' he told Grant.

'Yer Ma-jesty, dinna waste yer breethe damning the rifle. It was a verra ba-ad shot,' was the reply.

George V was keen that his sons should take to shooting and when they were young he would go out with them during the season to walk up the grouse although, curiously enough, he was not at his best in that form of shooting. However, George VI at any rate became skilled in it as he did in many things, in his own good time.

KING GEORGE VI

King George VI, it was said, set off with greater zest to his home at Balmoral than to any other, partly because his holiday there in the autumn came at a time when it was most appreciated. Partly too because he was a new sort of shooting monarch.

On his visits to Glamis before his betrothal to Lady Elizabeth Bowes Lyon he had learned there was more to the sport than just standing in the butts and firing at the birds: it could also involve observation about the wind and weather, the habits of birds and the success or

The Duke and Duchess of York (later King George VI and Queen Elizabeth) at Glamis Castle
with their daughter Princess Elizabeth and a young relative for the Golden Wedding celebrations
of the Duchess's parents, the Earl and Countess of Strathmore, in 1931.

failure of certain drives. From that moment shooting took on a new aspect.

At his shooting parties George VI became, as it were, the author, producer, stage-manager and the leading man, all at once. Every detail of the arrangements, however elaborate or humble a shoot he was giving, became his concern. Nothing escaped him and this new attitude was never more apparent than at Balmoral where on a sand table-model of the moors and forests around, all the moves of a day's shoot could be worked out.

In his father's day there was little grouse-driving at Balmoral for George V preferred to spend his Scottish holiday visiting friends at Moy or Floors and by the time he arrived at his own home, stalking was beginning and formed his chief sport there.

George VI, however, preferred family holidays at home and the companionship of a few close friends. He leased some of the Invercauld moors, first Gairnshiel and later Cornadaur, so that within a mile or so of Balmoral he had some of the best grouse-driving in Scotland and he made the most of it: new keepers were engaged, a programme of heather-burning and drainage planned; new roads and bridges were gradually developed and many new butts added, based entirely on his observation. He personally largely planned the drive, first with experimental butts which could either by adopted or corrected.

A member of the Household at the time describes a day at Balmoral starting from the moment the King emerged from his room, punctual to the minute:

He always wore his own tweed, which he had devised for himself and his keepers, and for those members of his household who were fortunate enough to be given a length. In one hand would be a long walking-stick, in the other, very often, some special article of apparel of his own planning for combating any trick of the weather; a cap, a scarf or some ingenious kind of coat for he was always a great contriver.

We would all clamber into the bus which at once became full of chatter and, about once a week, whoever was nearest the door would lower the window a little in order to inspire the storm of imprecation which instantly followed an act of such suicidal folly. This and other familiar features assumed gradually a ritualistic virtue about the holiday. The site of the opening day of the season before driving really began; a rabbit shoot among the juniper bushes in the region known as 'Back of the Wood'; expeditions on Sunday afternoon either to the far end of Loch Muick, for tea in the Glassalt or some light-hearted trout-fishing in the Loch—or to the Queen's charming little cottage where a more serious and less reputable form of fishing often produced some salmon, bearing mysterious marks almost suggestive of foul hooking.

On driving days most of the house party joined the guns for luncheon which was always in the open—the habit of having luncheon set out and served by footmen was long abandoned. The luncheon baskets were left in a favourite spot; plaid rugs spread about the heather and bog myrtle, and since, by one of the most hallowed shooting conventions, the ladies were usually on the spot before the guns had descended from the hillside, they had often set out the picnic.

In retrospect the sun seems so continuously to have shone on these Lucullan festivals that many would have been content to prolong them almost indefinitely, but the King had a watchful eye on the afternoon's programme and in due course a busy repacking would begin.

At first the King was tempted to shoot every day of the week but later he had one day a week's rest which gave the keepers and drivers a break and allowed him and his guests a chance to catch up on their correspondence.

In a good year the King used to drive grouse throughout September and into October, when the frost had already begun to turn the leaves red and gold. All through the season a succession of guests stayed in the castle.

In an indifferent grouse year, such as 1945, by September several beats had been shot hard enough and there was a full team of guns in the castle. On 3 September came a break in the ritual when the King deployed the whole party to try and fill the game card with everything the Balmoral estate could provide. Three small parties were detailed to pursue victims whose habits led them off the beaten track; the King and a friend climbed Lochnagar in search of ptarmigan; Princess Elizabeth and a friend soon had a stag; someone else was detailed to produce salmon and trout and took a gun with him and returned with a duck and something unusual for any menu—a heron and a sparrow hawk.

On the King's next birthday the nine participants gave him a silver table mat engraved with their names around his cypher in the centre, as a reminder of a very happy day. The bag had been 1 pheasant, 12 partridges, 2 hares, 3 rabbits, 1 woodcock, 1 snipe, 1 wild duck, 1 stag, 1 roe-deer, 2 pigeon, 2 black game, 17 grouse, 2 capercailzie, 6 ptarmigan, 2 salmon, 1 trout, a heron and a sparrow hawk.

PRINCESS MARINA, DUCHESS OF KENT

One of the saddest royal visits to Scotland took place in August 1946 when Princess Marina, the widowed Duchess of Kent, accompanied by a few close friends went to the Duke of Portland's Caithness estate in the north-east of Scotland. They walked over the rough moorland to find a wooden post marking the spot where her husband, the Duke of Kent, had been tragically killed in a flying accident four years previously, seven weeks after the birth of their youngest son, Prince Michael of Kent.

Not until four years after the accident had the Duchess been able to bring herself to visit the place where her husband had died on active service during World War II although on the first anniversary of his death she had asked a friend to go there and say a prayer for him. On her first visit the Duchess found that most of the wreck of the aircraft had been cleared away but some bits of the machine still lay scattered among the rocks and heather. A long black scar, bleak and bare, showed only too clearly where the plane had landed. The sight revived the Duchess's grief so intensely that it was fifteen years before she could bring herself to visit the place again.

The accident had taken place early in the afternoon of 25 August, 1942, after a tender had taken the Duke, his secretary, his ADC and his batman from the RAF base at Invergordon, out to the Sunderland flying boat which was waiting for them on the wide water of Cromarty Firth. It was not a good place for take-off because the water was too flat; 'smooth like grey slate' as the only surviving member of the crew said later.

Princess Marina and Prince George, the Duke and Duchess of Kent.

The Sunderland was fairly heavily laden with full petrol tanks, some depth charges and a crew of ten and climbed with difficulty into the sky for the long haul round the coast of Scotland and northward to Iceland on a wartime mission.

What happened less than half an hour after take-off was described by the rear gunner, Flight Sergeant (later Flight Lieutenant) Andrew Jack, the only survivor:

> We ran into heavy cloud. It was rather low, and I remember thinking to myself, as I sat there with cloud all round me: 'what a silly day to fly.' I could feel the aircraft going down and I said to myself, 'We're going to see the coastline again.' If you're not flying a compass course you've got to be able to see the coast to follow it. Looking back now, I think we must have been drifting inland without realizing it, and that the captain, trying to get below the cloud, came down over land instead of out to sea. I didn't know any more until I woke up and found myself on the ground.

Flight Sergeant Jack never knew how long he was unconscious nor did he realize that his face and arms were badly burned and his hand was broken. He had been thrown clear of the impact which was of such force that pieces of wreckage were scattered over the gorse and heather and bracken and were quite unrecognizable. The huge scar marked where the Sunderland had hit the slope, turned over and slid for 200 yards on its back before breaking up.

When the flight sergeant's brain started functioning again and he saw the aircraft in little pieces he realized that the rest of the passengers and crew must be dead. He recognized the Duke's body by his uniform of air commodore. He staggered off along a shepherd's path by a burn. When darkness fell he lay down in the ferns. At dawn he struggled to a hill top and eventually reached a cottage.

Meanwhile a farmer and his son, rounding up their sheep in the thick mist, heard the noise of an aeroplane flying low overhead followed shortly by a tremendous explosion. The son set out for help and with a doctor and search party eventually managed to find their way through the dense mist to the wrecked aircraft. The bodies had to be carried for about five miles over rough and desolate moorland to reach the ambulance.

Air Commodore the Duke of Kent was buried in St George's Chapel, Windsor. In 1961 his widow went again to the scene of the crash accompanied by her elder son and her daughter Princess Alexandra. By then all traces of the wreckage had disappeared and the Duchess had arranged for a simple granite cross to be erected in memory of her husband and those who died with him.

Seven years later when the Duchess died, the Duke's body was reinterred and they were laid to rest together in the small private burial ground at Frogmore, close to the remains of Queen Victoria and the Prince Consort.

QUEEN ELIZABETH

Queen Elizabeth's great-great-grandmother Queen Victoria, the last and greatest monarch of the House of Hanover, loved the Highlands but shunned public appearances with the result that her affection for Scotland remained a comparatively private affair for most of her life. The House of Windsor, typified by the Queen today, have taken Scotland to their hearts and make no secret about it.

When the Queen was Princess Elizabeth, Scotland was a second home for she spent all the summers of her childhood with her grandparents, the Earl and Countess of Strathmore, at Glamis Castle. Later there were regular Scottish holidays at Birkhall and Balmoral with her parents, and eventually with her own children.

Meanwhile, her public involvement with this most northern part of her kingdom is indicated by the fact that she has already paid more public visits to

Queen Elizabeth
with Prince Charles and Princess Anne at
Balmoral in 1952, the year of the Queen's accession.

Edinburgh Castle by the Lord Lyon and Heralds, to the Palace of Holyroodhouse for the State Procession to the cathedral. It was a moment of living history as they were borne through the crowded streets in the fourth and fifth carriages followed by the semi-state landau taking the Queen and the Duke of Edinburgh drawn by four of the famous grey horses from St Cuthbert's stud. All were flanked by a file of Royal Archers of the Queen's Bodyguard for Scotland and escorted by mounted police, massed pipes and drums, massed military bands, detachments from the armed forces, the banner bearer and civic dignitaries.

From that moment tradition came to life in Edinburgh as the pageantry of age-old ceremonies mingled with garden parties, official openings and twentieth-century walkabouts.

Edinburgh Castle added another episode to the historic visit when the royal couple drove along the Royal Mile from the Palace of Holyroodhouse with a sovereign's Escort of Household Cavalry and a detachment of the Royal Scots Greys, to receive the key of the castle. At the drawbridge the Lord Lyon King of Arms in his velvet heraldic coat accepted the Queen's command 'to summon the Castle of Edinburgh to open its gates'.

A fanfare of trumpets was followed by a challenge from the battlements:

'Halt! Who goes there?' and then, after the establishment of the royal identity and a request for admittance had been made, ending with the time-honoured injunction:

'. . . an ye fail ye shall answer at your highest peril.'

Then came the second cry from the battlements:

'Advance, Her Majesty, all is well,' and the presentation of the castle key from the Keeper.

Early on the final day of the visit the Queen installed Prince Philip as a Knight of the Thistle. But for a hundred thousand people the midnight scene in Holyrood Park that night was the most memorable of the visit. Gathered on the hillsides approaching Arthur's Seat where a beacon blazed on the very top lit by six athletes with burning torches, the flames taken from the master torch lit by the Queen herself, they saw the Queen. A fairy-tale figure in an ermine mantle and diamond tiara, she watched from a floodlit dais and, as

Edinburgh than any other sovereign since her ancestor King James VI left for England in 1603. The first ceremonial visit took place within three weeks of her Coronation in Westminster Abbey when she paid a three-day visit to Edinburgh with Prince Philip.

For those three days the sun scarcely stopped shining from the moment when the new Queen was ceremoniously presented with the keys of the city by the Lord Provost, Sir James Miller, on her arrival at Caledonian Station.

The climax of the visit was the service in St Giles' Cathedral where, for only the second time since the Union, the Honours of Scotland, the Crown, the Sceptre and the Sword, were ceremoniously borne before the reigning monarch at a service of Thanksgiving and Dedication. Previously, for the first time in three hundred years, they had been taken from

Queen Elizabeth addressing a meeting of the General Assembly of the Church of Scotland
in the Assembly Hall, Edinburgh, in October 1960 in commemoration of the fourth centenary
of the Reformation of Scotland.

Queen Elizabeth and the Duke of Edinburgh leave St Giles' Cathedral, Edinburgh, in 1960
after a service to mark the fourth centenary of the Reformation of Scotland.

The Queen and her family at Balmoral during the Royal Silver Wedding year
of 1972.

the flames of the beacon burned more gently the crowds sang to her *Will ye no come back again?*

She came back again, to join the 1960 celebrations of the four-hundredth anniversary of the Reformation in Scotland. The slim figure in an ankle-length turquoise gown with matching feathers in her hair was the first reigning British sovereign to visit the General Assembly of the Church of Scotland since the union of the crowns in 1603. Moreover, from time to time, as the years passed, she returned to the openings of the General Assembly to re-affirm her original pledge to uphold the rights and privileges of the Church of Scotland.

She visited Perth, on the 750th anniversary of the day King William the Lion granted it a Royal Charter, and she commemorated it by opening the new Queen's Bridge over the River Tay. Then, feeling that Glasgow tended to be neglected on ceremonial occasions, her Silver Jubilee tour began there rather than in Edinburgh. There, pageantry and ceremony apart, it was the walkabout in George Square, crowded with more than sixty thousand people, the visits to the housing estates and factories, sheltered workshops and community centres, that won the hearts of the Glaswegians.

There was no mistaking the warmth of the welcome as she arrived to drive in procession in an open state coach to the cathedral, escorted by the Household

Cavalry making their first appearance in the city. Thousands of voices raised to greet her with the traditional song which has become one of the unofficial Scottish national anthems:

THE FLOWER OF SCOTLAND

O' Flower of Scotland, when will we see your likes again?
That fought and died for, your wee bit hill and glen?
And stood against them, proud Edward's army,
And sent him homeward, tae think again.

The hills are bare now, and autumn leaves lie thick and still,
O'er land that is lost now, which those so dearly held,
And stood against them, proud Edward's army
And sent him homeward, tae think again.

Those days are passed now, and in the past they must remain,
But we can still rise now, and be the nation again,
That stood against them, proud Edward's army,
And sent him homeward, tae think again.

PRINCE CHARLES

Childhood holidays at Balmoral apart, Prince Charles's initiation to Scotland was a hard one: from 1 May, 1962 he was, as he described, 'incarcerated' with four hundred other pupils in the Spartan world of Gordonstoun, his father's old school in the chilly wastes of northern Scotland. Nothing in the first fourteen years of his life could have prepared him for that three-year ordeal.

Ironically the eighteenth-century manor house set in three hundred acres of land had once belonged to Sir William Gordon Cumming, a lieutenant colonel in the Scots Guards who had involved Prince Charles's great-great-grandfather, the future Edward VII, in a notorious gambling scandal. He had been accused of cheating at baccarat when the Prince of Wales was dealing the cards. Gordon Cumming lost the subsequent slander case but the Prince, to his mother's and the nation's dismay, was forced to give evidence.

Eighty years later Prince Charles found himself in a school of unpainted dormitories with bare floorboards, naked light bulbs and spare wooden bedsteads where life must be endured both in short trousers and huts exposed to the North-Sea gales. 'Well, at least he hasn't run away yet,' was Prince Philip's reply when asked, after a few weeks, how his son was getting on there.

The daily routine started at seven o'clock with a run round the grounds in shorts and singlets followed by

the first of the two showers of the day. The tough life-style was designed to protect the boys from their increasingly urbanized home lives by testing their physical resources against the forces of nature on land and on sea and to introduce a sense of purpose and self-reliance added to one of duty and service. It was hard for Charles. A fellow pupil explained:

How can you treat a boy as just an ordinary chap when his mother's portrait is on the coins you spend in the school shop. . . . Most boys tend to fight shy of friendship with Charles. The result is that he is very lonely. It is this loneliness, rather than the school's toughness, which must be hardest on him.

It was. Whenever he could escape Charles visited the Queen Mother at Birkhall who, more than anyone, understood her grandson's unhappiness but she refused his pleas to intercede with his parents to take him away. Instead they became staunch fishing companions as she tried to help him through his first major ordeal.

Her success was evident when, later, the Prince admitted that he was glad of those three years at Gordonstoun. He told his biographer Anthony Holden:

The toughness of the place is too much exaggerated by report. It was the character of the general education there—Kurt Hahn's principles; an education which tried to balance the physical and mental with the emphasis on self-reliance to develop a rounded human being. I did not enjoy school as much as I might have, but that was because I am happier at home than anywhere else. But Gordonstoun developed my willpower and self-control, helped me to discipline myself, and I think that discipline, not in the sense of making you bath in cold water, but in the Latin sense—giving shape and form and tidiness to your life—is the most important thing your education can do.

When, in due course, Charles's brothers Andrew and Edward followed him to Gordonstoun, they had a much happier time because Charles had pioneered the way.

Prince Charles arrives at Gordonstoun school in May, 1962.
'How do you do, sir?' says the heir to the throne to his housemaster, Mr Robert Whitby.
On the left is the school's headmaster, Mr Robert Chew.

EARL OF CARRICK

Fourteen years later Prince Charles was back in Scotland for a poignant occasion. On a June Sunday in 1979 he went to Dunfermline to pay a simple act of homage to his illustrious ancestor, King Robert the Bruce. He attended a service in Dunfermline Abbey to commemorate the burial, six hundred and fifty years ago, of Robert the Bruce after his death at his house in Cardross at the age of fifty-five. For two years he had been suffering from a serious illness—possibly leprosy.

Promptly at eleven o'clock a fanfare of trumpets by the Royal Marines sounded for a moment of pure pageantry as the kilted Prince, resplendent in the uniform of Colonel-in-Chief of the Gordon Highlanders, entered the packed abbey in a colourful procession. There were the ornate tabards of the heralds and pursuivants of the Lyon Court; the unfurled royal banner and national flag of Scotland; and floral decorations in the Bruce colours of red and gold.

Prince Charles, Earl of Carrick, lays a wreath on the tomb of his ancestor, King Robert the Bruce,
Earl of Carrick, in Dunfermline Abbey in June, 1979,
during the 650th anniversary service of the King's burial.

As the choir and the congregation of two thousand began to sing the Prince took his seat in the royal pew adjoining 'the fair tomb' which the great King had ordered to be made in Paris after restoring the abbey in the early fourteenth century.

After prayers and a sermon delivered from the pulpit just above the tomb, by the Right Reverend Professor Robin A. S. Barbour, Moderator of the General Assembly of the Church of Scotland, Prince Charles, Earl of Carrick, stepped forward to lay the wreath, inscribed 'King Robert the Bruce, 1306–1329', at the tomb of that other Earl of Carrick and stood for a few moments in silent homage.

After a prayer and the Benediction, a fanfare of trumpets sounded once again for the royal procession slowly to wend its way out of the abbey. But Prince Charles paused yet again before the tomb, in thoughtful contemplation.

Coming out into the daylight he looked across the ruins of the neighbouring Dunfermline Palace to the town where another Prince Charles was born in 1600 and whose statue as King Charles I at Charing Cross, London inspired a nineteenth-century poet to write of 'the saddest of all kings'.

Vanquished in life, his death
By beauty made amends:
The passing of his breath
Won his defeated ends.

Brief life, and hapless? Nay;
Through death, life grew sublime.
Speak after sentence? Yea;
And to the end of time.

213

LORD OF THE ISLES

As Lord of the Isles the Prince descends at least three dozen times over from the paramount Macdonald chiefs (long the mightiest of all the clans) who were the original Lords of the Isles. Added to the rest of his Scottish lineage which includes more than two hundred direct lines of descent from King Robert the Bruce and thus from the ancient Celtic kings of the Picts and the Scots it is not surprising that a love for Scotland flows deep in his veins. It was activated, he recalled on a BBC television programme, when he read Queen Victoria's *Highland Journals* for the first time:

> They immediately struck a chord. For instance, her first impression of Balmoral when she wrote 'All seemed to breath freedom and peace, and to make one forget the world and its sad turmoils.' Exactly what I feel. If you know and love Balmoral and its neighbourhood as much as I do, you can instantly recognize the places she describes. . . . She hated leaving, much as I hate leaving this marvellous place.

In Scottish churches Prince Charles is prayed for as Charles, Duke of Rothesay, but when, like his father, the Duke of Edinburgh, his grandfather, King George VI, and other distinguished ancestors, he became President of the Highland Society of London, he was the first to do so under his most romantic Highland title, Lord of the Isles. In his presidential speech at the Bicentenary Banquet in June 1978, he admitted to being:

> . . . an unashamed and hopeless romantic whose heart is very much in the Highlands and whose spirit is stirred and profoundly moved by the sound of the pipes. My heart is in the Highlands to the extent that each time I escape there I feel instantly restored in mind and spirit.

His interest in Scotland is not confined to his regular holidays there. He is consistently concerned at the current problems of the Highlands and Islands, particularly the relation between freedom and development and the difficulty of making a prosperous living in those parts. This was evident at the Bicentenary Banquet when the practical in him kept pace with the romantic. He spoke of subsidies, the re-establishment of craft work and high-quality products on a cottage industry basis as a means of preserving small Scottish communities 'living in a way that human beings *should* live, in communion, as it were, with their surroundings; their life reflecting the true dignity of labour'.

> We ought to be more aware of our human requirements . . . we call them spiritual rather than material—and of the greater peace which stems from living in better harmony with nature. . . . Communities matter, and the more we destroy our communities, the worse *all* our problems will be.

He turned the clock back two hundred years to 'one of the society's noblest past achievements', their success in 1782 in getting a repeal of the Act prohibiting the wearing of Highland dress.

> Personally, I enjoy wearing the kilt, despite the fact that as a garment it is not ideal for stalking, and if fishing it tends to spread out on the surface of the water when wading, not to mention the shelter it affords for a myriad of midges when on the bank!

The society, he said, had helped to preserve other aspects of Scottish culture by encouraging piping, preserving ancient Gaelic manuscripts and supporting welfare activities and charities with Scottish connections.

Finally again, as a self-confessed romantic, he spoke of the ethos of that wider Highland Society—overlaid with marvellous myths and sentimentality:

> . . . the society which existed in Wales and beyond the pale in Ireland, a Celtic society out of the Heroic Age, unchanged by the Romans or the Normans, the civil wars or any of the forces in society in these islands for two thousand years . . . It was a society based on tradition, and revolving around cattle stealing and poetry. The clans stole cattle from each other and, in attendance, like sports writers, were the bards who wrote about the exploits. . . .

> It was a society which certainly bewildered those English who dared to venture into the Highlands.

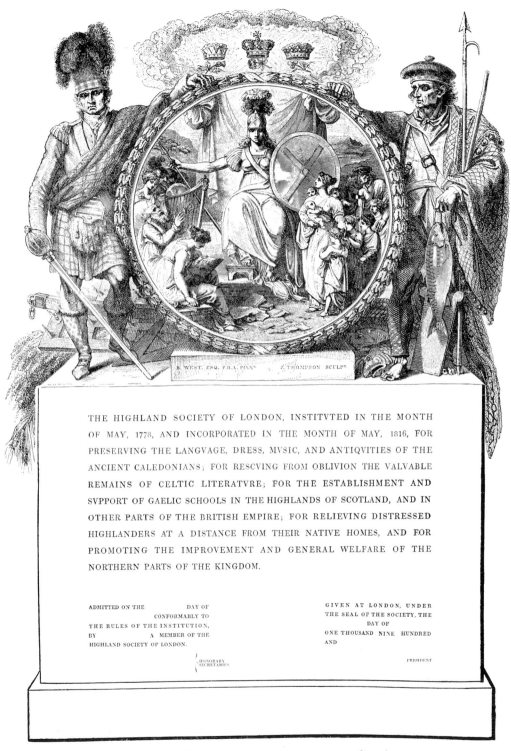

THE HIGHLAND SOCIETY OF LONDON, INSTITVTED IN THE MONTH
OF MAY, 1778, AND INCORPORATED IN THE MONTH OF MAY, 1816, FOR
PRESERVING THE LANGVAGE, DRESS, MVSIC, AND ANTIQVITIES OF THE
ANCIENT CALEDONIANS; FOR RESCVING FROM OBLIVION THE VALVABLE
REMAINS OF CELTIC LITERATVRE; FOR THE ESTABLISHMENT AND
SVPPORT OF GAELIC SCHOOLS IN THE HIGHLANDS OF SCOTLAND, AND IN
OTHER PARTS OF THE BRITISH EMPIRE; FOR RELIEVING DISTRESSED
HIGHLANDERS AT A DISTANCE FROM THEIR NATIVE HOMES, AND FOR
PROMOTING THE IMPROVEMENT AND GENERAL WELFARE OF THE
NORTHERN PARTS OF THE KINGDOM.

ADMITTED ON THE   DAY OF
                   CONFORMABLY TO
THE RULES OF THE INSTITUTION,
BY   A MEMBER OF THE
HIGHLAND SOCIETY OF LONDON.

GIVEN AT LONDON, UNDER
THE SEAL OF THE SOCIETY, THE
          DAY OF
ONE THOUSAND NINE HUNDRED
AND

HONORARY
SECRETARIES.

PRESIDENT

Commission of membership of the Highland Society of London,
founded in 1778 and one of the oldest
Highland Societies in Britain.

Like William Sacheverell, one-time governor of the Isle of Man, who wrote that there appeared in all their actions a certain generous air of freedom and contempt for these trifles, luxury and ambition, which we so servilely creep after. There is still just a lingering taste of such an attitude in the Highlands today.

Enough, it seems, to lure this descendent of Kenneth mac Alpin, Robert the Bruce and the great kings and queens of Scotland, to take his young bride back to the Highlands for part of their honeymoon. She shares his Scottish heritage from the time of James VI, is one of the nearest living relations of Bonnie Prince Charlie and her mother, the Hon. Mrs Shand Kydd, farms on the Isle of Seil. Here indeed is a true Scottish princess.

It was in the wild loneliness and peace of the Scottish Highlands in September 1981, that their first child, William Arthur Philip Louis, was conceived, to extend the fragile mystery of monarchy, a mixture of power and limitation, that has endured down the centuries from those earliest kings who claimed their descent from the gods. Here is a prince born, no doubt, to play his part, in another century, in the history of Royal Scotland.

The Prince and Princess of Wales with their son, Prince William Arthur Philip Louis of Wales, born on 21 June, 1982 and christened at Buckingham Palace on 4th August, six days after his parents' first wedding anniversary.

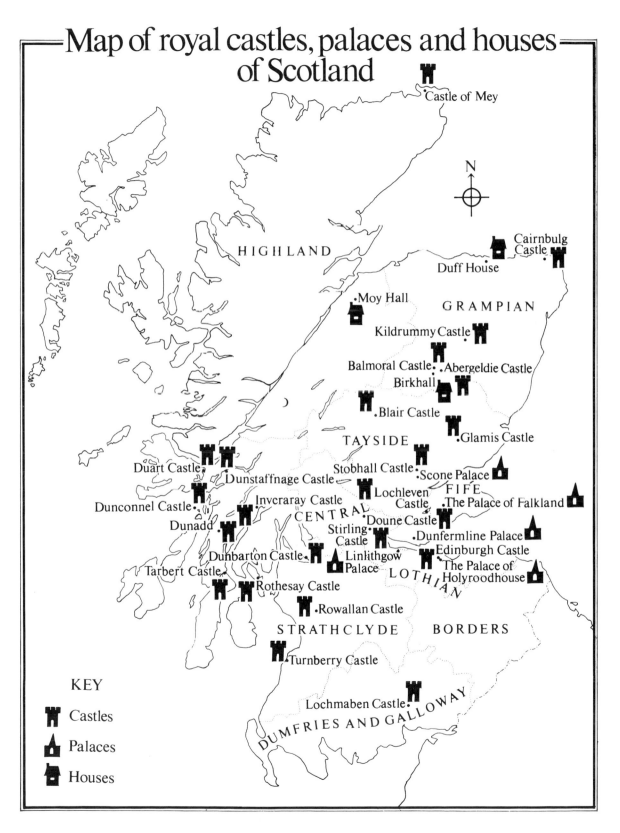

Map of royal castles, palaces and houses of Scotland

Castle of Mey

N

HIGHLAND

Cairnbulg Castle

Duff House

Moy Hall

GRAMPIAN

Kildrummy Castle

Balmoral Castle · Abergeldie Castle

Birkhall

· Blair Castle

TAYSIDE

· Glamis Castle

Duart Castle

Stobhall Castle

Dunstaffnage Castle

Scone Palace

FIFE

Lochleven Castle

The Palace of Falkland

Dunconnel Castle ·

Inveraray Castle

CENTRAL

Dunadd

Doune Castle

Stirling Castle

· Dunfermline Palace

Dunbarton Castle ·

Linlithgow Palace

Edinburgh Castle

Tarbert Castle ·

LOTHIAN

The Palace of Holyroodhouse

Rothesay Castle

· Rowallan Castle

STRATHCLYDE

BORDERS

· Turnberry Castle

Lochmaben Castle ·

DUMFRIES AND GALLOWAY

KEY

Castles

Palaces

Houses

217

MONARCHS OF SCOTLAND SINCE AD 1005

The Roman numerals in quotation marks show that these numbers refer to the English succession, not to the Scottish (i.e., after the Union of the Crowns in 1603).

Malcolm II	1005–34
Duncan I	1034–40
Macbeth	1040–57
Lulach	1057–8
Malcolm III 'Canmore'	1058–93
Donald Ban	1093–4
	1094–7
Duncan II	1094
Edgar	1097–1107
Alexander I	1107–24
David I	1124–53
Malcolm IV	1153–65
William I 'The Lion'	1165–1214
Alexander II	1214–49
Alexander III	1249–86
Margaret, Maid of Norway	1286–90
John Balliol	1292–6
Robert Bruce (Robert I)	1306–29
David II	1329–71
Robert II (the Stewart)	1371–90
Robert III	1390–1406
James I	1406–37
James II	1437–60
James III	1460–88
James IV	1488–1513
James V	1513–42
Mary (I)	1542–67
James VI (James I of England)	1567–1625
Charles I	1625–49
Charles II	1649–85
James VII (James II of England)	1685–8
William II and Mary II	1689–94
William II (III of England)	1694–1702
Anne	1702–14
George I	1714–27
George II	1727–60
George III	1760–1820
George IV	1820–30
William 'IV'	1830–37
Victoria	1837–1901
Edward 'VII'	1901–10
George V	1910–36
Edward 'VIII'	1936
George VI	1936–52
Elizabeth 'II'	1952–

BIBLIOGRAPHY

Alexander, Marc, *Haunted Castles* F. Muller, 1975

Atholl, KT, John, 7th Duke of, *Chronicles of the Atholl and Tullibardine Families. I* (privately printed), 1908

Barrow, G. W. S. *Robert Bruce* Eyre & Spottiswoode, 1965

Brown, Ivor, *Balmoral* Collins, 1955

Buxton, Aubrey, *The King in his Country* Longmans Green, 1955

Court, Alex, *The Romantic Castles of Scotland III* Jarrold, 1979

Daiches, David, *A Companion to Scottish Culture* Edward Arnold, 1981

Duff, David, *Victoria Travels* F. Muller, 1970

    Albert and Victoria F. Muller, 1972

    Elizabeth of Glamis F. Muller, 1973

    Eugenie and Napoleon III Collins, 1978

    Alexandra, Princess and Queen Collins, 1980

    Queen Victoria's Highland Journals (edited by David Duff) Webb & Bower, 1980

Farr, A. D., *The Royal Deeside Line* David & Charles, 1968

Fenwick, Hubert, *Scotland's Castles* Robert Hale, 1976

Flower, Sibylla Jane, *The Stately Homes of Britain* Debrett/Webb & Bower, 1982

Fraser, Antonia, *Mary Queen of Scots* Weidenfeld & Nicholson, 1969

    King James VI of Scotland; I of England Weidenfeld & Nicolson, 1974

    King Charles II Weidenfeld & Nicolson, 1979

Gore, John, *King George V, A Personal Memoir* John Murray, 1941

Gunn, Douglas, *The Romantic Castles of Scotland I & II* Jarrold, 1974

Hay, Ian, *The Royal Company of Archers* Wm Blackwood, 1951

Hibbert, Christopher, *Edward VII* Allen Lane, 1976

Holden, Anthony, *Charles Prince of Wales* Weidenfeld & Nicolson, 1979

Irvine, Douglas, H., *Royal Palaces of Scotland* Constable, 1911

Johnson, Edgar, *Sir Walter Scott, I & II* Hamish Hamilton, 1970

King, Stella, *Princess Marina, Her Life and Times* Cassell, 1969

Lindsay, Maurice, *The Eye is Delighted* F. Muller, 1971

Lindsay, Patricia, *Recollections of a Royal Parish* John Murray, 1902

Longford, Elizabeth, *Victoria R.I.* Weidenfeld & Nicolson, 1973

Macgibbon, David & Ross, Thomas, *The Castellated & Domestic Architecture of Scotland from the Twelfth to the Eighteenth Century. I–V* David Douglas, 1887–92

Magnus, Philip, *King Edward VII* John Murray, 1964

Mackie, R. L., *A Short History of Scotland* Oliver & Boyd, 1930

MacPhail, I. M. N., *Dunbarton Castle*, John Donald, 1979

Middlemas, Keith, *The Life & Times of Edward VII* Weidenfeld & Nicolson, 1972

Mitchison, Rosalind, *A History of Scotland* Methuen, 1970

Moncreiffe of that Ilk, Sir Iain, *The Highland Clans* Barrie & Rockliff, 1982

Munro, R. W., *Highland Clans & Tartans* Octopus, 1977

Oman, Carola, *Elizabeth of Bohemia* Hodder & Stoughton, 1938

Plumb, J. H. & Wheldon, Huw, *Royal Heritage* BBC, 1977

Plumptre, George, *Royal Gardens* Collins, 1981

Ponsonby, Sir Frederick, *Recollections of Three Reigns* Eyre & Spottiswoode, 1951

Pope-Hennessy, James, *Queen Mary*, George Allen & Unwin, 1959

Ryan, Peter, *The National Trust and The National Trust For Scotland* J. M. Dent, 1969

Sanderson, M. A. & Melville, Lewis, *King Edward VII Vol. V* Gresham, 1910

Scott-Moncrieff, George, *Scotland's Dowry*, Richard Paterson, 1956

Simpson, W. Douglas, *Scottish Castles* HMSO, 1959

Skene, William F., *Celtic Scotland I* Edmonston & Douglas, 1836

Tayler, Alistair & Henrietta, *The Book of the Duffs*, William Brown, 1914

Tranter, Nigel G., *The Fortalices and Early Mansions of Southern Scotland*, Moray Press, 1935
   The Fortified Homes in Scotland Vols I–V Oliver & Boyd, 1962–7

Victoria, Princess of Prussia, *Queen Victoria at Windsor and Balmoral* George Allen & Unwin, 1959

Wentworth Day, James, *The Queen Mother's Family Story* Robert Hale, 1967

Windsor, HRH The Duke of, *A King's Story* Cassell, 1951

Other sources: *Tales from Scottish Lairds*, Jarrold Colour Publications
                The Times
                North, magazine of the Highlands and Islands Development Board

ACKNOWLEDGEMENTS

For a Sassenach to have the opportunity of collaborating with as knowledgeable a Scot as Sir Iain Moncreiffe of that Ilk when writing about his country is an impressive and illuminating experience and one I should hate to have missed. His understanding, in every sense, has been infinite.

I am also particularly grateful to David Duff for his advice and for allowing me to quote freely from many of his royal biographies as listed in the Bibliography, and to Alan Delgado and Joyce Dunford for help with the research and also to R. J. Unstead for valuable advice and to Anne-Marie Ehrlich, a most knowledgeable picture researcher.

My sincere thanks also go to the owners and keepers of the historic properties featured in the book and to many other Scots mentioned in it, for their ready co-operation. Here I am particularly indebted to the Countess of Mansfield who supplied me with relevant information far beyond her own territory of the Palace of Scone.

Among those who have allowed me to quote from their work I am indebted to Lord Buxton, Anthony Holden, J. H. Plumb and Huw Wheldon, George Plumptre and James Wentworth Day. I have also received help from the Highland Society of London, the National Trust for Scotland, the National Library of Scotland, the London Library and the Norwich Central Library, which I much appreciate.

PICTURE CREDITS

The authors and publishers would like to thank the following for supplying illustrations:

COLOUR

Reproduced by Gracious Permission of Her Majesty The Queen 11, 79, 91, 98 above, 102/3, 122 above and below, 123 above and below, 127, 156, 163 above; J. & C. Bord 19, 23; British Tourist Authority 52; Camera Press/Patrick Lichfield 130, 131 left and right; Company of Merchants of Edinburgh/Tom Scott 167; Crown Copyright/Her Majesty's Stationery Office 160; Grampian Regional Council/Andrew Llanwarne 111; Tim Graham 131 above; Michael Holford 26; Anwar Hussein 163 below; Jarrolds 31; A. F. Kersting 95; National Portrait Gallery 91, 98 right; Octopus Books/Sir Ian Ogilvy 90; Tate Gallery 178/9; Pilgrim Press, Derby 6/7, 115, 145, 148 left; Peter Roberts Collection 2/3, 142; Scottish Development Department 64; Scottish Tourist Board 49, 86, 118; Sotheby's Belgravia 99; Spectrum Colour Library 14/15, 52, 53, 118, 119; Strathmore Estates/Photographic Records Ltd 148 right; Syndication International Ltd 152 above and below, 153; Eileen Tweedy 18.

BLACK AND WHITE

Reproduced by Gracious Permission of Her Majesty The Queen 9, 45, 76 above, 50 left, 79, 97 right, 100, 108, 109, 121, 127, 133, 134 above, 136, 137, 138, 139, 165 above and below, 176, 187 above and below, 189, 196, 200; Aerofilms 82; Duke of Atholl Collection/Bridgeman Art Library 76 below; BBC Hulton Picture Library 135, 195, 197 above and right, 199, 201, 202, 208; J. & C. Bord 24; British Museum/Eileen Tweedy 21, 97 right, 181; British Tourist Authority 70 above, 77, 78, 89, 92, 104, 150,/K. M. Andrew 40, 48,/E.T. Archive 34; Marquis of Bute/Irwin Photography Ltd 67; J. Allan Cash 36 below, 88, 93; Camera Press 175, 210, 216; Central Press Photos 141, 147, 204; Peter Clayton 56; Master and Fellows of Corpus Christi College, Cambridge 39,/Octopus Books 47; Cowper & Co. 105 below,/Sir Iain Moncreiffe of that Ilk 158/9; Crown Copyright Reserved/Victoria and Albert Museum, London 134 below; Drummond Families 63; Dunfermline Press 213; E.T. Archive 30 above, 105 above; College of Arms 42; Fox Photos Ltd 177; the Highland Society of London 215; Jarrolds 28; Duke of Hamilton 171; Anwar Hussein 132; A. F. Kersting 35 above; Mansell Collection 20 below, 128, 174, 191, 192/3, 194; Derry Moore/Debrett's *The Stately Homes of Britain* 73; National Galleries of Scotland 30 below, 45, 50 right, 55,/Tom Scott 43, 70 left, 71, 74, 87, 110; National Museum of Antiquities of Scotland 25; National Portrait Gallery 79, 107 below; Courtesy Sir David Ogilvy 59; Parker Gallery 186; Pilgrim Press, Derby 117, 120,/Sydney Newbery 116; Popperfoto 129, 155, 209 above and below; Private Collection 146 right,/Eileen Tweedy 107 above; Lady Saltoun 112; *The Scotsman* Publications Ltd 169; Scottish Development Department 66, 68, 106; Scottish Record Office 48 below, 57; Scottish Tourist Board 29, 32, 37, 60, 70 right, 84; Spectrum Colour Library 33, 101; Syndication International Ltd 143, 146 left, 203, 212; Victoria and Albert Museum, London/Bethnal Green Museum 80; Weidenfeld and Nicholson Publishers Ltd 20 below, 35 below, 41.

INDEX

Page numbers in italics refer to illustrations.

Abercorn, Marquis and
Marchioness of 187, 188
Abercrombie, Mr 200, 203
Aberdeen University 112
Abergeldie Castle 124, 136 40,
136, 198, 201
Abernethy, Abbot of 29
Abernethy, Lord 161
Adolphus of Teck, Prince 198
Aedan, King of Dalriada 23
Albany, Murdach, Duke of 20,
71, 87
Leopold, Prince, Duke of 135
Alexander Stewart, Duke of
35 6
Robert Stewart, Duke of
68 9, 87
Albert, Prince Consort 75, 77 8,
102 3, 120 21, *121,* 132 4, 138,
150, 176, 188, 190, 197, 207
Albert Victor, Prince *see* Clarence,
Duke of
Alexander I, King of Scots 10, 34,
40, 48, 85, 172
Alexander II, King of Scots 12,
28, 40
Alexander III, King of Scots 12,
46 7, *47,* 79, 170
Alexander VI, Pope 159
Alexandra, Duchess of Fife,
granddaughter of Edward VII
107
Alexandra Feodorovna, Czarina of
Russia 126 8, *127, 128*
Alexandra, Princess (Hon. Mrs
Angus Ogilvy) 207
Alexandra, Queen of Edward VII
108 10, *109,* 126, 133, *138,*
154, *174,* 194 8, 200
Alfred, Prince, Duke of
Edinburgh and Saxe-Coburg 189
Alice, Princess, Grand Duchess of
Hesse 126
Alt-na-guithasach ('The Hut')
133 4, *134*
Andersen, Hans Christian 38, 40,
100
Anderson, Meysie 200
Andrew, Prince *210, 212*
Angus *19,* 144
Anne, Princess (Mrs Mark
Phillips) *131, 208, 210*
Anne, Queen of James VI 45, *50,*
56, 93
Anne, Queen of Scotland and
England 162, 171, 173
Antrim, Countess of 184
Archers, Royal Company of
162 3, *163, 165,* 172, 182 3,
190, 208
Argyll 12, 16, 21 3, *23*
Argyll family and Clan Campbell
8, 12, 17, 25, *30,* 65, 81, 84, 92,
116 17, 119 20, 161
Jean, Countess of 92
9th Duke of 6 7, 113 14

12th Duke, Hereditary
Master of the Household
168; Keeper of
Dunstaffnage 171
see also Louise, Princess
Armstrong-Jones, Lady Sarah *131*
Arran, Isle of 62, 65
Athlone, Earl of 135
Princess Alice, Countess of 135
Atholl Highlanders 78
Atholl, House of 10, 58, 72 5, 78,
87, 184
Hon. Jane Cathcart, wife of
4th Duke 77
John, 1st Marquis of 75
John, 4th Duke of 76

Balliol, House of 10
Balliol, John, King of Scots 12,
28, 46, *57,* 58, 63, 68, 81, 159
Balmoral *2 3,* 13, 107, 120, 122 32,
122, 123, 135 6, 138 9, 176,
183, 190, 194 5, 197 8, 200,
205, 207 8, 210 11, *210, 214*
Ban, Donald 34 5
Battles:
Alnwick 35
Bannockburn 38, 40 1,
61 2, 110, 160, 168, 181
Carham 12
Culloden 75, 104 5, *105,* 180
Flodden 44, 53 4, 95, 162, 168
Killiecrankie 137
Langside 80
Nevill's Cross 35, 168
Pinkie Cleugh 137
Sauchieburn 42
Sheriffmuir 145, 174
Beatoun, Cardinal 88
Elisabeth 92
Beatrice, Princess (Princess Henry
of Battenberg) 176, 185, 188 90
Beaufort, Lady Joan, Queen of
James I 53
Berwick Castle 29, 61
Birkhall 132, 133 8, *133,* 207, 211
Blair Castle 72 8, *73, 76, 87,* 150
Blair, William 138
Bothwell, Countess of 44
James Hepburn, 4th Earl of
38, 55, 79, 100, 151
'Wizard Earl' 93
Bowes-Lyon family:
Lady Elizabeth *see* Elizabeth,
the Queen Mother
Lady Janet (née Douglas)
141, 144
Sir David *143*
Lyon, John (son of Sir John)
141
Lyon, Sir John, Thane of
Glamis 141
1st Lord Glamis 141, 147 8
7th Lord Glamis 141
19th Lord and Lady Glamis
148

20th Lord Glamis 148
1st Earl of Strathmore and
Kinghorne 144
3rd Earl of 144, *145*
5th Earl of 145
6th Earl of 145 6
9th Earl and Countess (Mary
Eleanor Bowes) of 146, *146*
11th Earl of 147 8
14th Earl of *146,* 207
15th Earl of *146*
16th Earl of *146*
17th Earl of and family 149
Braemar Castle 176
Braemar Gathering 173 7, *174, 175*
Braemar Highland Society 174, 176
Bride, legendary Pictish goddess 72
Brown, John 125, *134,* 185, 195
Bruce, House of
Adam, elder son of Robert
de Brus 57
Alexander, Dean of Glasgow
62
Christian, Countess of Mar
(sister of Robert I) 58, 61
Edward, King of Ireland 62
Marjorie, Countess of Carrick
(mother of Robert I) 61
Marjorie (daughter of Robert
I) 55, 58, 61, 67
Mary 58, 110
Robert de Brus 57
Robert, gt-grandfather of the
'Old Competitor' 57
Robert, King of Scots *see*
Robert the Bruce (Robert I)
Robert, the 'Old Competitor'
57 8
Robert, 5th Lord of
Annandale 61
Sir Neil (brother of Robert I)
58, 61
Thomas (brother of Robert I)
62
Bruce of Kinross, Sir William 100
Buccleuch, Duke of 182, 190
Buchan, Earls of 110
Isabel, Countess of 29, 61
Bunnock, William 51, 53
Burns, Robert 33, 46, 120, 162
Bute, Isle of 65
Bute, Marquises of 65, 67, 93;
Hereditary Keeper of Rothesay
Castle 171

Cairnbulg Castle 110 13, *111*
Caledonia and Caledonians 12, 16
Cameron, Mr *139,* 194
Campbell, Arthur 25
Campbell, Clan *see* Argyll
Carlisle 62
Carrick Castle 81
Carrick, Marjorie, Countess of *see*
Bruce, Marjorie
Carrick, Neil, Earl of 61
Cathcart, Hon. Jane *see* Atholl,

House of
Cawdor, Thane of 140
Ceretic (or Coroticus), King 17,
19, 22
Charles I, King 38, 46, 48, 51,
64 5, 93, 100, 158, 161, 182, 213
Charles II, King 10, 29, *30,* 46,
51, 93, 95, 100, 120, 161, 180
Charles Edward Stuart, Prince 16,
31, 38, 56, 74, 83, *98, 99,* 100,
104, 124, 216
Charles, Prince of Wales 10, 16,
67, *131,* 135, 168, *175, 208, 210,*
211 16, *212, 213, 216*
Chew, Robert *212*
Churchill, Lady 185, 188
Clarence, Duke of, Prince Albert
Victor *137, 138,* 195 8, *195, 197*
Clark, Sir James 121, 133
Clinog Eiten, King 34
Coel Hen, King (Old King
Coel) 17, *18*
Colquhoun, Iain, 10th of Luss 20
Comgall, King 23
Conall, King of Dalriada 82 3
Connaught, Duchess of *128, 176*
Dukes of 108
Prince Arthur, Duke of 108,
113, *127,* 176, 190
Princess Margaret of *128, 176*
Princess Patricia of *112,* 113,
128, 176
Crawford, Earls and Lords of *147,*
160, 173
Crichton-Stuart, Major Michael 94
Ninian, John 94, 171
Croker, John 180
Cromwell, Oliver 28, 93, 120,
144, 161
Culzean Castle 17
Cumberland, Dukes of 56, 105
Curle, Lady Elizabeth 97
Curtis, Sir William *181*

Dalkeith Palace 182
Dalriada 10, 16, 22, 23, 82 3
Dalrymple Hamilton, Colonel 164
Dalton, Canon 200
Darnley, Henry Stuart, Lord 21,
36 7, 45, 55, 58, 79, 95 6, *96,*
97, *98,* 151
David, Earl, grandson of David I
58
David I, King of Scots 16, 19, *20,*
34, 35, 40, 51, 55, 57 8, 61, 94,
168
David II, King of Scots 20, 25,
29, 35, 48, 53, 63, 65
de Bunsen, Sir Maurice 108
de Witt, Jacob 75, 100, 144
Diana, Princess of Wales *175,* 216,
216
Dinnie, Donald 174, 177
Disraeli, Benjamin 6 7, 126
Donald, King in Islay 12
Donald, Prince of Scotland 19

Donaldson, David 173
Donaldson, Professor Gordon 173
Dornoch Cathedral 151
Douglas family 12, 29, 30, 141,
  151, 161
  Archibald, Earl of Angus 92
  David, brother of 6th Earl 35
  George 79–80
  Hugh, Earl of Ormond 42
  James, Sir 50
  Janet *see* Bowes-Lyon
  Lady Margaret 79
  William, Sir 79–80
  William, 6th Earl of 35, 36
  William, 8th Earl of 41–2
Doune Castle 14–15, 69, 70, 71
Doune, Dowager Lady 69, 71
Dreux, Count of 46
Drostan, Pictish king 27
Druids 22
Drummond family 63
  Annabella, Queen of Robert
    III 63
  Euphame 63
  John of Stobhall 63
  Margaret ('The Diamond of
    Delight') 44, 63
  Margaret, Queen of David II
    see Logie, Margaret
  Mary (née Montfichet) 63
  Sybilla 63
Duart Castle 83 5, *81*
Duff House 106–10, *106*
Duff, William 'Dipple' 106
Duff, William *see* Fife, 1st Earl
Dunadd Castle 22 6, 82
Dunbar Castle 55
Dunbar, Sir Patrick 151
Dunbarton 17 22, *21*, 44, 171
Dunblane Cathedral 40, 63
Duncan I, King of Scots 19, 34, 140
Dunconnel Castle 82 3, *82*, 171
Dundee, Earls of 13, 137
  11th Earl, Henry James
    Scrymgeour, Hereditary
    Royal Banner Bearer 170
Dunfermline 12, 46
  Abbey 40, *48*, 212 13
  Abbot of 159
  Palace 46 51, 213
Dunoon Castle 81
Dunottar Castle 161
Dunrobin Castle 150
Dunstaffnage Castle 10, 22 5, *26*,
  28, 171
Dunvegan Castle 12, 17, 124

Edinburgh 12, *37*, 44, 46, 51,
  55 6, 96, 100, 170, 173, 208,
  209
  Castle 33 8, *33*, *34*, 53, 94,
    141, 161, 166, 171, *179*,
    181 2, 208
  St Giles' Cathedral 160, 166,
    172, 208, *209*
  St Margaret's Chapel *35*, 38
Edinburgh, Prince Philip, Duke
  of 16, 22, 129, *131*, 132, 166,
  208, 210, 211, 214
Edingight, Malcolm Innes of (The
  Lord Lyon King of Arms) *169*
Edward I, King 12, 28 9, 40, *41*,

46, 48, 51, 58, 81, 110, 159
Edward II, King 12, 58, 61–2, 65
Edward VII, King 107, 126–32,
  127, 138, 154, *165*, 166, 174,
  190–5, *191*, 192, 194, 198, 211
Edward VIII, King 129, 139–40,
  200, 201
Edward, Prince 210, 212
Edwin, King of Northumbria 34
Elisabeth, Queen of Bohemia (the
  'Winter Queen') 45, 50, 56
Elizabeth I, Queen 21, 36, 44,
  92–3, 100
Elizabeth II, Queen 10, 12–13, 22,
  27–8, 32, 67, 85, *129*, 135, *141*,
  160–1, *163*, 166 8, *167*, 203, 204,
  205, 207, 208, *208*, *209*, 210, *210*,
  211
Elizabeth, Queen of Roumania
  (Carmen Silva) 126
Elizabeth, the Queen Mother 22, 135,
  141, *143*, 146, 147, *148*, 149, 150,
  154, 155, 166, *175*, 177, *204*, 211
Elizabeth (2nd Queen of Robert
  the Bruce) 58, 61
Erroll, Countess of 161
  Earls of 182
  12th Earl of 158, *158*
  24th Earl of, Lord High
    Constable 13, 168
Erskine family including Earls of
  Mar and Kellie 20, 44 5, 58,
  133, 174
  Hereditary Keepers of Stirling
    171
  Margaret, mistress of James V
    88
Eugénie, Empress 75, 77, 138, 184

Falkland Palace 55, 63, 85 8, *86*,
  88, *89*, 92 4, *93*, 171
Farquharson Clan 124, 128, 174,
  176
Fergus Mor, King of Dalriada 10,
  23, 24, 100
Fergus, Prince of Galloway 61
Ferguson, Adam 183
Fife, Earls and Dukes of 28 9, 61,
  85, 107, *107*, *108*
  Isabel, Countess of 85, 87
  1st Duke of, 107, *108*, 177
Fleming, Lady 20
Fleming, Lord 21
Floors Castle 205
Forbes, Bishop Robert 154
Francis II, King of France 20, 36,
  44, 95
Frankie, Mr and Mrs Willie 138
Fraserburgh, town and university
  112
Fraser, Donald 104
Fraser family:
  Simon (Canadian explorer)
    112
  Sir Alexander (Chamberlain
    of Scotland) 110
  Sir Alexander (the Chamber-
    lain's grandson) 112
  Sir Simon (the Chamber-
    lain's brother) 112
Frederick Henry, Prince 45
Frederick, King of Bohemia 50

Frederick, Prince of Wales 165
Frederick William, Prince of
  Prussia 125

Gabran, King 23
George I, King 50
George II, King 38
George III, King 10, 55fn, *165*
George IV, King 9, 100, 120,
  160–1, 162, 164, 173, 179,
  180–3, *181*, 190
George V, King 16, *105*, 126, 128,
  135, 137–40, *137*, *138*, 164, 166,
  171, 197–203, 199, 201, 202, 203
George VI, King 12, 22, 28, 135,
  146, *147*, 166, 177, 200, 201, 203,
  204–6, *204*, 214
Glamis Castle 140–1, *142*, 144 9,
  145, 154, 204, 207
Glasgow 210
Gloucester, Duke of 50
Gloucester, Prince Henry, Duke of
  201
Gloucester, Prince Richard, Duke
  of 10
Gordon, Capt Charles 133
Gordon Cumming, Sir William
  211
Gordon family:
  Alexander 124, *137*
  John 151
  12th Earl of Sutherland 151
Gordon, Joseph and his wife
  Elizabeth 133
Gordon, Mrs Glen 56
Gordon, Sir Robert 121, 124
Gordonstoun 211 12

Haakon, King of Norway 40, 65
Hall, Sydney 6, 7, 119, 137
Hamilton, Dukes of 29, 100, 161
  15th Duke of, Hereditary
    Keeper of the Palace of
    Holyroodhouse 170, *171*
Hamilton, Lord Claud 188
Hanover, Elector of 50
Hanover, House of 10
Hansell, Mr 139
Hay family 12
Hay, Sir Gilbert, 5th Baron of
  Erroll 168
Helena, Princess, Duchess of
  Albany 135
Helena Victoria, Princess of
  Schleswig-Holstein *108*
Hélène of Orleans, Princess 195 8,
  197
Henry III, King 79
Henry IV, King 53
Henry V, King 53
Henry V, King 88
Henry VII, King 44, 63
Henry VIII, King 20, 44
Hesse, Louis, Grand Duke of 195
Highland Society of London 214
  Commission of membership 215
Holyroodhouse, Palace of 56,
  93 103, 95, *101*, *103*, 144,
  160 1, *163*, *165*, 170, 172, 182,
  189, 208
Home, Earl of (Sir Alec Douglas-
  Home) 161, 166

Honours of Scotland 158–61, *160*,
  182, 208
Huntly, House of 144

Ingrid, Queen of Denmark 112
Inveraray Castle 17, 113–20, *114*,
  118, *119*
Iona, Isle of 82
Isabel of Mar, 1st Queen of Robert
  the Bruce 58, *59*
Islay, Isle of 12

Jack, Flt-Sergeant Andrew, RAF
  207
James I, King of Scots 20, 48, 53,
  63, 65, 69, 71, 87, 100, 162
James II, King of Scots 20, 35, 41,
  58, 63, 71 2, *87*, 94, 182
James III, King of Scots 35, *42*,
  53, 56, 71, 83, 88, 94
James IV, King of Scots 25, 36,
  42–4, *43*, 53 4, 58, 63, 65, 81,
  83, 88, 94 5, 159, 162, 168, 171
James V, King of Scots 20, 44,
  53, 55, 56, 65, 72, 79, 88, 89,
  90, 92, 94–5, *98*, 99, 141,
  159–60, 166, 168, 171
James VI, King of Scots and I of
  England 10, 13, 21–2, 28, 31,
  36, 38, 45, 44 5, 46, 50, 55, 69,
  79, 85, 91 3, *92*, 96, *98*, 100,
  112, 137, 141, 144, 161, 171–2,
  208, 216
James VII, King of Scotland and
  II of England 64, 100, 166
James Edward Stuart ('Old
  Chevalier') 8, 10, 31, 74, 104,
  145, 174
Joan, Princess, 1st Queen of David
  II 20
John, Prince 201
Johnson, Dr Samuel 113, 117

Kanne, J. J. 184 5
Kennedy, Lady Jane 97
Kennedys of Culzean 17
  Sir Thomas 67
Kenneth mac Alpin, 1st King of
  united Picts and Scots 10, 19,
  25, 27, 216
Kent, Prince George, Duke of *201*,
  206 7, *206*
Kent, Princess Marina, Duchess of
  206 7, *206*
Kent, Prince Michael of 206
Kent, Victoria Maria, Duchess of
  76, 138, 176
Kilconquhar, Adam, Lord of 61
Kildrummy Castle 58, 60, 61
Kintyre, Isle of 12, 62, 81

Landseer, Sir Edwin 124 5, 132
Lang, Dr Cosmo, Archbishop of
  Canterbury 200, 203
Lauderdale, Earls of (Hereditary
  Saltire Bearers) 170
Lennox family and Earls of 12,
  20 21, 45, 50 51, 65, 71, *98*
Leven and Melville, the Earl of 166
Lindsay, House of 148
Lindsay of the Mount, Sir David
  88, 94

Lindsay, Patricia 138, 140
Linlithgow and Linlithgow Palace 44, 51, 52 6, *52, 53, 54*, 92
Livingstone, Lords 20, 56
Lochleven Castle 79 80, *80*
Lochmaben Castle 57 8
Logie, Margaret (née Drummond) 2nd Queen of David II 63
Longair, Professor Malcolm 173
Lord Lyon King of Arms (The) 13, 30, 56, 88, 166, 169–71, 208
Lorn, King of Dalriada 10, 23
Lothian, Marquis of 190
Loudoun, Earl of 104
Louise, Princess, Duchess of Argyll 113, *115*, 117, 119 20, 185, 188, 191
Louise of Wales, Princess, Duchess of Fife 6–7, 107 8, *108, 128, 138, 176,* 195
Louis Napoleon, the Prince Imperial 138

Macbeth, King of Scots 16, 19, 28, 34, 46, 140 1
MacCrimmon, Donald Ban 104
Macdonald Clan 12, 82, 214
   Angus of Islay 12
   Donald, 2nd Lord of the Isles 83
   John, 1st Lord of the Isles 82–3
   John, 4th Lord of the Isles 83
   Mary, daughter of the 1st Lord and wife of Lachlan Lubanach 83
Macduff Clan 28, 30, 107 8
Macfarlane, Mrs 188
MacGregor Clan 128, 183 4
McIntyre, The Very Rev. Prof. John 172
Mackay Clan 151
Mackintosh Clan:
   Mackintosh, Lachlan 104
   Mackintosh, Lady ('Colonel Annie') 104
   Mackintosh of Mackintosh *104*
   Mackintosh of Mackintosh, Vice-Admiral Lachlan 105
   M'Kyntosh, Malcolm 104
Maclean Clan 85, 171
   Lubanach, Hector 83
   Lubanach, Lachlan, 5th Clan Chief 83–4
   Sir Charles, 11th Baronet of Duart 85
   Sit Fitzroy, 10th Baronet of Duart 85
   Sir Fitzroy, 1st Baronet of Dunconnel 171
Macleod Clan 12, 17, 104
Macnaghten, Sir Stewart and Lady Emily 184–5, 188
Madeleine, 1st Queen of James V 44, 88, *90, 94*
Magnus, King of Norway 65, 81
Malcolm II, King of Scots 140–1
Malcolm III, 'Canmore', King of Scots 19, 34 5, *35*, 46, 72, 81, 173
Malcolm IV, King of Scots 20, 85
Man, Isle of 65, 216
Mansfield, Earls of 27

8th Earl and Countess and family *31, 32*
Mar and Kellie, Earls of *see* Erskine
Margaret of Denmark, Queen of James III *42*, 71, 94
Margaret, Princess, daughter of Alexander III 46
Margaret, Princess, the Countess of Snowdon 135, *141*
Margaret, Queen of Alexander III 79
Margaret, Queen of Malcolm III (later St Margaret) *35*, 46
Margaret, 'the Maid of Norway' 12, 46
Margaret Tudor, Queen of James IV *44*, 53 5, 63, 71, 88, 95 6
Marie, Grand Duchess of Russia 189
Marie Louise, Princess of Schleswig-Holstein *108*
Mary of Guise, 2nd Queen of James V 44, 55 6, 88 9, 92, 141
Mary, Princess Royal, Countess of Harewood *200, 201, 202*
Mary, Queen of George V (Princess May of Teck) 16, *108*, 128, 138, 164, *176*, 198, 200, *201, 202, 203, 203*
Mary, Queen of Scots 16, 20–2, 28, 36–7, 45, 54–6, 58, 71–2, 74, *79, 91*, 92, 95, *96, 97, 98*, 100, 144, 151, 171
Maud of Wales, Princess, Queen of Norway 107, *108*
Melfort, Earl of 64
Melrose Abbey 48
Mey, the Castle of 140, 149 51, *150, 152, 153*, 154, 194
Moncreiffe of that Ilk, Sir Iain (Albany Herald) 8, 13, 172
Moncreiffe, Sir Mathew of 12
Montfichet, Mary 62 3
Montrose, Earls and Marquises of 120, 137, 151, 182
Moray, Elizabeth, Countess of 69
   James, 1st Earl of 44, 69, *70*, 144
   James Stuart, 2nd Earl of (Lord Doune) 69, *71*
Morton, James Douglas, 4th Earl of *50*
Moy Hall 104 5, 205
Muir family 67
   Elisabeth, daughter of Sir Adam and 1st wife of Robert II 67
   Sir Adam 67
Mull, Isle of 12
Murray family 10, 12, 151
   Lord George 74–5, *74*
Murray, Gilbert of 58

Napoleon III, Emperor of France 75, 164
Nicholas II, Czar of Russia 126, *127, 128*
Norway 12, 65

Olaf V, King of Norway 166

Oliphants of Gask 133, 151
Orkney, Isle of 16

Paris, Comte de 195, 198
Pearson, Brigadier A. S. 171
Peart, Mr James 155
Perth, 12, 63, 210
Perth, Earls and Dukes of 63–4
Picts 10, 12, 16, 17, *19*, 22, 27, 72, 150 1, 166, 214
Playfair, Dr Lyon 190–1
Ponsonby, Sir Frederick 194
Ponsonby, Sir Henry 135, 185–6
Portland, Duke of 206
Pottinger, John (Don) (Islay Herald) 172

Raeburn, Sir Henry 162, 183
Ragnhild, Norse Princess, Queen of King Somerled 65
Ramsay, Lady Patricia *see* Connaught, Princess Patricia of
Ramsay of Balmain, John, Lord Bothwell 88
Ramsay of Mar, Capt Alexander 110, *112*, 113
Reid, Sir James *139*
Riccio, David 36, 96, *97*, 100
Richard III, King 172
Robert the Bruce, Robert I, King of Scots 10, 12, 16, 20, 25, 29, 34, *36*, 38, *48, 49*, 53, 58, *59*, 61, 62, 81, 110, 151, 160, 168, 170, *212, 213*, 214, 216
Robert II, King of Scots 53, 56, 61, 65, 67, 72, 85 6, 141
Robert III, King of Scots 53, 56, 63, 65, 68 9, 87
Rob Roy 117, 120, 183
Romans 16, 17, 22, *25*, 40
Rose, David 200
Ross, Earl of 110
Rothesay Castle 65 7, *66*, 171
Rothesay, David, 1st Duke of 63, 65, 68
Rowallan Castle 67 9, *68*
Roxburgh Castle 61, 87

St Andrews, Bishop of 28
   Cathedral 40
St Clair Erskine, Lady Sybil 198
St Columba 82, 119
St Malachy O'Morgair 57
St Patrick 17, 22
Saltoun family 113
   Saltoun, Lady (née Fraser), wife of Capt Alexander Ramsay of Mar 110, *112*, 113
   Saltoun, Lady, wife of 19th Lord *112*
Scone and Scone Palace 10, 27–32, *29*, 58, 100, 107, 120, 161
Scott, Sir Walter 8–9, *9*, 62, 68, 71, 85, 93, 117, 146 7, 161, 162, 180 3, 184
Scrymgeour, Sir Alexander 170
Seton, Lord 80
Seton, Mary 79–80
Shakespeare, William 19, 140
Sinclair family 151

12th Earl of Caithness 154
14th Earl of Caithness 154
15th Earl of Caithness 154
Skye, Isle of 12
Solemn League and Covenant 50
Somerled, local King of Argyll 65
Sophia, Princess of the Rhine 50
Spens, John 172
Spens, Dr Nathaniel 162
Stair, the Earl of 172
Steward, Walter the 55, 58, 61
Stewart, House of 10; *see also* Stuart
   David, Duke of Rothesay, son of Robert III 87
   Jean *see* Argyll, Countess of
   Lord James, Earl of Moray, natural son of James V 21, 88
   Lord John, natural son of James V 21
   Lord Robert, Earl of Orkney, natural son of James V 21
   Sir John, natural son of Robert II 65
   Walter, 2nd son of Robert II 85
Stewart, Donald 200
Stirling and Stirling Castle 10, 38 46, *39, 40*, 51, 55 6, 92, 159, 161, 171, 172
Stobhall Castle 62–5, *64*
Stone of Destiny 10, *28*, 58
Strathclyde 12, 16, 19
Stuart, House of 10; *see also* Stewart

Tarbert Castle 80–81, *81*
Teesdale, Sir Christopher *199*
Thistle, Order of the 64, 166 8, 172, 208
Tullibardine, William, Marquis of 74
Turnberry Castle 61–2

Union, Act of 38, 158, 161, 208

Vanbrugh, Sir John 114, 182
Victoria Adelaide, Princess 125
Victoria of Wales, Princess *108, 138, 139, 197*
Victoria, Princess of Prussia 183
Victoria, Queen 9, 10, *31*, 36, 75, 77, 100, 110, 113, 114, 117, 119, 120–1, *121*, 127–8, 132–5, 138, 150, 154, 174, 176, 183–90, *186, 187, 189*, 191, 195, 197–8, 207, 214

Wallace, Sir William 12, 22, 170
Wentworth Day, James 149, 150
Whitby, Robert *212*
Wilkie of Foulden, John 190
William IV, King (III of Scotland) 170
William 'the Lion', King of Scots 63, 210
William of Wales, Prince 216, *216*
Windsor Castle 181, 183, 198, 207
Windsor, House of 10

Yolande, Queen of Alexander III 46
Young Cameron, Sir David 173